UNDERSTANDING COUNSELING AND PSYCHOTHERAPY

Fourth Edition

By
Thomas R. Coleman, Ed.D.
with
Jaynie E. Coleman, M.S, LDT-C
and
Maxine Bradshaw, Ph.D., MBA, MEd.

ISBN 978-1-0980-7448-7 (hardcover)
ISBN 978-1-0980-7449-4 (digital)

Christian Faith Publishing, Inc.
832 Park Avenue
Meadville, PA 16335
www.christianfaithpublishing.com

Printed in the United States of America

Contents

Contents

+++

ACKNOWLEDGEMENTS

This fourth edition of ***Understanding Counseling and Psychotherapy*** was worked on by many people. We are grateful for their assistance and inspiration. First, we would like to thank Dr. Maxine Bradshaw for her encouragement and valuable contributions to the book. Next, we would like to thank Dr. David Schroeder for his pertinent suggestions and advice. The help of Dr. Wayne Dyer for his cooperation in expediting the book was significant. Additionally, we thank Professor Roger Cunningham for his insightful contributions to the chapters on Group Counseling and Therapy, Dream Table, and Addictions and Recovery, and to Dr. Hilde Dyer for her astute contributions to the chapter on Family Counseling. We gratefully thank Shari Franco for her many hours of transcribing the original manuscript. Kudos also to Dr. Joanne Noel for her professional editing. Finally, to my faithful wife, Jaynie, who labored hundreds of hours to fact check, grammar check and organize the whole book to prepare it for publication.

Regards,

Dr. Thomas R. Coleman
January 2020

CHAPTER ONE

THE SUCCESSFUL COUNSELOR-PERSONALLY & PROFESSIONALLY

In the first edition of this book I wrote about how to succeed as a counselor. I then realized that a person cannot fully separate his or her counseling life from his or her personal life. That is one reason to address this chapter to the individual as a counselor, as well as a person. Over the past decades of working in this field, I have witnessed the burnout of many mental health workers and psychologists. This has helped me realize that if I were to be partially responsible for my students' future successes and failures, it was also my obligation to impart some basic principles to help them succeed as mental health clinicians. One story that comes to mind was the rapid rise of a promising bright woman from the role of counselor to supervisor of a large mental health agency. Upon entering her office, I was immediately aware of her dictatorial ways of responding to her workers and her abusive way of talking to people on the phone. When I tried to broach the subject of more effective people management, she sternly made it clear that she had the situation under control and that she didn't need any advice. It was then that I realized that I should have reached her on those issues of social skills when she was an eager student and open to listening. Soon after this the woman lost her supervisor's job and has since left the field of mental health.

It is my goal to have the student reader understand that this chapter is the most important one in the book. Knowing how to work effectively with people is vital both as a professional and as a private person, and as a spiritual being. Publicly and privately, at work, at home, and in church, these cannot be separated.

Just because a research study or a book has been written more recently, it doesn't mean that it is more helpful or more scientific. For instance, the Bible was written over thousands of years ago and is full of stories and sayings that are used as guidelines for millions of people. We Christians believe that it is by far the most valuable therapy book, not only to get us through this life, but also to help us find the narrow path into the hereafter.

Another timeless book that became required reading for my students, after the unpleasant experience of the above example of the graduate student's rise and fall, that is, lose her job, because of poor social skills, is Dale Carnegie's *How to Win Friends and Influence People.* First published in 1936, it has sold well over fifteen million copies and still remains on every major bookshelf, and teaches relevant principles of working with people. It helps everyone realize the importance of developing positive relationships with clients, colleagues and all others in our lives.

The term *counselor* is often used in a variety of disciplines, not just in psychology. There are tax counselors and camp counselors as well as guidance counselors and drug counselors. With that, the educational requirements for a psychological counselor can vary from no formal education to a doctorate degree. The characteristics listed below, while certainly not comprehensive, are research based as well as experiential.

A SUCCESSFUL COUNSELOR IS:

1. Moral and Ethical

   "An honest witness tells the truth, but a false witness tells lies. The words of the reckless pierce like swords, but the tongue of the wise brings healing." (Proverbs 12:17–18)

   Counselors are in very powerful positions when they come into contact with a client. Whether the client is paying for this service or not, the client is dependent on the counselor. Therefore, it should be clear that the counselor should be a person with healthy internalized moral values and boundaries. If counselors were to act unethically by having sexual relations, stealing from clients or not respecting their right to confidentiality, this would severely undermine the trust that counselors need to build with clients, as well as possibly have other severe psychological and personal and legal ramifications. If you are moral and ethical, your supervisor will tend to trust you to take care of your job and not to cheat the organization or to do anything unethical to disgrace anyone or the organization. If a superior wants you to falsify records or do something illegal say, "No." You may have to find a new job, but an unethical supervisor or agency does not stay around forever and the truth usually comes out. If you are a trustworthy, moral, hardworking individual you will find that when the time comes for promotion you will be the more likely candidate because you can be trusted with the funds and resources. When you commit to do the right thing, while some people may not like you, at least you will have a clear conscience. Practice ethical and moral behaviors in your everyday life, and thrive to be law abiding. Know who you are and be true to yourself.

2. Knowledgeable

   **"Choose my instruction instead of silver, knowledge rather than choice gold, for wisdom is more precious than rubies and nothing you desire can compare with her."
   (Prov 8:10–11)**

   It is vital to be current with the recent findings in the field. A good counselor attends workshops, seminars, classes and reviews current literature. If you are deficient in some areas, it is important to refer the client to a professional who is more adept in that area while you study that area. Since a good counselor is always exploring new research and learning, he or she is open to new ideas and approaches. One of the dangers in this field is the counselor that acts like a "know it all." Above all, practice within your sphere of expertise, where your education, training and experience will give you the confidence to best serve your clients.

3. Empathetic

   > If I can stop one heart from breaking,
   > I shall not live in vain.
   > If I can ease one life the aching,
   >   or cool the one pain,
   > Or help one fainting robin
   >   unto his nest again,
   > I shall not live in vain.
   >
   > Emily Dickinson

"Therefore, as God's chosen people, holy and dearly loved, cloth yourselves with compassion, kindness, humility, gentleness, and patience. Bear with each other and forgive whatever grievances you may have against one another. Forgive as the Lord forgave you." (Col. 3:2)

Counselors should care about their clients. *Say what you mean, mean what you say, but don't say it mean.* How would you like it if you had a problem and the counselor acted as if he or she did not care about you? You would find it difficult to open up and be honest. Empathetic and concerned counselors develop trusting relationships more quickly than non-caring ones. The healing qualities of this type of relationship are superior. *People don't care how much you know, until they know how much you care.* Empathy (putting yourself in the shoes of others) is not the same as sympathy (feeling sorrowful or pitying someone.) Counselors should be aware that empathy is different from getting so involved with the client that the objectivity toward the client is lost. Sometimes counselors not only lose their objectivity, they become social friends with clients, even to the point of developing a romantic bond. Dual relationships such as these are unethical and should be avoided at all costs. These are called boundary violations and are serious breaches of practice. (See the issues surrounding dual relationships in the chapter on ethics.)

4. Mature

"You are the salt of the earth: but if the salt has lost its savor, wherewith shall it be salted? It is thenceforth good for nothing but to be cast out, and to be trodden under foot of men… You are the light of the world. A city set on a hill cannot be hid. Neither do men light a candle, and put it under a bushel, but on a candlestick: and it gives light to everyone in the house. In the same way, let your light so shine before men that they may see your good works and glorify your Father which is in heaven." (Mathew 5:13–16)

Maturity entails being a responsible, sensible, and reasonable individual. Maturity and responsibility are signs of emotional stability. If the counselor has attained these qualities, they can be taught to the client. Additionally, the counselor should be taking the same advice that is being given to the client. It is hypocritical if the counselor tells the client to be honest, but then the client catches him or her in a lie.

One important characteristic of a mature person is that he or she is in touch with and can express appropriate feelings. Counselors encourage clients to express their feelings. A mature person can express the full range of emotions, not just anger. This means that a good counselor should be open to working on his or her own problems and is able to express pain and get in touch with feelings. This includes crying. Research shows that crying can improve your relationships, your health, even your career. People often feel better after crying because their tears actually remove stress chemicals that build up in the body. "The expression *to cry it out* might literally be true," says Dr. William Frey, a biochemist and researcher director of the Dry Eye and Tear Research Center at Saint Paul's Ramsey Medical Center. "Emotional tears contain about 24% more protein than tears shed when the eye is irritated, which shows something unique is happening when we cry emotional tears. Tears also contain two hormones, prolactin and adrenocorticotropic hormone (ACTH), that are produced by the pituitary gland and released into the bloodstream in a stressful situation. This suggests that tears may be an adaptive response to stress, serving to remove those built up hormones in the body. How much we cry may determine how susceptible we are to stress related illnesses," says Dr. Frey. "Tears are literally necessary to our health," says Dr. Margaret Crepeau, a psychotherapist in Milwaukee. In a study comparing the crying habits of healthy men and women to those people with colitis and ulcers, she found that "healthy people cry more often and view tears more positively than those who can't or won't cry." (Coleman 1999) The counselor, if handicapped in an ability to express his or her own feelings, may squelch the feelings that the client is trying to express. Often a counselor will take the client only as far as therapeutically as he or she has personally gone. There is a saying—*If you're going to talk that talk, you must learn to walk that walk*. In other words, practice what you preach.

5.   Optimistic

> **"Finally, brothers and sisters, whatever is true, whatever is noble, whatever is right, whatever is pure, whatever is lovely, whatever is admirable—if anything is excellent or praiseworthy—think about such things." (Phil. 4:8)**

A positive outlook is important for a counselor. Consider the psychologist who has a negative view of the world, is chronically depressed, and maintains an office that is dark and messy. Are you surprised to find that person has difficulty gaining and keeping clients? Would you choose such a counselor? Studies suggest that optimism is good for your mental and physical health. Without a positive outlook about the client's problem, one may impede the resolution of the problem. If not positive, the counselor should refer the client to someone who can be more optimistic about particular issues.

6.   Aware of Limitations

> **"Rebuke the discerning, and they will gain knowledge." (Prov 19:25) "For I say to everyman…not to think of himself more highly than he ought to think, but to think soberly." (Romans 12:3)**

A counselor must be aware of what he or she can and cannot do. A person that has not had courses in sex counseling cannot represent or treat a client for sexual disorders. It is important that a counselor whose only knowledge and experience is in working with substance abuse clients not attempt to treat a person who has a severe psychiatric problem. It is dangerous when counselors act as if they know more than they really do. Psychology, as a science, in many ways is still in its infancy and one needs to be aware that there is much still unknown.

7.   A Good Listener

> **Encourage others to talk about themselves. (Dale Carnegie)**

"When people are in crisis, one of the first steps is to give them an opportunity to fully express themselves. Sensitive listening, hearing, and understanding are essential at this point. Being heard and understood helps ground people in crisis." (Corey, 2005, p. 176)

Do you want people to like you and your clients to be cooperative and loyal to you? The solution is simply to **be a good listener.** Show your client that you are listening. The most commonly used words in the English language are **I** and **me**. Humans are hopelessly egocentric and far more interested in themselves than in others. When learning to be interested and enthusiastic in what others are doing and saying, a counselor will find that clients engage and cooperate more readily. It is vital to learn to listen and to relate to others where they are. A good reflective listener uses the Socratic Method. With this method one learns to ask good questions so the client can express his or her ideas, beliefs and feelings. With proper questioning, an effective counselor can direct the session in order to obtain information necessary for a proper assessment.

A good counselor does far more listening than talking. Clients like the sound of their own voices best. The most beautiful words that a person can hear is the sound of his or her own name. Remember the person's name and say it often.

This technique is also important in your personal life. Many people boast to others how wonderful they are and then later wonder why no one likes them. If you want friends, learn to listen, and be quiet except when you ask questions to stimulate the person to express him or herself.

One time on a job interview I spied a picture of an interviewer's family on his desk. I inquired about his family and the ages of his children. The interviewer talked almost an hour about his family and their accomplishments. At the end of the hour the manager asked me when I wanted to start working and what salary I would like. He knew little about me, but he liked me. Active listening skills show good social skills. Learn to take genuine interest in others and their welfare.

8. Never too Serious

"God resists the proud but gives grace to the humble." (James 4:6)

It is important to be serious about yourself and your responsibilities as a counselor, however, is not helpful if you take yourself so seriously that you cannot sometimes laugh at yourself or admit when you are wrong. We all make mistakes and can learn from them, but not if we act as if we are infallible. A good counselor learns appropriate laughing. Laughing with a client is sometimes helpful, especially after the client has talked about a deeply depressing subject. After a client has had a good cry over something that has bothered him or her deeply, one can sometimes feel relieved and find these experiences amusing and more bearable, thus able to laugh. A word of caution here—while it makes sense "to laugh with those that laugh and weep with those that weep," if the client is suffering from intense pain, it may be inappropriate to lighten up too quickly. It is difficult to try to get a person to laugh if he or she has not fully worked through the painful feelings.

Counselors need to use their intuition to find the correct response to a client's feelings. It is important not to be too serious. If you want to find two people that are too serious, listen to two people who are arguing. They are trying hard to get the other to see their point of view. It is nearly impossible to "win" an argument with another person. Even if people tell you that you are right and they are wrong, you will find that secretly they have often become more entrenched in their attitudes than they were before, or sometimes a person's feelings may be hurt so badly that they want revenge. This is one of the reasons that Carnegie says never argue, condemn or complain. Arguing, condemning or complaining can be negative self-defeating behaviors.

9. Humble

"Arrogance will bring you down but if you are humble you will be respected." (Proverbs 29:23)

At first consideration it might seem that those who boast about themselves are the ones that get ahead. While it is important to be confident about what you can do, instead of bragging about what you can do, it is better if you simply go about your business quietly and get things done. Let others take credit for your work. The people around you will ultimately see who the competent ones are. Anyone can brag; it is the humble competent person that usually wins out.

There are few things that people hate more than a person that tells you how wonderful and fantastic they are. Nobody likes an egotist. Let others give you the credit; you don't need to do it for yourself if you are competent. Likewise, it is important to be able to admit when you are wrong or to apologize when you have crossed someone. Finally, let others have room to save face. Do not expect others to apologize or admit they are wrong and do not keep rubbing it in if you find that they have made a mistake, but let the person off the hook gracefully. Others will often be grateful, even if they cannot admit it.

10. Organized

"All hard work brings a profit, but mere talk leads only to poverty." (Proverbs 14:23)

Educators have found a positive correlation between students' organization of their materials and their grades. The students that are the most organized are the ones with the higher grades. It is helpful to be organized and have carefully maintained files and complete paper work correctly and on time. Pay your bills, and return calls and correspondences as soon as possible. Carry a calendar with you and record all appointments.

11. Punctual

Being on time is an essential for a professional. If you promise something—deliver. If you make an appointment—be there on time. Remember when you keep people waiting you are spending their most valuable commodity-time. If you are running late for an appointment, call ahead and explain the situation. People remember your promises, so make them few. Learn how to communicate and apologize if you need to change your plans.

12. A Positive Reinforcer

Give honest and sincere appreciation. (Dale Carnegie)

Carnegie advises, "Let's cease thinking of our accomplishments, or wants. Let's try to figure out the other person's good points. Forget the flattery. Give honest, sincere appreciation. Be hearty in your approbation and lavish in your praise and people will cherish your words and treasure them and repeat them over a lifetime. Yes, they will repeat them years after you have forgotten them."

Psychology books are full of studies that document the power of using rewards. A reward can come in many forms, such as praise, a pat on the back, a gift, or simply a smile. People are highly motivated to attain positive reinforcement and live for this feedback. If you want people to admire you and be loyal to you, find out what they desire and help them attain it.

Unfortunately, people are too quick to criticize and not quick enough to praise. A person who has excellent social skills praises lavishly and sincerely. Since everyone has feelings of inadequacy, they usually respond positively to rewards such as praise. Even listening to someone intently is a powerful positive reinforcer. Another often overlooked positive reinforcer is cheerfulness and smiling. Even though some grouches will be irritated by your cheerfulness, most people will respond affirmatively.

Someone once said, "I met a person without a smile so I gave him mine." Friendly, warm, and cheerful people are more likely to get ahead in business than the aggressive individuals. Another good reinforcer is to remember a person's name, birthday and other things about them. When you make someone feel special and important, you will also benefit.

13. Able to Cope with Stress

"So, we say with confidence, the Lord is my helper: I will not be afraid. What can man do to me?" (Hebrews 13:6)

It is vital for your mental and physical health to know yourself. Learn ways to reduce and cope with stress. Stress management includes, first, focus on what you want to learn and learn to say **No** to things that distract you from what you want. Learn how to relax, get sleep, and find someone with whom to talk. Exercise regularly, let your feelings out, take regular vacations and ask God to help you.

Counseling is much more stressful than most people realize. Not managing hostility and other negative emotions can exhaust a person quickly. It is, therefore, important to take care of your mental health. If you burn yourself out, you will be of little value to others. You can become anxious or depressed, and not only lose your effectiveness on the job, but also learn to hate your job. It is important to maintain your vitality. Additionally, stress can tear down your immune system and make you susceptible to disease. Studies suggest that stress is one of the biggest killers in the United States. The American Psychological Association states that most Americans are suffering from stress, with concerns about money, work, and the economy (2011).

14. Well-Groomed

Dress the way you want to be addressed. (Bianca Frazier)

A person's first impression of someone tends to become a lasting impression. This includes the way you dress. How would you feel if you walked into a counseling room and your male counselor was wearing shorts and had his wrinkled shirt open so that you could see his hairy chest and the tattoo of his girlfriend? Would you feel comfortable with a physician with long, ungroomed hair, a couple of days' growth on his chin, and blood on his white coat from his last patient? People tend to judge competence by how one dresses and how one maintains the surroundings. While it might be premature to judge a professional by appearance, why put yourself in a disadvantage by dressing improperly at work? Dirty clothes and poor hygiene are not acceptable. You need clothes in which you feel comfortable and appear professional.

15. A Good Networker

Someone with a warm smile and cheerful greeting, and if you so desire, a big hug, is easy to like and pleasant to be around. When this person is also an excellent networker, if he or she lost a job today there would be others who would choose to hire him or her immediately. Learning to meet people and getting to know them is important in any occupation, and the competent person who can do so will rarely be unemployed for long. Many jobs are gotten through who you know. People who have faith in you are likely to help you network if you are looking for a new job, but those you have offended will often harm your chances of moving on. Most people are fired not because of technical skills but because they show poor social judgment. In other words, they don't get along well with others. It is important to remember to treat everyone well because you never know when you might meet again.

16. An Interesting Speaker

No one is enthusiastic about a boring person, even if he or she has something important to say. People need to be enthusiastic and vibrant. Everyone wants others to find them interesting and to take notice of what they have to say. A counselor should explain ideas in a lively manner and use body language as well as clear verbal skills. At times, counselors may be asked to talk to a group of people. Think of the best speakers that you have heard. What are they like? You might find that they dramatize what they say and use clear interesting illustrations and stories. With a little practice and confidence, you can also learn to excel. To be a good speaker, practice in front of a mirror or a group of friends who will give you productive feedback.

17. Non-judgmental and Accepting

"Judge not, that ye be not judged." (Matt 7:1)

Dale Carnegie says, "Don't criticize, condemn or complain." It is often too easy to notice what is wrong with other people, but we must realize that we also are not perfect. If we gossip about others, it ultimately gets back to that person and creates bad feelings. We may not agree with someone's lifestyle, but it does no good to condemn the individual. Often you can help a person to a more positive lifestyle through acceptance and warmly helping him or her find a way to what works better. Likewise, it is not good to criticize a person directly; as you will learn, Carl Rogers used the Socratic Method of asking questions. Well thought-out questions help clients to examine the folly of their ways and sometimes help others to correct these behaviors on their own. When clients learn that the solutions to their problems are their own, they are more likely to follow through on the solution. Helping others discover their own solutions help them claim ownership to these solutions.

Once a male client was complaining about how fat his wife was getting after they married. He said that the more he criticized her, the more defensive she became, and the more weight she gained. Through effective questioning the husband learned to realize that his criticism was not working. Consequently, he decided to accept her the way she was. Interestingly the more he complimented her, the more she criticized herself. The result was that this accepting atmosphere made her feel more confident. She then developed more self-control, and she lost the needed weight.

Obviously, the above example doesn't always work because criticizing can be very self-defeating. All too often it drives a person toward the negative behavior that one wants to eliminate. This is called the "forbidden fruit syndrome." Remember Adam and Eve? They were told they could eat any fruit of the garden except one tree. That forbidden fruit tree was the one which Eve became enamored by. A general precept in psychology is that if something is forbidden, we are often more curious about it. Sometimes the more forbidden it is, the more curious we are about it. Therefore, if we severely criticize someone for something, we often drive them to want it more. This principle is seen clearly in children. Sternly tell a two-year-old that he cannot touch a vase and then promptly leave the room. Often the young child will make a beeline to the vase. Young children cannot control their impulses and often wish to do what they have been forbidden to do.

Finally, an accepting person is open-minded and flexible. As people get older, they are often closed to new and innovative ideas. It is vital that one never stops learning and becomes so rigid that one cannot change or grow.

18. Empathic: Able to get behind another person's eyes

A coach is someone who can give correction without causing resentment. (John Wooden)

Obviously, no one can view the world through another person's eyes, but a successful counselor is always trying to understand what the client's view is. Then, you can better know what questions to ask to get the client to open up and to confide. When you can see the world as a client sees it, you sometimes can help come to a satisfying solution to a problem. When you respect another person's individuality, and learn their interests and views, you show more willingness to understand and to be trusted.

19. Spiritual

On our American coins and the dollar bills are the words "In God we trust." The heritage of this country is built on a deep trust in God. Two of the reasons for this country's greatness is believed to be that God has blessed us, and that our moral code is built upon the Judeo-Christian ethic. Psychologists Carl Jung and Viktor Frankel both explain that a person that has hope and meaning in one's life is a healthy person. One of the most powerful ingredients in Alcoholics Anonymous and Narcotics Anonymous is the belief in a Higher Power, which most members choose to view as God. God has gotten more people off drugs and alcohol than all the drug programs combined.

Even though there is a breakdown in the morals of the society, most Americans still profess to believe in a God. When it comes to counseling the sick and dying, psychology has little vision of the beyond and traditional therapy is of little help for the dying. A strong belief in a loving God and heaven has given many a dying person strength, courage and new meaning. Numerous books are giving documented evidence as to the reality of the hereafter. Many people that have had near death experiences come back with reports of visiting heaven or hell. As one ages or is dying, a strong belief in God sustains a person more than the latest psychological techniques.

20. Dedicated Learner

You are never too old to learn and you can never learn enough.

We live in an ever-changing environment where information evolves rapidly. As twenty first century practitioners, we must become dedicated to keeping up with the information, research and tools that are current and relevant to the field of counseling. Attend workshops, become a member of the professional organization in your area of interest, subscribe to professional journals, and most importantly, do not resist changing your ideas when more relevant and proven methods become available. Your willingness to learn and pursue knowledge will empower you towards becoming your best self and an asset to your peers and clients.

21. Multiculturally Aware

"The rich and poor have this in common. The Lord is the maker of them all." (Prov. 22:2)

We live in a pluralistic society and everyone is unique. Counselors who counsel clients from one world view are in danger of failure as a counselor as well as failing the client in his or her time of need. Each client must be understood in the context of the culture he or she represents. Goals and techniques used must be sensitive to the client's culture. For example, the dominant culture emphasizes eye contact as a mark of confidence, but you cannot expect individuals from Asian and Caribbean cultures to be comfortable maintaining eye contact, as this is a mark of disrespect in some of those cultures.

Finally, becoming the best you can be means to tap into all the dimensions of your humanity: a tripartite being. While for the most part, when people place great emphasis on the social aspect of human nature, striving for companionship and the desire to feel loved and appreciated, they often neglect the spiritual self. As such, pay particular attention to taking care of your bodies, with an equal mix of social and spiritual or God connections. Only then can you achieve your full potential.

References

American Psychological Association. (2011, January). *Stressed in America*. Retrieved from www.apa.org. 42, (1).

Brammer, Lawrence. (1979). *The helping relationship: Process and skills*. Englewood Cliffs, NJ: Prentice-Hall, Inc.

Carnegie, Dale. (1998). *How to win friends and influence people*. New York: Pocket Books.

Coleman, Thomas. (1999). *Understanding counseling and psychotherapy* (3rd Ed.) Acton, MA: Copley Publishing Co.

Corey, Gerald. (2005). *Theory and practice of counseling and psychotherapy*. Belmont, CA: Brooks/Cole Publishing Co.

Frazier, Bianca. www.goodreads.com.

Larson, S., and Londono-McConnell, A. (2019). Protecting your privacy: Understanding confidentiality. *The American Psychological Association*. Retrieved from www.apa.org/confidentiality.

Lichtenstein, E. (1980). *Psychotherapy: Approaches and applications*. Monterey, CA: Brooks/Cole Publishing.

Rawlings, Maurice. (1993). *To hell and back*. Nashville, TN: Thomas Nelson Publishers.

Schmidt, Stuart. (1987, November). The perils of persistence. *Psychology Today*.

Sundberg, Norman, et al. (1983). *Introduction to clinical psychology*. Englewood Cliffs, NJ: Prentice-Hall, Inc.

U.S. Department of Health and Human Services. (2019). *HIPAA privacy rules and sharing information related to mental health*. Retrieved from www.hhs.gov/sites/hipaa-privacy-rule.

Study Questions

These pretests and posttests, or study guide questions, are very important in helping to remember and to clarify some of the ideas and values that are developing within you. Take these evaluations thoughtfully and realize that in some cases there are no absolutely correct or incorrect answers.

1. What do you believe is the most important characteristic a successful counselor should possess?
2. If you were to seek counseling, what three characteristics would you believe are vital for the person that counsels you?
3. As a counselor, what is your strongest attribute?
4. List some fears you may have about becoming a counselor. Explain why you have some of these fears.
5. What must you do now to prepare yourself to be an effective counselor?
6. Should a counselor use humor in counseling? Explain.
7. If your client were to commit suicide, how would you feel? What would you do?
8. Should a counselor use silence in a session? Explain.
9. Think of a person in your life who has helped you in the past. What personality characteristics did that person have?
10. What is the role of feelings in counseling?
11. What do you see as the role of spirituality in counseling?
12. In what areas do you need more training to be a good counselor?

CHAPTER TWO

ETHICAL AND LEGAL ISSUES

Knowledge without morality creates a menace to society. (Theodore Roosevelt)

You shall know the truth and the truth will set you free. (John 8:32)

A counselor must become familiar with the complex problems that one can encounter in therapy work. There are few absolutes in the area of ethics and sometimes there are situations where the law conflicts with ethical considerations. Also, sometimes spiritual values can clash with legal and ethical values. Sometimes there are alternative decisions that a counselor may consider in certain situations. There are few hard and fast rules in many circumstances, but personal and professional integrity and virtue remain paramount. There are professional organizations that publish ethical guidelines, and it is important to familiarize yourself with their standards.

A professional counselor or psychologist should be a member of the Association for Counseling and Development (AACD), the American Counseling Association (ACA), or the American Psychological Association (APA). Other organizations that also publish materials on ethics include:

The American Academy of Psychotherapists
The National Association for Social Workers
The American Personnel and Guidance Association
The American Psychiatric Association
The American Association of Marriage and Family Therapists
The American Association of Christian Counselors

These organizations publish ethical and legal guidelines that counselors and therapists should study and integrate into their practices. Several suggestions are included below that could help prevent an ethical mistake that could possibly jeopardize your career, or that could prevent you from facing ethical or legal sanctions.

1. Attend workshops that present the HIPAA laws and the legal and ethical guidelines of your area.
2. If you work for an institution or business that may have an ethical violation find what the guidelines are for reporting unethical or illegal issues.
3. If you work independently, consult with your peers or colleagues concerning the ethical implications of an uncertain situation.

4. Be clear that not all spiritual, legal and ethical experts will be in agreement on all legal and ethical issues.

SIGNIFICANT LEGAL AND ETHICAL ISSUES

1. Confidentiality

The trust of the client is vital to an effective counseling relationship; therefore, it is important that counselor-client confidentiality be kept as much as possible. It is an ethical obligation that the client be told the areas in which confidentiality can be breached, such as recording the session with the client or discussing the case with a supervisor. Generally, it is not a breach of confidentiality if you discuss the client's issues with your supervisor. A client must agree before any session is recorded or viewed through a one-way mirror. When you break confidentiality (i.e. transfer files to another agency, or discuss a client's issues with his or her spouse), you must have written permission from the client. Your office should have prepared release forms that the client signs. Also, an ethical requirement is that the clients' records be kept secure to protect them from theft or unwarranted search.

Confidentiality can be a controversial issue. Many counselors believe that confidentiality should be maintained under every circumstance, but what if the client has a gun and fully intends to kill someone as soon as the counseling session is over? What would you do? The general rule is to talk the person out of the behavior, but if he or she leaves your office you should notify the future victim, and if that is not possible, notify the police. There are no easy answers because the person may be bluffing, but the wrong decision can have devastating consequences. Therefore, counselors need to know the legal and ethical ramification of their decisions. (See items 6 and 7 following.)

Children, especially adolescents, have rights to confidentiality and this should be respected as much as possible for the sake of the trust between client and counselor. However, with very small children, the restrictions of confidentiality are not as rigid nor as dire. Many times, it is advantageous to work with a responsible parent to help the child cope with issues.

In group it is vital that all group members be aware of the HIPAA laws about confidentiality. They may talk about what they themselves said, but they may not talk about what another group member said. A member who gossips outside of the group can be detrimental to the group's trust.

2. Boundary Violations

A boundary is a wall or barrier that one builds in relationships with others. Obviously, these boundaries are good or bad depending on whether they breach legal and/or ethical issues. Psychologist and attorney Bryant Welch explains that boundary violations are a major source of licensing board complaints and litigation. Litigation means being involved in a law suit. Welch advised that there are three main areas where a therapist can unwittingly get caught in a boundary violation. They are: (1) Counter transference with borderline patients. (2) The personal needs of the counselor. (3) Experimentation with alternative therapies.

A well-intended therapist can feed an unrealistic fantasy through a misguided attempt to try harder to help a borderline patient. Perhaps by spending extra time talking with the patient, or agreeing to a reduced fee the therapist may be at risk. When the client realizes that a more personal relationship won't happen, the client may become angry. There have been situations when a therapist has been stalked, harassed, accused or sued.

As a therapist, one must take inventory of unresolved personal issues, conflicts and feelings. If a therapist is experiencing some personal deprivation in his or her own life, one is more prevalent to a boundary violation. Something may be missing—a loved one is lost, a personal problem unresolved, or there may be a feeling of inadequacy or loneliness. The therapist may feel isolated and become vulnerable to the attention of a patient. The patient's wish for a more intimate relationship may become the therapist's wish as well. Obviously, a serious boundary violation is having sex with a client, which should be avoided at all cost. Even if the client has sex willingly with the counselor, it is totally illegal and unethical and the person can easily sue you.

A therapist cannot be too careful. If you tend to be a touching person by nature, be aware that different people take touching differently. It is important to be aware of whom you touch and how you touch. A simple hug could be misinterpreted as sexual interest by a client or third parties that do not know you. Do not mislead the client by non-verbal behaviors.

Generally, it is advisable not to touch a client in a private session, but touching can be used more in group therapy where there are other objective observers around. In this setting the client is less likely to be able to accuse the therapist of boundary issues. A good rule: Do not open yourself to even the appearance of impropriety. In other words, do not do anything that will even look like you are breaking a boundary issue.

Finally, a counselor has to be careful when experimenting with new therapies that overstep people's boundaries. Without knowledge and training in alternative therapies, a therapist should not experiment without client approval. While new ideas in any field are necessary for the advancement of that field, therapists should exercise caution for the safety and protection of all involved.

3.   Improper Representation

Represent yourself for what you are and do not mislead the client to believe that you are more certified than you are. Put any degrees, certifications, or licenses you have earned on display in your work area for clients to examine. Also give no guarantees for your services. In this field there are no "sure solutions" and if you guarantee a "cure" for the client, you are making a clear ethical violation.

4.   Counselor Competence

Counseling and psychotherapy are constantly changing and expanding. It is incumbent on the counselor to strengthen his or her abilities and knowledge in the field.

It is good for a counselor to be sensitive to the ideas, beliefs and attitudes of others. Clients can sense when one makes value judgments. Counselors and psychotherapists should examine their own values and attitudes and not try to impose them on others. Sometimes a counselor that has used divorce in his own marital relationship might try to impose this solution on a couple who might not otherwise have considered this alternative.

As a counselor, you should know your area of competence. It is unethical to act like a "know it all" and attempt therapeutic techniques that are beyond your training. Do not attempt to treat a client with a problem that is beyond your area of expertise. The client should be referred to a person who is more competent to handle the problem. You may listen to the client, act as a sounding board, but do not treat. For example, if the client is clearly bipolar, he or she also may need the care of a psychiatrist who can prescribe medication.

You are a role model and your behavior, in and out of the therapy session, will have an effect on the client. If the client has a drug problem and he or she finds out that you smoke marijuana, the client may lose respect for you or may possibly relapse.

Just like the clients, counselors have personal problems and should admit to them and get professional help for them. Too often counselors attempt to help clients with problems that they have not resolved for themselves.

5. Negligence in Practice

As a counselor you have a professional responsibility and it should be taken seriously. Malpractice occurs if you fail to provide the client with professional, legal and ethical standard of care. The counselor should be extremely careful not to use the client for selfish purposes and be mindful not to make any unreasonable financial or service demands on the client. Because the client is coming for help, this person is somewhat dependent. A counselor that is power hungry might foster that dependence and then "use" the client for the counselor's own selfish gains. This should be guarded against.

Dual or multiple relationships with a client should be avoided. It is a good rule to not mix business and pleasure, or violate boundary issues. It is usually best not to socialize with clients you are seeing. Obviously, it is a clear ethical violation to have a sexual relationship with a client. Welch (1999) said, "Sex with a patient or former patient? **Don't. The codes are explicit even in this regard, and in many states, it is a felony carrying a prison term**." Each year psychologists and psychiatrists lose their licenses and are subject to law suits because of having affairs with clients. Even if the client is completely willing to have an affair with the counselor, it is still a clear ethical and legal violation. Besides, such relationships are usually traumatic for the client and destroys the client's trust for the counselor. Remember that the client is dependent on the counselor for help and a sexual relationship is of no therapeutic value.

Other dual relationships, such as business partnerships, are also to be avoided. It should be noted that it is never a good idea to offer counseling to a relative. For comparison, consider that you are a brain surgeon and your daughter needs surgery for a brain tumor. Would it be ethical for you to perform the surgery? Because you are too emotionally involved with the patient, it is unethical. Likewise, a therapist is not to be a therapist to a relative. Emotional involvement often interferes with objectivity and productivity in therapy. A client will be less honest to a therapist that is at the same family gatherings and within the same family "grape vine."

Finally, it is important to know when to terminate therapy. Generally, it a good to terminate or refer elsewhere if it is evident that the client is not benefiting from therapy. Another practice is to terminate therapy when the client has reached his or her goals and objectives. Also, terminate therapy if the client desires to do so, or he or she is no longer willing to cooperate.

6. Clients that are Dangerous to Others

The controversy continues between professionals and the courts concerning confidentiality and when it should be breached. In California in the 1970's a university student told a psychologist that he was going to kill his ex-girlfriend, Tonya Tarasoff. The psychologist told the police at the university and they attempted to arrest the client. The client was released and later killed Miss Tarasoff. The parents of the girl sued the university because they said that they should have been told of the client's intent. The parents won the case because it was ruled that the psychologist's job is first to protect the public. The Tarasoff case has ramifications for all professionals. Generally, the law states that if a person is severely dangerous to self or other then confidentiality must be breached. Of course, this case also has implications concerning how candid clients can be with their counselors. Many counselors simply tell the client in which cases confidentiality must be breached so they do not hear something from a client that they would have to report. Often it is difficult to tell what degree of danger a client is showing. If you judge that the client is dangerous to someone, your first obligation is to notify that someone whose life is in danger. If you cannot contact the person in danger, you must then report your concerns to the authorities, i.e. the police. Whenever there is the slightest question the counselor should discuss it with a supervisor. Also, the counselor may discuss the case with colleagues for a better understanding of it.

A counselor should be able to do a homicide assessment. While no assessments are perfect, one needs to be aware of the deviousness of **intent**.

Homicide Assessment

A. Emotion and Intent

How angry is the client at the victim? How serious is he or she about harming this person and does the client have a plan of when to hurt this person? Does this person believe that revenge is a solution to an interpersonal problem?

B. Personal History

Does this person have a bad temper? Has this person acted violently with someone else in the past? Has he or she manifested violence towards people or animals? If this is a pattern in the client's past, then the seriousness of the circumstances increases. Sometimes a psychological test can help the therapist gauge a person's potential for violence. For example, the hostility scale or a psychopathic deviate scale of the Minnesota Multiphasic Personality Inventory (MMPI) can give a better indication of the client's potential for violence.

C. Family History

Does this person come from an environment or family where violence or abuse is or was prevalent? Has any family member killed or acted violently toward someone? Has any family member had a drug problem or record of incarceration?

D. Method

If the client says he or she is intent on killing another, ask how this will happen. If the person has a gun and shows you the bullets, take the threat very seriously. Allow the client to relate the anger and then try to persuade the person to hand over the bullets. If the client leaves the office to execute the murder, then it is necessary to take appropriate action. First, alert the intended victim and/or contact the police. **Always take every homicide threat seriously.**

7. Clients that are Dangerous to Self

As with the client who is dangerous to others, you take all precautions, including questioning to ascertain if suicide is being considered. If someone is serious about suicide, try to get this person to self-admit to a hospital, which is not always easy to do. It may be helpful to discuss an oral or written contract with this client. If someone leaves your office having clearly not resolved the suicide issue, your responsibility is to notify the next of kin so that he or she can watch the person and possibly talk the client into going to the hospital. If the person is severely suicidal, antidepressant drugs might be helpful in altering the dysphoric mood that the client wants to escape through suicide. Even though alerting the family is a breach of confidentiality, you might later be thanked for saving someone's life.

Doing a suicide assessment is similar to doing a homicide assessment. Sometimes a client can be both suicidal and homicidal as seen in cases where the person kills a spouse and then commits suicide. Additionally, in the US the number of suicides is about twice the number of homicides. In 2016 the number of suicides was 44,965. The suicide rate has increased 24% from 1999 to 2014. (National Institute of Health Statistics, 2019)

Suicide Assessment

A. Emotion and Intent

If the person is severely depressed, ask if he or she is interested in "harming" him or herself. Obviously the deeper the depression the more likely the suicide, but that is not always true. Sometimes the person will deny that he or she is suicidal and even act cheerful. Often a suicidal person will give his or her favorite possessions away. Watch for this. A good way to gauge the depth of a depression is by using the Beck Depression Scale, or the depression scale of the MMPI. Generally, the deeper the depression, the more you have to be careful of suicide. **Always take every suicide threat seriously.**

B. Personal History

Ask the person if there have been previous attempts to harm oneself. Has he or she taken pills, cut wrists, or used other methods? If the response is "I cut my wrists" ask to see the wrists and notice how serious the scars are. Obviously the worse the mutilation, or the more times the stomach was pumped, the more likely the person is to commit suicide.

C. Family History

Ask if any family members have a history of depression or Bipolar Disorder. (There is a genetic link to depression and suicide that can be passed down in family members.) Ask if any other family member has attempted or committed suicide. If there are suicides among family members, then the chances of your client committing suicide are higher.

D. Method

It is important to determine if the person has a plan of how they intend to commit suicide. If the client says that he or she is going to commit suicide and is carrying around fifty sleeping pills, you ask to see the pills and then try to talk the person out of taking the pills. Next, try to persuade the person to go to the hospital for his or her own protection. Clients that choose more lethal methods, such as firearms or explosives, are usually more serious about suicide. The counselor must listen closely and try to determine the seriousness of the intent. If it is clear the person wants to die and refuses further help or will not voluntarily go to the hospital, it is imperative to notify the client's family.

8. Duty to Report

Professionals who are aware that a minor or an elderly person is being harmed or at risk for abuse have a legal obligation to report to the authorities. This is true even if you seriously <u>suspect</u> that a child or an elderly person is being abused. It is best to err on the side of caution than never to report and later discover that your suspicions were correct. In these cases, **if you know something, say something.**

The HIPAA laws and most state laws also require that you report any cases of child abuse and the child agency will decide whether to investigate or prosecute. Know the statutes of your state. Generally, states are becoming stricter in the laws that pertain to child abuse. All states legally require counselors to report any cases of suspected or known abuse or neglect to the appropriate authorities. Often what constitutes child abuse is again a problem of interpretation. If the child tells you that he or she has been abused, it is best to question the child carefully before jumping to conclusions. In one case, a nine-year-old told school personnel that she was abused by her father. The girl noticed that an abused girl on a television drama had gotten quite a lot of attention. As a result, the girl concluded that saying that she too was abused by her angry father would be a good way to get attention. The result was that the father was arrested until the truth of the case was revealed. The current caution that the authorities and agencies are taking in the cases of child abuse, however, is usually justified because of the terrible abuses that have happened and have previously gone unreported. Historically, children were looked upon as more the property of parents than individuals with rights. If you know of a case of child abuse and have checked it out with your supervisor and/or colleagues, you are required to report it. This is especially essential if the incident happened recently or is likely to happen again.

9. Conflicts with Institutions

At times, institutions, such as schools, have policies with which a counselor may disagree. For example, if the student confesses that she is using drugs, or is pregnant, the counselor may be required to inform the student's parents. Obviously, this can radically interfere with confidentiality. There are many sides to this argument. Some counselors say that students will not talk to them, because they do not trust them, because of breaches of confidentiality in the past. The school administration and the parents demand to know if the student has a problem. Generally, it is best to follow the policy of the institution where you work, while also knowing and complying with federal and state guidelines. Counselors can make serious ethical and legal errors and later discover the ramifications of some of their inappropriate decisions or actions.

In conclusion, we live in an age where individuals who succeed by dishonest means are sometimes admired and seen as role models. While we must adhere to the ethical standards of the profession, and conform to legal dictates of society, there must be a commitment to a personal standard of conduct that transcends professional and legal requirements. Holding oneself to a higher standard of conduct than that required by state and secular organizations will make you a champion on multiple levels. **Be true to yourself as you excel in your conduct before God and people.**

References

APA Code of Ethics: //http://www.apa.org/ethics.

Ethical standards. (2019). American Personnel and Guidance Association. Washington, D.C.

Ethical standards of psychologists. (2019). American Psychological Association. Washington, D.C.

Corey, G., Corey, M., and Callanan, P. (2017*). Professional and ethical issues in counseling and psychotherapy.* Monterey, CA.: Brooks/Cole.

Fretz, B., and Mills, D. (1980) *Licensing and certification of psychologists and counselors.* San Francisco: Jossey-Bass.

Welch, Bryant. (1999). *Boundary violations in the eye of the beholder insight.* Amityville, NY: American Professional Agency, Inc.

Study Questions

For each question discuss the best ethical alternatives.

1. What do you believe is the most important ethical issue in therapy? Support your answer.
2. A client expresses that she is in love with you and wants to marry you. How would you handle this situation?
3. Your client is so pleased with the results of the therapy that he hands you a check for $5000 extra and insists that you keep it. What are you to do?
4. A client invites you to his home to meet his wife and have a drink. What would you do?
5. In what situations would you clearly break confidentiality?
6. A client comes to you with severe sexual problems. How would you handle this situation?
7. A twelve-year old girl confesses that her uncle has sexually molested her. She pleads with you not to tell her mother. What would you do?
8. A twenty-five year old woman tells you that her father molested her on many occasions when she was a preteen. What would you do?
9. Just as he is leaving your office, a client tells you that he is going to commit suicide. What do you do?
10. A female client says that she is going to kill her ex-boyfriend and that she has the loaded gun in her purse. What would you do?
11. One of your manipulative clients tells your supervisor that you had sex with him/her. What do you do?
12. What situations of child abuse should be reported to authorities?
13. Under what conditions would you terminate therapy with a client?
14. What is your view on counseling friends?
15. In counseling, to whom do you believe is your primary responsibility?
16. Under what conditions would you refer a client to another professional?
17. What is your primary motivation as a counselor?
18. Your supervisor asks you to report that several clients have been attending sessions with you, when they have not. What would you do?
19. Your supervisor wants you to record a session with a client. What would you do?
20. What is a boundary issue? Name some important boundary violation problems.
21. What kind of counter transference can a counselor displace to a client?
22. Describe how to do a Homicide Assessment.
23. Describe how to do a Suicide Assessment.
24. Explain how the personal needs of a counselor can interfere with a client's boundaries. What makes you believe you can effectively counsel others?

CHAPTER THREE

PSYCHOANALYSIS

The school of Psychoanalysis was founded by an Austrian physician named Sigmund Freud (1856–1939). As a doctor, Freud noticed that most of his clients' physical symptoms could not be explained by underlying organic pathologies. Hysteria is one of those illnesses in which that is true. Hysteria is an illness where the person shows the symptoms of a physical disorder (blindness, paralysis, deafness, loss of skin sensation) but the underlying organic pathology is not found. Freud studied hypnosis and he found that he could eliminate many people's hysterical symptoms by using hypnosis.

Later, however, Freud became dissatisfied with the use of hypnosis because he believed it did not get to the root of a person's problem. Not everyone can be hypnotized and cured, and some clients would develop other types of problems. Just before the turn of the last century Freud met another physician named Joseph Breuer who helped a client (Anna O.) overcome a hysterical paralysis of her arm by using the method of catharsis, or what they called the "talking cure." In her sessions with Dr. Breuer, Anna would talk about her psychological conflicts and eventually her paralysis disappeared. Freud developed this talking approach into what he later called his method of free association. Throughout his searching for the causes of hysteria and other related disorders, Freud became convinced of the tremendous influence of the unconscious mind in developing psychological disorders.

FREUD'S PSYCHODYNAMIC THEORY

In 1900 Freud wrote *The Interpretation of Dreams*. In this first book Freud emphasized the importance of the unconscious. He discussed that the easiest way to gaze into the unconscious was to have people relate their dreams. There are two types of dream content. The manifest content is what the dreamer remembers (a monster chased him down the street) and the latent content is what the dream really means (the monster might symbolize the client's authoritarian father.)

Freud divides the mind into three parts: the conscious, the preconscious, and the unconscious. The conscious mind is our center of awareness and the unconscious is from where all of our basic primitive drives, or instincts, come. Also, in the unconscious are repressed thoughts, feelings and memories that the person found anxiety arousing and therefore pushed or repressed them into the unconscious. In essence the person forgets this repressed material.

The preconscious mind is the boundary between the conscious and the unconscious minds. Thoughts, feeling and memories that are pushed into the preconscious mind are said to be suppressed. Suppressed materials can be retrieved at any time. Sometimes materials will slip from the preconscious to the unconscious and this material then becomes repressed. As a result, it is less harmful to suppress than to repress.

Later, Freud postulated three other parts of the personality. The first he called the id; it is the part of the personality that is inborn. After id, the ego and the superego develop. The ego and superego are learned.

THE ID

Freud said that the id is totally unconscious. Since a child is born with an id, to understand the characteristics of the id, one should look at the behaviors of small children. Children are selfish and put their own needs above the needs of others. Freud used the philosophical theory of hedonism to explain that the id works under the pleasure principle meaning that the id wants the greatest amount of pleasure and the least amount of pain. The id is very selfish, narcissistic, and amoral. Obviously, the id is unsocialized.

Freud said the id has feelings of omnipotence—that is, the id (child) believes that it is superior to others. Therefore, Freud explains that inferiority feelings and unselfish feelings are learned and are not from the id. The pleasure principle is the most important principle in the primary process.

The id is a reservoir of psychic energy which means it contains all of our basic or primary drives (instincts). These drives, such as hunger, thirst, sexual drives, and even reflexes, come out of the id.

Another significant characteristic of the id is not only does it not know reality, but it cannot make the distinction between fantasy and reality. This concept is important because people constantly project their feelings onto others often with disastrous results. For example, instead of saying, "I am mad at you," one might say, "You make me mad." The anger is within the person but one thinks the other person is the cause of her or his anger. Freud said this type of giving in to the id is very dangerous and distorts a person's understanding of reality.

THE EGO

The ego is the executive of the personality. The ego is located in the conscious and the preconscious, and has its roots in the unconscious mind. It works on the reality principle. It is concerned with satisfying the id in reality. This reality principle is the most important principle in the secondary process. Like the id, the ego is also amoral. It is not concerned with morality but is only concerned about real consequences and it learns these consequences from real life situations. (You steal something, you can get caught and you can get punished.)

Because the superego is the part of the personality that is concerned with morality, the person that has only an id and ego is called a psychopathic personality, an antisocial personality, or a sociopath. These individuals are not mentally ill; they are morally ill. Generally antisocial personalities are not found in mental hospitals, but in jails. As people grow their egos should mature from learning about the world. Generally, people identify more with their ego than any other part of their personality.

THE SUPEREGO

The superego is the internalized parent that every socialized person possesses and is the part of the personality concerned with developing morality. The superego, like the ego, is located in all three parts of the mind (conscious, preconscious and unconscious.) The morality of the superego may have little to do with society's standards and more to do with the conditioning and influence of parents or other role models on an individual. For example, although brushing one's teeth in the morning may have little to do with morality and more to do with hygiene and conditioning, often a person that forgets to brush his or her teeth may feel guilt (sometimes disguised as the fear of bad breath) and be very uncomfortable until able to brush them.

The superego is divided into two parts: the ego ideal and the conscience. The ego ideal is the part of the personality that tells a person when one has done something morally right. It can also reward the individual. In other words, the ego ideal contains the "thou shalts." It may tell the person that one should always be honest, kind, considerate, and unselfish. As a child when we did something that our parents labeled as morally right, they might have rewarded us with a hug or some other type of positive reward. The rewards then became internalized into our ego ideal. Even though our parents may be gone, when we do something that our ego ideal says is morally right, we still feel good. Along with feeling good, our ego ideal might reward us by even pleasing ourselves outright, i.e. buy ourselves something.

The conscience is the other side of the moral coin. The conscience is on a continuum from the ego ideal, in that for every "thou shalt" there is a "thou shalt not." The conscience tells us when we have done something morally wrong and it can also punish us. The most common form of punishment from the conscience is guilt. When we were young and we did something that our parents labeled as morally wrong, they punished us (withdrew love, spanked, or sent us to our rooms.) Today when we do something that we have been taught is morally wrong, we feel guilt. Many times, however, we many not want to accept our conditioning and realize that we feel guilty. We might then repress the guilt and rationalize that we don't feel poorly about what we have done.

Freud believes that unconscious guilt can punish more than conscious guilt. Some of the unconscious punishments from the conscience are mental illness (especially depression), inferiority feelings, accidents, mistakes, and physical ailments. The conscience can act powerfully and irrationally even to the extent of getting a person so depressed that one might commit suicide. With understanding the functioning of the conscience better, much mental illness can be eliminated.

ANXIETY

Anxiety is the reason why people have nervous breakdowns, abuse drugs, fight with others, and do other neurotic things. Generally speaking, Freud looked at anxiety as a signal that repressed thoughts, feelings and memories are trying to become conscious. The goal of the therapist is to help the person become conscious of as much repressed material as possible in order for the person's anxiety level to be reduced. Freud identified three types of anxiety.

REALITY ANXIETY

Fear is the same thing as reality anxiety. If a dog were to ferociously attack and bite you, you would be afraid and the fear would be very appropriate. This is reality anxiety. This type of anxiety has nothing to do with repressed feelings. However, most of our internal fears are interpreted as being reality anxiety, when in fact, they are really moral or neurotic anxiety.

NEUROTIC ANXIETY

This anxiety is fear of the id. At one time or another everyone experiences "wicked thoughts and feelings" (the most common being sexual or aggressive) that they fear will get out of control. Often people have the feelings so repressed that they do not even know what the impulse is that they are having; all they know is that they are anxious and afraid of losing control.

MORAL ANXIETY

Another term for moral anxiety is guilt. This is fear of the conscience. The person may not realize that he or she is suffering from unconscious guilt and think that something in the external world is causing the pain rather than one's own moral anxiety. However, because of the id's and the conscience's inability to make the distinction between fantasy and reality, people believe that they are suffering from reality anxiety when in fact they are suffering from moral and/or neurotic anxiety.

THE EGO DEFENSE MECHANISMS

Ego defense mechanisms are mechanisms that everyone uses unconsciously to reduce anxiety. Just like a person might drink alcohol to reduce anxiety, everyone uses defense mechanisms to do the same. Even though defense mechanisms may reduce anxiety, in the long run they distort reality and, in fact, aid in the repression of more feelings, which over time causes an increase in anxiety. As a result, defense mechanisms are not healthy. Generally, it would seem that the more mentally ill the individual, the more a person uses defense mechanisms.

REPRESSION

Repression is the most common defensive mechanism, and it involves pushing anxiety arousing thoughts, feelings and memories into the unconscious mind. The goal of psychoanalysis is to bring these repressed materials back into consciousness, thereby reducing anxiety. Be aware that all (with the possible exception of suppression) defense mechanisms work unconsciously; therefore, people don't know they are using them.

SUPPRESSION

Suppression is the healthiest defense mechanism because it can be performed consciously. Suppression happens when a person pushes thoughts, feelings and memories into the preconscious mind. Suppressed materials can be retrieved at any time. If you have a dentist appointment today and I ask if you have one, you will deny it if you have repressed that fact, but you will remember it if you have suppressed it.

REACTION FORMATION

This mechanism happens when a person tries to reduce anxiety by acting the opposite of the way she or he may really feel. A person that feels inferior in social situations may try to over compensate by acting superior to others. This mechanism is active in many types of prejudice.

DISPLACEMENT

In displacement the person tries to reduce anxiety by redirecting the feelings from a goal or object that is thwarted or blocked to one that is safer and more attainable. In the case of displaced aggression, the person may want to hit the boss, but instead goes home full of feelings and kicks the dog. In the case of love, a little boy may have love feelings toward his mother, but because this mother won't marry him, he represses the feelings and later finds a girl just like Mommy to marry.

SUBLIMATION

Sublimation is a type of displacement, but not all displacements are sublimations. Freud gave the example of Leonardo DaVinci, the famous painter, who did not have a mother. Because he sublimated his intense longing to have one, he spent much time painting Madonnas. He displaced those longing feelings onto his paintings. Note however that sublimations are not fully constructive because as with other defense mechanisms, sublimation works unconsciously. The person may not be not aware that he or she is sublimating.

PROJECTION

This is undoubtedly the most dangerous defense mechanism. Projection is a way of reducing anxiety by perceiving one's own unacceptable feelings onto others. For instance, a boy may hate his father but represses the feelings because he is afraid of him, and then may project the hostility for his father by saying, "Daddy, you hate me!" Often a person who commits murder explains that it was simply done in self-defense.

RATIONALIZATION

This is a way of reducing anxiety by giving false or at least partly false excuses for one's conduct. In other words, it is false self-justification. Someone might steal something from work and then rationalize that it was justified because the person didn't get the perceived deserved raise.

REGRESSION

Regression is a way of reducing anxiety by acting childish. A person that can't have one's own way may have a childish temper tantrum. In a psychiatric hospital there are wards where they keep "severely regressed" patients. In these wards many of the clients are not toilet trained and may eat with the fingers just like little children.

FANTASY

Sometimes a person will try to reduce anxiety by substituting fantasy for reality. There is nothing wrong with <u>fantasizing</u> occasionally, but when a person starts believing these fantasies and substituting them for realty, then one could develop severe psychological problems. One of the characteristics of schizophrenia is that the person substitutes fantasy for reality. For example, a male paranoid schizophrenic may believe that he is God.

DENIAL

This is similar to repression, but an aspect of the reality of the situation is ignored. People in southern California know that a devastating earthquake is inevitable but the real estate prices right over the faults are just as high as other places. Denial is probably the biggest mechanism with alcoholics. They may know they drink in excess but refuse to believe that they have a problem and explain that they can stop at any time.

TECHNIQUES OF PSYCHOANALYSIS

FREE ASSOCIATION

The belief behind free association is that we all censure what we say because we are afraid of facing our repressed materials. In this way we carefully, but unconsciously, avoid the real painful issues in our life. Because in Freudian psychoanalysis relaxation is so important, the client usually lays on a couch. With free association the person relaxes and talks about whatever comes into his or her mind. One is encouraged to say anything, no matter how embarrassing or painful. The theory is that eventually the unconscious will become clean of repressed feelings and the person's anxiety level will then be lowered.

Freud looked at repressions like balloons held under water. It takes physical and psychological tension or pressure to keep repressed materials unconscious and as soon as the tension is relaxed, the repressed materials automatically surface. That is why relaxation is stressed. As soon as the person learns to relax, the door to the unconscious opens and repressed materials surface.

DREAM ANALYSIS

Freud called dreams "the royal road to the unconscious." He believed that dreams are the quickest way to find out what is going on in the unconscious mind. There are two types of content to a dream. The first is the dream's manifest content, which is what the dreamer remembers. Take the example of a witch chasing someone down the street. This manifest content points symbolically to hidden meanings or to the latent content of the dream. The latent content is what the dream really means. In this case, the witch could be the negative memories the person has toward his or her mother.

ANALYSIS OF RESISTANCE

Often when a person comes close to remembering a painful repression, he or she might use defense mechanisms or evasive tactics (come late to a session, change the subject or not talk about certain subjects) so that the painful material doesn't have to be faced. It is important for a therapist to be aware of such tactics in order to encourage the client to recognize these resistances and to learn to let one's guard down and to accept the painful issues.

ANALYSIS OF TRANSFERENCE

Often a client may feel toward the therapist the way he or she has felt toward some significant person, such as a parent. The person will displace the feelings toward someone from the past onto the therapist. If the historical person was rejecting, the transference onto the therapist could be a healing process in which the client works through this problem and comes to a better understanding of feelings and helps resolve this internal conflict.

Freud believed that it is important to understand that a therapist also brings conflicts and repressions to the therapy session and that therapists can transfer their feelings onto the client. This counter transference, as Freud called it, can interfere with the therapy of the client. This is why Freud recommended that every psychoanalyst should also undergo psychoanalytical therapy.

Newer psychodynamic therapists have infused more vigor and vitality into Freud's ideas. Because psychoanalysis is often viewed as a long-term investment, the newer analysts have developed Brief Psychodynamic

Therapy, or BPT (Messer and Warren 2001). BPT is becoming more popular and is starting to put more emphasis on developing a closer therapeutic alliance between client and therapist. Additionally, BPT is putting an emphasis on positive therapeutic outcomes, making therapy more economical, and having shorter time limits. Another improvement is that they are working on developing new treatments for different psychological disorders.

A CHRISTIAN PERSPECTIVE OF PSYCHOANALYSIS

Every American psychologist has been substantially affected by the influence of Psychoanalysis. There is much about the functioning of the human mind that can be construed from Freud's theories, including his conceptions of the Conscious, Preconscious, and Unconscious, and his Ego Defense Mechanisms. On the other hand, Christians and others object to his ideas for numerous reasons:

1. Freud rejected any idea of a supernatural realm and a belief in God.
2. Freud depicted the prime motivation of the id as sexual.
3. Freud strongly objected to people, including Adler and Jung, who criticized his work or suggested other alternatives to his ideas.
4. There is no clearly articulated ethical system presented in Psychoanalysis. Jones and Butman quoted Vitz, "Psychoanalysis is essentially an agnostic or atheistic system, since religion is treated as an illusion. Genuine religious motivation and the spiritual life are ignored or treated negatively in psychoanalysis." (1991 p.77)
5. Vitz also documented that Freud dabbled in the occult. It is insinuated by Christian counselors that people have lost their faith in Jesus Christ after studying the writings of Freud. As a result, numerous Christian psychologists totally disregard the teachings of Freud. He does, however, give us some insight into the mechanics of the human psyche. The Christian counselor must remain careful to test Freud's ideas against the teachings of the Bible.

References

Brenner, C. (1955). *An Elementary textbook of psychoanalysis.* New York: Doubleday.

Browning, D. (1987). *Religious thought and the modern psychologies.* Philadelphia: Fortress Press.

Freud, S. (1949). *An outline of psychoanalysis.* J. Starchey, trans. New York: W.W. Norton.

Freud, S. (1952). *An autobiographical study.* J. Starchy, trans. New York: W.W. Norton.

Freud, S. (1962). *The ego and the id.* J. Rieviere, trans. New York: W.W. Norton.

Freud, S. (1965). *The interpretation of dreams.* J. Starchy, trans. New York: Avon Books.

Freud, S. (1977). *Five lectures in psychoanalysis.* J. Starchey, trans. New York: W.W. Norton.

Jones, S., & Butman, R. (1991). *Modern psychotherapies: A comprehensive Christian appraisal.* Downer's Grove, IL.: InterVarsity Press.

Hall, C. (1955). *A primer of Freudian psychology.* New York: The American Library. Hurding, R. (1985). *Roots and shoots.* London: Hodder and Stroughton.

Messer, S.B., and Warren, C.S. (2001). Brief psychodynamic therapy. in R. Corsini (Ed.) *Handbook of Innovative Therapies.* New York: Wiley, 67–85.

Vitz, P. (1988). *Sigmund Freud's Christian unconscious.* New York: Guilford.

Study Questions

1. Fill in the blanks with the correct answers.

   a. What a dream really means is called the dream's _____ content.
   b. What the dreamer remembers is called the dream's _____ content.
   c. The most commonly used defense mechanism is called _____.
   d. The most dangerous defense mechanism is called _____.
   e. Acting the opposite of the way you really feel is _____.
   f. A man acts childish whenever he is frustrated. This defense mechanism is called _____.
   g. _____ is the most selfish and narcissistic part of the Freudian personality.
   h. The _____ is called the executive personality.
   i. The _____ is referred to as our internalized parents.
   j. The _____ and the _____ _____ are parts of the superego.
   k. The _____ and the _____ cannot make the distinction between fantasy and reality.
   l. The _____ lives in fantasy.
   m. Freud called _____ the "royal road to the unconscious."
   n. When a person relaxes and talks about whatever comes into his mind, this is called _____ _____.
   o. The feelings a client displaces onto the therapist is called _____.
   p. The feelings a therapist displaces onto a client is called _____.
   q. A client is reluctant to talk about a certain topic and changes the subject whenever he comes close to that topic. Freud calls this defensiveness _____.
   r. A man is on a date and has anxiety because he is afraid of the urge that he will rape his date. This is called _____ anxiety.
   s. A child steals money from his mother but his mother is not likely to find out. Still the child feels badly about it. The child is feeling _____.
   t. A little boy is afraid of a bully at school who keeps picking on him. The boy is afraid of _____ anxiety.

Answer each of the following questions in about 200 words.

2.   What is anxiety? Identify and explain each of the three types of anxiety. Give an example of each.
3.   What is a defense mechanism? Name and define seven defense mechanisms. Give an example of each.
4.   Explain the basic components of Freudian Psychoanalytic Therapy. Include the conscious, preconscious, unconscious, ID, EGO and SUPERGO and discuss how they are interrelated.
5.   List 4 defense mechanisms that you use the most and explain when you use them.
6.   Name 3 situations that make you the most anxious and try to explain what repressions are behind the anxiety.
7.   Try to remember a dream. Try to interpret its unconscious message.

CHAPTER FOUR

INDIVIDUAL PSYCHOTHERAPY

Alfred Adler (1870–1937) was the founder of the school of Individual Psychology. Adler, who lived outside of Vienna, Austria, was very sickly as a child, and at three witnessed the death of his brother. Even though he struggled in school in his early years, Adler overcame his circumstances to become a medical doctor. Both his early experiences and Freudian concepts influenced his ideas about psychotherapy. However, unlike Freud who stressed biology, and the sexual basis of many psychological disorders, Adler stressed conscious influences, rather than unconscious ones. Where Freud stressed the past experiences as being most important (an approach called <u>determinism</u>), Adler saw humans as having future looking, goal directed, purposeful behaviors. The therapist that uses this approach is using a <u>teleological approach</u>. In Freud's therapy, the psychoanalyst tends to look upon his or her role as more parental, but in Individual Psychology, the therapist views him or herself as an equal and not as superior to the client.

BASIC INFERIORITY AND STRIVING FOR SUPERIORITY

Inferiority feelings, Adler postulates, are at the bottom of much of human striving. Adler believes that we all possess inferiority feelings and the root of these feelings grows out of childhood. As children we are helpless and know very little about reality. We are physically small and more at the whim of environmental forces. Because of these inept and helpless feelings as children, we all develop anxiety arousing <u>inferiority feelings</u>. As a result, many people try to find some way to <u>compensate</u>, or overcome, their inferiority feelings.

In compensating the person finds one's own way to <u>strive for superiority</u>. In this striving for superiority the person seeks to be more powerful, more perfect, and more complete. In Adlerian analysis the therapist helps clients explore their inferiority feelings and to try to find the unique ways in which they can strive for superiority.

In his own life, Adler became a doctor, possibly because of his brother's death, and because of his own sickness. Teddy Roosevelt is another example of someone striving for superiority. As a child Roosevelt was also very sickly, however, he went on to not only overcome his illnesses, but also to become a famous soldier and President. Other examples include runner Wilma Rudolph and swimmer Mark Spitz. Both these athletes had polio as children, overcame their handicaps, excelled in their sports, and won numerous medals in the Olympic games.

STYLE OF LIFE

Adler call the individualized way people develop views of life as one's style of life. People have a unique style of life that depends partly on the way they chose to understand the experiences they have had. Through examining the person's style of life and goals, a person can develop insight into his or her personality and readjust this style of life to be more socially effective.

Adlerian therapy is generally interactive. The client usually sits in a chair facing the therapist and at times the therapist can use confrontation. Similar to the more modern cognitive behavioral therapies, Adlerian therapy examines the person's thinking and helps the client find more constructive ways in which to view and work in the world.

Like Adler, who overcame the challenges of his early beginnings and dedicated his life to use the disadvantages of his past to influence the growth and development of others, you too need not be hindered by setbacks in your childhood or at any stage of your life. Learn from your challenges and perhaps you too could write the next theory birthed from the challenging circumstances of your life.

A CHRISTIAN VIEW OF INDIVIDUAL PSYCHOLOGY

Adler was a believer in individual choice and his therapy was short-termed and quite directive. Adler was an adult convert from Judaism to liberal Protestantism and perhaps leaned toward socialistic Protestant views.

"Few psychologists disagree with Adler because we all grow up from helpless and unknowing beginnings, we do develop inferiority feelings and most people do struggle to overcome these universal feelings (compensation). Adler looked at "neurotic symptoms" as protecting people from having to struggle with their discouragement, as they can passively wait for the problems to dissipate, or can search for someone to cure them. They can protect their fragile self-esteem by not demanding much of themselves while they are thus indisposed." (Jones, pp. 242–243)

Jones further explains that there is "compatibility between Christianity and Individual Psychology. In Adler, we find an approach that respects human responsibility, rationality, individuality, social inter-connectedness and capacities for change." (p, 243)

While Adler's ideas are helpful, insightful and anxiety reducing, they do not provide for eternity. If you are looking for a Savior named Jesus, to whom you can surrender and who died on the cross for your sins, you won't find that in Adlerian Psychology.

References

Adler, A. (1963). *The practice and theory of individual psychology*. P. Radin, trans. Paterson, NJ: Littlefield, Adams & Co.

Adler, A. (1958). *What a life should mean to you*. New York: Capricorn.

Adler, A. (1964). *Social interest: A challenge to mankind*. New York: Capricorn.

Brink, (1977). Adlerian theory and pastoral counseling. *Journal of Psychology and Theology*, 5. 143–149.

Corey, G. (1986). *Theory and Practice of Counseling and Psychotherapy* (*3rd ed.)* Monterey, CA: Brooks/Cole.

Jones, S., & Butman, R. (1991). *Modern Psychotherapies: A comprehensive Christian appraisal*. Downer's Grove, IL: InterVarsity Press.

Study Questions

1. Fill in the blanks with the correct answer.

    a. Adler believed that the future is more important than the past. A person that uses this approach is said to use a _____ approach.
    b. Adler said that we all develop feelings from our childhood that we later overcome. These feelings are called _____ feelings.
    c. The unique way each person overcomes inferiority feelings is called _____ for _____.
    d. Everyone develops a unique way of dealing with life. This Adler calls _____ of _____.
    e. The mechanism by which a person overcomes inferiority feelings is called _____.

2. Examine your own life. In what areas you have developed inferiority feelings?
3. How have you compensated and in what areas have you striven for superiority?

CHAPTER FIVE

ANALYTIC PSYCHOLOGY

Carl Gustav Jung (1875–1961), like Adler, was a follower of Freud. Also, like Adler and Freud, he was a medical doctor and psychiatrist. Freud, impressed by Jung's personality and knowledge, appointed Jung head of Freud's Psychoanalytic Congress. Later, Jung, like Adler, broke from Freud's teachings partly because he believed that Freud stressed the role of sexuality in neurosis too heavily.

Jung, the son of a Protestant minister, throughout his life maintained his religious faith. However, at the same time Jung traveled all over the world to study other cultures and religions, especially Hinduism and Buddhism, in order to understand them in relation to the unconscious mind.

Jung is quoted as saying, "My life is a story of the self-realization of the unconscious." Jung never tried to over systematize what he had learned; he realized that learning and life were extremely complex and very open ended. Jung consistently developed new ideas and new insights.

JUNG'S CONCEPTIONS OF THE PERSONALITY

Jung divides the personality into three parts.

1. The conscious mind
2. The personal unconscious mind
3. The collective unconscious mind

Like Freud, Jung perceives the unconscious mind as the most important part of the mind. However, Jung's conceptions of the unconscious are very different from Freud's view of the unconscious.

THE CONSCIOUS MIND AND THE EGO

Jung uses the terms <u>conscious mind</u> and ego almost synonymously. The conscious mind is a small part of the mind but the part that the average person identifies with and consists of our awareness of the outside world. Jung believes that the conscious mind is in existence from birth and that it grows daily from everyday experiences. When the average person in society says "I" or "me," Jung says one is referring to the ego. The ego is the gate keeper to the conscious mind and it keeps unwanted thoughts, feelings and memories out of consciousness. In this way the conscious mind is not overwhelmed by the complex and varied processes of the unconscious.

THE PERSONAL UNCONSCIOUS MIND

The personal unconscious is the part of the mind that contains both thoughts, feelings and memories that have been suppressed, repressed, forgotten, ignored, and also materials that are too weak to make a conscious impression. By the use of the word "personal" Jung means that it is private to the individual. This differentiates it from the collective unconscious. The collective unconscious is the foundation of the personality and contains universal elements found in all humans. In the personal unconscious mind are located what Jung calls complexes. A <u>complex</u> is a <u>group or constellation of thoughts, feelings, and memories that are associated around a basic theme</u>. Even though complexes are in the collective unconscious, there is one that is mainly conscious, called the ego. The ego's roots are in the collective unconscious and the theme of the ego is centered on the "I" identity. Just like the ego, the unconscious complexes can become so large and powerful that they can become little personalities in their own right. The roots of all complexes go through the personal unconscious and into the collective unconscious.

THE COLLECTIVE UNCONSCIOUS MIND

The collective unconscious mind is the foundation of the personality. Just like the Freudian id, the collective unconscious is inborn and unlearned. Where Freud used the term instincts (drives) to describe the inner forces of the id, Jung used the term <u>archetypes</u> to describe the workings of the collective unconscious. Jung refers to archetypes as being prepotentials in the personality. Just like a person is born with the "knowledge" or ability to have a hunger drive or sex drive or sucking reflex, so an archetype is the <u>prepotential</u>, or potential knowledge, with which a person is born. While a baby in its mother's womb is floating in a liquid, that neonate is developing lungs with the prepotential to be able to breath air. In a like manner Jung believes that down through the generations people have developed inborn prepotentials that become deeply ingrained into the personality. Think of archetypes as the foundation of a building, and complexes as the structure built upon that foundation. For every complex there is an archetype underneath.

Jung looked at humans as spiritual as well as physical beings. Jung believed that the symbols of a culture were expressions of the collective unconscious. He constantly looked for commonalities in all cultures and religions. One universal symbol he found was the circle, which is called the <u>mandala</u>. Jung believed that circular symbols represented a person's striving for unity or self-actualization.

COMPLEX ARCHETYPES

Other complex archetypes, besides the ego, are the:

1. PERSONA
2. SHADOW
3. ANIMA-ANIMUS
4. SELF

These complexes are also archetypes because they are universal in all cultures. The complexes are unique to each person because of individual personal experiences. The persona, shadow or anima-animus are unconscious in the average person. The self-complex is the only archetype that has not been developed in most people because it has to do with the integration of the other three complexes.

1. PERSONA

The theatrical masks worn by actors in ancient times were called in Latin "personae." In Jung's use, the persona is the face we show the world, or the social mask we adopt. It is determined largely by the special roles we play. Such social roles are heavily based on social expectations and customs and are essential for social living.

However, when the ego identifies too strongly with the persona, the individual becomes more involved in the role he or she is playing rather than being one's real self. The person becomes phony and simply reflects the expectations of others. This identification with the persona eventually means loss of individuality and not being true to oneself. A person can lose individuality by only doing what is pleasing to others.

There are two reasons why a person develops a persona: acceptance and protection. Jung explains that everyone wants to be liked, appreciated and needed by others; therefore, people act in ways that are pleasing or accepting to others. Protection is the second function of the persona; it helps the person hide vulnerable feelings and secrets behind this mask so that others cannot see the hurt and fear inside. The person that has a "boiler plate" persona does not know how he or she really feels inside because feelings are so deeply repressed. Likewise, a person that has a "thick" persona is incapable of intimacy.

2. SHADOW

The shadow is the animal part of human nature. It is repressed because it can act very unsocialized. Jung says that the shadow can be the source of great creativity or it can simply be a demon that haunts the personality. Jung calls it the shadow because it hides behind the persona, literally in the "shadows" of the persona. People hide their shadow because they fear others will reject them if they show their raw, "wicked," primitive nature. Just as most people are unaware of their persona, people are also oblivious of their shadow. Because the principle of compensation is active in Jung's conceptions of the personality (Jung's conception of compensation is similar to Adler's), the stronger the repressions of the shadow, the more the persona will attempt to compensate and will act the opposite of the feelings of the shadow.

Convicted murderers are some of the nicest individuals in the prison population. Many of these people do not realize that they are repressing materials into their personal unconscious and making their shadow stronger until it builds up enough strength to overcome the ego.

3. ANIMA-ANIMUS

Jung viewed humans as bisexual; both the male and the female secrete both male and female hormones. On a psychological level as well, both sexes manifest masculine and feminine aspects of their personality. This happens because one identifies with and models one's self after individuals of the opposite sex as well as people of the same sex. Generally, people, particularly men, repress the identifications with individuals of the opposite sex because they believe that it will make them more likely to become homosexual.

Each female has her animus and every male has his anima. The anima and animus are archetypes that stem from the collective experiences of man and woman living together throughout thousands of generations. These complexes are complexes because everyone lives and is influenced by individuals of the opposite sex.

There is a saying that states: <u>Most men spend most of their time trying to prove something that is obvious</u>. This can be observed in the male <u>machismo</u> of the Latin culture, but is also evident in most other societies. Many believe that the anima may be man's biggest hang up and why some men are sexually addicted, have to be in control, or in other ways feel compelled to <u>prove their identity</u> when it is so obvious.

When a man is aware of the nature of his anima, but incorrectly assumes that it is the totality of his personality, he may become homosexual. The same is true of a woman who over identifies with her animus.

There are distinct advantages for persons to be aware of their anima-animus. Jung explains that when a man is aware of the true nature of his anima, it helps him to be more creative and to understand and relate to women better; likewise, when a woman integrates her animus into her personality, it helps her understand and relate to males better. The price of not realizing one's complexes consists of numerous psychological and interpersonal problems.

4. SELF COMPLEX ARCHETYPE

Jung's conception of the <u>self</u> is quite different from other conceptions. Jung's self is something that most people in society have not achieved and will never achieve. While a person is born with an archetype or pre-potential to develop a self, Jung believes most people never achieve the <u>self-complex.</u> Attaining the self comes through integration of the personality. By integrating the personality, Jung means that the person must become conscious of the persona, the shadow and any other complexes that have been developed in life.

In attaining the self, the person's ego must realize that it has company and that it is only a small part of the personality. The ego must then "move over" as the conscious mind expands to accommodate the other complexes into the personal unconscious. In integrating the other complexes into the personality, the person gains more maturity and becomes <u>self-actualized</u>. In other words, the person learns to use more of self to find out and live up to his or her potential and become all one can be in this life. This Jung calls the <u>individuation process</u>.

While a person can have multiple complexes, Jung explains that the self-complex is something that is strived for, but is rarely reached on one's own. One of the ways that Jung believes a person can work toward the self is through Analytic Therapy.

JUNGIAN ANALYTIC PSYCHOTHERAPY

Similar to Adler, Jung looks at the therapist as a collaborator and not superior to the client. A Jungian therapist engages the client by recording into a daily log one's thoughts, feelings, experiences, dreams, spiritual experiences, and whatever else the individual deems relevant to record.

One aspect of Analytic Therapy is that a person does not need to have neurotic or psychotic symptoms to enter into therapy; on the contrary, a "normal" person can get "analyzed" and work toward his or her self-actualization issues.

Like Freud, Jung devoted much time to concentrating on dreams. Jung believed that dreams are constantly pointing toward actualization, but that individuals often don't know how to learn from these dreams. A Jungian therapist once had an unhappy female lawyer come for analysis. The woman reported consistently dreaming of watering flowers. The therapist suggested that she find a place where she could water flowers, so she went to a local botanical garden and asked a gardener if she could water the flowers. As she watered the flowers she was caught up in the beauty and excitement of the plant world and was fascinated to learn about and care for plants. She had repressed the desire to be a botanist because she had spent so many years studying to be a lawyer. She could not admit to herself that she hated law. When she went back to school, studied botany, and worked with plants, she found that much of the unhappiness she had suffered disappeared.

Jung's analytic psychology is proof that one can integrate all aspects of our being—spirit, soul and body—into a viable theory and practice within the profession. Be true to who you are. As you ponder how best to utilize your experiences, knowledge and skills to make this a better world, you too can become the next theorist in the field of psychology. Each person is born with talents and gifts. Do not deny your God-given abilities as you seek to work with those in need of positive mental health.

A CHRISTIAN PERSPECTIVE OF ANALYTIC PSYCHOLOGY

"Jung's father was a Protestant minister in the Calvinistic tradition. By his own telling, Jung was pro-foundly affected by his father's vacillating and doubt-filled faith. Jung was also influenced by personal and professional encounters with the occult. His grandmother was a medium, his mother had psychic experi-ences, his medical thesis was on occult phenomena, and he had repeated mysterious encounters with 'spirits' throughout his adult life. He was a serious student of comparative religion, especially Eastern religions and the occult…. Jung seemed to find Christianity useful in promoting the larger quest for meaning, but he clearly did not embrace the cross and the resurrection as historical facts. "(Jones, p. 129)

Because Jung had a deep faith in evolution and world religions, some theologians have accused him of missing the point of creationism. Also because of his research into "Eastern religions" others have accused him of awakening psychology to the inclusion of the beliefs of Eastern religions into psychology.

Authorities also have explained that the study of the complexes is very useful for understanding the per-sonality for a client in psychotherapy. However, in contrast to biblical teaching, Jung had too much "faith" in the human psyche and less faith in the God of the Bible.

References

Browing, D. (1987). *Religious thought and the modern psychologies*. Philadelphia, PA: Fortress.

Bryant, C. (1983). *Jung and the Christian way*. London: Darton, Longman & Todd.

Existential Psychotherapy: http://www.existential-analysis.org.

Hall, C. (1973). *A primer of Jungian psychology*. New York: New American Library Inc.

Jacobi, Jolande. (1959). *Complex, archetype, symbol in the psychology of C.G. Jung*. New York: Pantheon Books.

Jung, C.G. (1963). *Memories, dreams and reflections*. New York: Random House.

Jung, C.G. (1958). *The undiscovered self*. New York: Little, Brown and Co.

Jones, S., and Butman, R. (1991). *Modern psychotherapies*: *A comprehensive Christian approach*. Downer's Grove: IL: InterVarsity Press.

Stein, M. (1985). *Jung's treatment of Christianity*. Wilmette, IL: Chirion.

Study Questions

1. Fill in the correct answer.

    a. The mask that we hide behind Jung calls the _____.
    b. The animal part of the personality is called the_____.
    c. A man over identifies with his _____ and thinks that it is the totality of his personality. This man is in danger of believing he is homosexual.
    d. The prepotentials located in the collective unconscious mind are called _____.
    e. A constellation of thoughts, feelings and memories is called a _____.
    f. The part of the unconscious that is more learned is called the _____ unconscious.
    g. The part of the unconscious that is inborn is called the _____ unconscious.
    h. After a person has matured and fully integrated the unconscious aspects of his or her personality with the conscious parts, the _____ process has occurred.
    i. A person who has fully integrated his or her personality and achieves its potentials has achieved the _____ complex.
    j. When people say "I" or "me," they are referring to their _____.
    k. The _____ complex is located in the conscious mind.
    l. The male part of a female's personality is called the_____.
    m. The complex in your personality that has given you the most anxiety is_____.

CHAPTER SIX

PERSON CENTERED THERAPY

Carl Rogers (1902–1987), an American psychologist, caused controversy in the psychological community when he expounded the belief that the client knows best and that the therapist is no more than a sounding board for the client. Roger's concept of human nature is that people are basically good, and if they are brought up in the proper type of accepting atmosphere, they will learn to do actualizing things with their lives.

Person Centered Therapy or Rogerian therapy is the most <u>nondirective</u> of all of the therapies. In most therapies, therapists are directive to varying degrees as they interpret, give homework, or instruct the client. Rogers, on the other hand, preached that the person knows best and really all a therapist can do is help create a trusting atmosphere, through questioning, where the client feels as if he or she is really heard and understood. Many have lauded Roger's work as being multicultural in focus. His principles have international appeal.

BASIC CONCEPTIONS OF PERSON CENTERED THERAPY

1.   INCONGRUENCE AND CONGRUENCE

Rogers believed that a client enters therapy in a state of incongruence; that is, there is a great discrepancy between the person's self-perception and his or her experience of reality. Put another way, there is a big division between the person's <u>real</u> self-concept and the <u>ideal</u> self-concept. An example of this occurs when a high school student wants to go to Harvard University, but has only average grades in high school.

The goal of therapy is to help the client gain congruence and become more self-accepting. This, however, is the job of the client and not the therapist. In the therapeutic process the client learns to take increasing responsibility for feelings and behaviors. Rogers had such a deep faith in human nature that he believed that the person will ultimately arrive at the best decisions for his or her own life.

2.   UNCONDITIONAL POSITIVE REGARD

Because Rogers believed that the person is far more significant than the problem, he suggested that the relationship the therapist has with the client is very important. Rogers stressed the idea that no matter what the person says, the therapist, should, as much as possible, accept, like, and, refrain from making judgments about the client and what is said.

Implicit in Rogers's ideas seems to be the notion that people develop problems in part because they are judged, rejected and disliked. The unconditional acceptance that the therapist shows toward the client should help to heal the wounds and help the client develop more self-confidence.

3.   EMPATHETIC UNDERSTANDING

While everyone wants to believe that he or she is understood, many people confess in both in life and in therapy that they have never felt understood. For this reason, Rogers stated that it is important for the therapist to set aside his or her own ideas, beliefs, prejudices and preconceptions about the person and become immersed, actively and continuously, in the private world of the client. To do this, therapists give feedback on what they perceive the client is saying or feeling. In this way, the therapist will act as a <u>mirror of feeling</u>. This approach is called <u>reflective listening</u>. To illustrate the therapist reflects as follows:

THERAPIST: What I hear you saying is that you seem to be very sad about the death of your best friend.
CLIENT: Yes, I am sad but I am also angry because she left me all alone.
THERAPIST: I see, you are both angry and sad. Would you like to talk more about this anger?
CLIENT: How could she die and leave me all alone? I have struggled so hard to develop this friendship with her and then she goes and dies.
THERAPIST: Making friends is a very difficult task for you and now you feel lost and alone.
CLIENT: Exactly, and now I don't know what to do…

As seen above, first, the therapist works to understand what the client is saying and then repeats back to the client the underlying meaning being expressed. If the therapist is wrong in the interpretation, the client will correct him or her immediately. In the same example a therapist from another school of thought might confront the client that it is irrational to blame a deceased person, who did not intend to die, for dying. However, implicit in Rogerian Therapy is the assumption that the client will ultimately realize this faulty thinking, and develop on their own, more responsibility for the feelings. The client finally realizes the solution to his or her own problems. The goal of the therapist is to be used as a sounding board.

The following poem demonstrates some of the basic tenets of <u>reflective listening</u> for the suffering person. New counselors often make the mistake of not fully listening and too quickly giving advice to the client.

ON LISTENING

When I ask you to listen to me
and you start by giving advice,
you haven't done what I asked.
When I ask you to listen to me
and you begin to tell me why I shouldn't feel
that way, you are trampling on my feelings.
When I ask you to listen to me
and you feel you have to do something to
solve my problem, you have failed
me, strange as it may seem.
Listen! All I ask is that you listen,
not talk or do… just hear me.
When you can do something for me that
I can do for myself, you
contribute to my fear and inadequacy.
But when you accept as simple fact that
I do feel what I feel, no matter how
irrational, then I can quit trying to
convince you and get about the
business of understanding what's
behind this irrational feeling. And
when that's clear, the answers are
obvious and I don't need advice.
Perhaps that's why prayer works, sometimes for some people…because God is
mute, and He doesn't give advice
or try to fix things. God just listens and
lets you work it out yourself.
So, please listen and just hear me.
And if you want to talk, wait a minute for
your turn, and I'll listen to you.

Ralph Roughton

LIMITATIONS OF PERSON CENTERED THERAPY

If the client wants advice from the therapist, a Rogerian therapist may not be the one to see. When counselors do not listen reflectively and decide what is important in the client's communications, a client can be scared away by the "know it all" who is going to "tell it straight." The overly zealous counselor needs to work from the client's frame of reference and not preach or direct; it is the client that needs to decide to integrate new behaviors and ideas. A counselor can come up with all kinds of alternatives for the client's life, but if the client is resistant to changing those individual aspects then the counselor's urgings will be futile.

Many experienced therapists use a Rogerian approach when they first start seeing a client. This often not only helps the client learn to like and trust the counselor, but also aids in helping to raise the client's self-esteem by having someone really "listen"—without judging. After developing a rapport, in later sessions, the therapist may use other more directive approaches.

Always be aware in the person centered approach that the client is only giving one side of the story. Often people distort reality in their own favor to try to look good, sometimes at the expense of others. Others may use blaming games to make themselves look good and others look poorly. Some clients may try to explain that others are responsible for the misery they suffer. Be clear that the <u>truth</u> can be very different from what the client relates.

There are always at least three sides to each story.

1. your side
2. my side
3. the truth (what really happened)

Often in the telling of one's story, the client will try to lead the counselor to give a certain type of advice, but counselor beware. Sometimes advice can severely backfire, cause conflicts, or, even worse, lawsuits. Therapists should be wary of clients who may try to shift life changing decisions onto the therapist and then hold the therapist responsible for any repercussions from that decision.

CLIENT: My wife constantly disrespects me and she has even hit me. She has turned my friends against me by saying untrue things about me. She even went out and spent most of my paycheck on clothes for herself.
THERAPIST: You seem angry.
CLIENT: You're damn right I'm angry! Wouldn't you be angry? Should I divorce her, should I?
THERAPIST: What do you want to do?
CLIENT: I asked you a question and I want an answer, should I divorce her? I told you about all of the bad things that she does to me. Should I divorce her? Why don't you answer me?
THERAPIST: It seems like you want me to say that you should divorce her…

This example illustrates how an inexperienced counselor may advise that he should divorce his wife, but what the client may not have revealed is that he is an alcoholic and that he has done worse things <u>to</u> his wife. This person might even be more miserable after his divorce and return to blame the therapist for saying that he should have divorced. This illustrates why Rogerian therapists are very careful about not giving advice.

Finally, Rogerian therapy works best with rather verbal, highly intelligent, self-aware individuals, and often is not very effective with those from lower socioeconomic backgrounds, for those with drug abuse, or for those with conduct disorders. These clients generally expect and even demand more directive interactions from the therapist and can get very frustrated when a strictly person centered approach is adhered to. Reflecting on what they are saying is often misunderstood by them and they sometimes think that the therapist is mocking them or parroting back their statements.

In conclusion, Rogers captured the concept of the importance of the individual's self-determination toward good. As a student who desires to work with those facing mental distress, never forget that a person's mental or physical disability does not determine his or her worth. Rogers' concepts can be coined within the Golden Rule: Treat others in the same way you wish others to treat you.

A CHISTIAN PERSPECTIVE OF PERSON CENTERED THERAPY

Person centered therapy assumes that people are basically good and that they are generally trustworthy. When the therapist "reflects back" to clients what they are saying, the clients will grow towards self-understanding and self-actualization.

The Bible says something different. It explains that humans were created innocent but have fallen into sin and self-deception because of Adam and Eve's rebellion. Their sin caused the whole of humanity to fall into sin (Romans 5:12), and now we are all sinful and deceitful, and we desire that which is evil (Galatians 5:17–21). A therapist cannot redeem us; it is through the sacrificing blood of Jesus that we can be saved for eternity, and this is by the work of the Holy Spirit. (2 Corinthians 5:17–21 and Ephesians 4:22–24)

We all need salvation. When we examine Person Centered Therapy it points to "self-actualization," which could mean being selfish and egotistical. The Bible teaches that we need redemption and salvation so that the Holy Spirit can come into our hearts and fill us with God's gift of love and service. We don't need to "find ourselves"; we need to surrender to Jesus. Human nature teaches us to be self-centered and put ourselves first. The Bible tells us to obey God. (Philippians 2:4). We need to seek God, and the Holy Spirit will reveal to us the purpose for our lives. (John 17:17)

There is, however, a valuable lesson that we can learn from Person Centered Therapy. Dietrich Bonhoeffer said it this way, "The first service one owes to others is that fellowship consists in listening to them. Just as love to God begins with listening to His Word, so the beginning of love for the brethren is learning to listen to them." Often Christians are talking when we should be listening. Bonhoeffer warned, "It is little wonder that we are no longer capable of the greatest service of listening that God has committed to our brother's confession…We should listen with the ears of God that we may speak the Word of God." (pp. 97–99)

References

Bonhoeffer, D. (1954). *Life together*. New York: Harper and Row.

Carl Rogers: http://www.carlrogers.info.

Evans, R. (1975). *Carl Rogers: The man and his ideas*. New York: Dutton.

Rogers, C. (1942). *Counseling and psychotherapy*. Boston: Houghton Mifflin.

Rogers, C. (1951). *Self-Centered Therapy*. Boston: Houghton Mifflin.

Rogers, C. (1957). The necessary and sufficient condition of therapeutic personality change. *Journal of Consulting Psychology*, 21, 95–103.

Rogers, C. (1961). *On becoming a person*. Boston: Houghton Mifflin.

Rogers, C. (1980). *A way of being*. Palo Alto, CA: Houghton Mifflin.

Rogers, C. & Wood, J. (1974). Client-centered theory: Carl Rogers. In A. Burton (Ed.), *Operational Theories of Personality*. New York: Brunner/Mazel.

Study Questions

1. Summarize the basic ideas of Person Centered Therapy.
2. What are the strengths and weaknesses of Person Centered Therapy?
3. What would you do with a client whom you found hard to like, and had to show an unconditional positive regard towards?
4. What aspects of the Rogerian approach might you integrate into your counseling methods?
5. As a counselor, what can you do to get clients to open up and to tell you their secrets?

CHAPTER SEVEN

GESTALT THERAPY

Gestalt therapy was founded by Fritz Perls (1893–1970), a psychiatrist of German Jewish descent who spent his later life in the United States and Canada. As a psychoanalyst, Perls was a highly creative individual who soon departed from the psychoanalytic orthodoxy. Perls was influenced by Jung, especially by Jung's Individuation Process. Other influences on Perls were from Eastern religions and existentialism. Later in Perls' life and "before his death in 1970, Perls made considerable use of ideas from Zen Buddhism, Taoism and the human-potential movement. For years he was a resident 'guru' in workshops and retreat centers across North America." (Jones, 1991)

VIEWS OF HUMAN NATURE

Perls looked at human nature in a similar manner as Carl Rogers. He believed that humans are capable of making healthy decisions within this "insane" world. The objective of Gestalt Therapy is not to teach the person to conform, but to help one reach self-actualization in this insane world. Similar to Jung's and Adler's principle of compensation, Perls believed that the personality is made up of polarities and the goal of therapy is the midpoint, or the integration, of these opposites.

HERE AND NOW

In a Gestalt Therapy session, one might observe that the people are talking in a strange way, because everything is being said in the present tense. Instead of a woman saying, "When I was three, I was sexually abused by my father," she would say, "I am three and I am sleeping in bed. I hear the bedroom door open…"

By talking in the present tense, the past becomes more real and the person is encouraged to experience the past events. To experience means to be open and to process unresolved conflicts in one's life. These conflicts are called unfinished business. Unfinished business is usually some unexpressed emotion, such as guilt, pain, anger, shame, or rejection.

Gestalt Therapy places much emphasis on the expressing and experiencing of feelings that the person has kept inside. Perls explained that there are dire consequences to holding feelings in and to not expressing them. In the case above, the price for unexpressed feelings about her sexual abuse is anger, pain, interpersonal distrust, and manipulation of men. With the expression of the "now" in Gestalt Therapy, that past is gone and the future is not yet here. Through the process of expressing past feelings, which are only "psychological realities," a person can heal from them and then integrate his or her personality more fully.

In addition, Gestalt Therapy teaches that if a person has unfinished business, often blaming games are played. Blaming games involve projection. These games enable the client to take responsibility off him or herself. Often people in jail and first admissions to drug programs show excessive use of blaming games. This means that the person is attributing his or her fate to external factors, which is a type of thinking called external locus of control. External locus of control thinking is not helpful because it causes a person to put responsibility for one's actions on others. Unsuccessful people have this external locus of control. If therapy is to be successful the person must develop an internal locus of control, which means helping the client learn to take responsibility for these actions. Thus, the goal of Gestalt Therapy is to help the client take responsibility for these behaviors, or to develop an internal locus of control.

Another reason that some clients do not progress in therapy and do not face their unfinished business, is because they have catastrophic expectations. These are expectations about what will happen if they experience problems. For example, one might say, "I am not going to enroll in college because I might fail and that would destroy me." They have irrational beliefs that the fear and these catastrophic expectations will severely limit them living up to their potential. The person might falsely believe, "I will be rejected," "I will lose my mind," or "I will not be loved." Clients are encouraged to face these irrational expectations and resolve these conflicts by expanding their awareness and experiencing their emotions.

LOOSE YOUR MIND AND COME TO YOUR SENSES

Perls said, "Loose your mind and come to your senses." Often, when caught up in mind games, people develop what Perls called "holes in our personality." In other words, people live in their minds and use various defense mechanisms (such as intellectualization, and reaction formation) to survive. As a result, not only do they get out of touch with their emotions, but also do not use, or limit the use of one or more of their senses (smell, touch, etc.) Gestalt Therapy teaches that humans should learn to smell the flowers, listen to sounds, feel textures, and enjoy eating a good meal. Children can do it easily, but often adults lose the ability to experience fully the world around them. People can lose an ability to experience joy when there are these "holes in our personality."

Along with coming to one's senses is the goal of awareness expansion in Gestalt Therapy. The more awareness is expanded, the more the person is aware of emotions and reality. Gestalt Therapy requires the peeling back of layer after layer of defensiveness until the person becomes fully alive and explodes with joy, sorrow or pain. Perls believed that under those layers of defensiveness an authentic person is hiding.

In Gestalt Therapy the therapist is not superior to the client; in fact, the therapist should be open to change just as much as the client. One of the important points that a Gestalt therapist tries to get clients to realize is that there are an infinite number of choices in this world and the clients can take responsibility for changing their own lives. Perls summarizes his ideas with the following equation:

NOW = EXPERIENCE = AWARENESS = REALITY

TECHNIQUES OF GESTALT THERAPY

Gestalt Therapy is very dramatic and active. Psychodrama, role playing, fantasy trips, and other types of exercises to help the person become more authentic are used. This is always done in the present tense because the client is there to live his or her problems, not to recall them. Since this type of therapy is often dynamic, the person that engages in Gestalt therapy must be highly verbal and imaginative. A Gestalt therapist attempts to help the client eliminate but and can't vocabulary and change the negatives to the affirmative will. The goal is for individuals to take more responsibility for their behaviors.

AVOID QUESTIONS

One technique that a therapist uses is to <u>not</u> allow questions. Instead, the therapist asks the client to change all questions into statements. For example, the client might be asked to alter, "Why are you asking me to do this role play?" to "I am not sure I want to do this role play." In this way, when the person changes questions into statements, one stops rationalizing, starts realizing what the real motives are, and starts taking responsibility for the feelings.

Gestalt therapists teach clients to avoid <u>WHY</u> questions, and are instead directed to ask <u>WHAT</u> or <u>HOW</u> questions. Gestalt therapists believe that <u>WHY</u> questions lead to intellectualizations and can make the person very defensive.

Gestalt Therapy does not allow <u>you</u> or <u>it</u> language. The client is requested to change <u>you</u> or <u>it</u> statements into <u>I</u> statements. Instead of saying, "You make me angry," the client is urged to say, "I am angry because…" Instead of saying, "This stomach of mine is killing me," one is encouraged to say, "I am killing me." These types of statements help people learn to take responsibility for their behaviors.

DREAM WORK

Gestalt therapists teach clients to act out and experience their dream fantasies rather than interpret them as the psychoanalysts do. A client in therapy once had a dream of a witch chasing him down the street.

THERAPIST: Now, you be yourself and tell what you experienced.
CLIENT: I am walking down the street and a horrible looking witch is running after me and laughing. I am trying to get away but I can't run very fast. I just can't seem to get away from her. She is getting closer and closer…
THERAPIST: Very good, now you be the witch.
CLIENT: I am the witch and I am running after Joe because I don't like him. I am going to eat him up because he is more use to me as meat than he is getting all the attention away from me alive…

Gestalt dream work makes for lively sessions that allow people to identify feelings. Perls explained that every <u>dream symbol</u> is a facet of the personality that needs to be expressed. A dream symbol in dream work can be anything in a dream—a body part, a child's swing, any element of the dream. In the case above, Joe had a long history of self-destructive behaviors, with the female part of his personality trying to destroy him. After he became aware of this self-destructive side and integrated it into his personality, he gained more control over his self-destructive tendencies.

MAKING THE ROUNDS

Making the rounds is done in groups and can be done by asking the group to stand. One person in the group is then requested to turn to face the person on the right and hold that person's hands and make eye contact. The first person is then given a sentence such as "Right now I feel…" The person might say "Right now I feel afraid." After person number one finishes the sentence, the second person is requested to finish the same sentence. Then the second person will turn to the next person on the right (person number three) and the process will repeat again with each person finishing the "Right now I feel…" sentence. This process will continue around the circle twice until everyone has repeated "Right now I feel…" This process requires each person in the group to express a personal feeling.

A person that is not participating in the group might be asked to go to each person and finish the following sentence, "I am not involved with this group because..." or the person might be required to ask each person, "Do you know how I feel about you? I feel..." There are many variations in which making the rounds can occur. In groups, clients can go to the several people they most trust and say, "The therapeutic issue that I need to work on the most is ..." Then the person may repeat the same statement, and talk about his or her own issue.

MAY I FEED YOU A SENTENCE?

Sometimes when a counselor believes that a client is conveying an attitude (such as anger), he or she will ask the client to finish a sentence. For example, the client may be asked to say, "The reason I have not said anything is because I don't trust anybody." If the counselor is correct, clients often gain some insight into their behaviors. If the counselor is wrong, clients are encouraged to finish the sentence in the manner that reflects more accurate feelings. For instance, a person may say, "The reason why I have not said anything in the group is because everybody else's problem seems more serious than mine."

Then the group leader might simply feed a client an incomplete sentence to give the group information about how that client feels. Examples of sentences that a therapist might use include: "I wish..., I fear..., I love..., I want...."

I TAKE RESPONSIBILITY FOR

An important function of Gestalt Therapy is for the client to learn to take responsibility for his or her own behaviors. A therapist will often encourage the client to stop blaming others and make a statement that ends with, "...and I take responsibility for it." For example, a person who may be angry at someone will be encouraged to say, "I am angry at you and I take responsibility for my anger." Or the person might say, "I take responsibility for being bored in this group and not getting involved." This often gives the therapist insight, but, more importantly, it reinforces the client to <u>become</u> responsible and acknowledge and accept his or her own feelings.

EXAGGERATION GAME

This game helps the client become more aware of individual behaviors. If the client is constantly fidgeting nervously in the seat, the therapist might ask the client to exaggerate that fidgeting and put words to the nervousness such as, "I want someone to notice me can so I get this feeling off my chest." In the exaggeration game the therapist will take any noticeable behavior to help bring the unconscious motives for the behavior to the surface.

With stammering, for example, a client is asked purposely to stammer as much as possible. Because a stammerer is spending most of the time trying <u>not</u> to stutter, it often relieves psychological pressure to go in the opposite direction of the natural inclinations. Some clients have actually learned to stop stammering by "practicing stammering." This technique is similar to a technique called <u>paradoxical intention</u> used by behavior therapists (See the chapter on Behavior Therapy).

I HAVE A SECRET

With this technique, clients are asked to think about their darkest secrets and imagine how others would react if they were exposed to these secrets. Often clients realize that others would not reject them if they were to know the secrets. In the group when one person becomes honest about a secret, others also become more honest about their secrets.

A modified form of secrets group is to have each group member anonymously write his or her secret on a card. The group leader collects the cards, shuffles them, and passes them out to the other group members. The leader explains that if some people get their own secret, they should pretend that they are reading someone else's secret. The members then each read the secret and tell a story about that secret as if that secret was theirs. After the person tells the story about that secret, others in the group may also respond non-judgmentally. In most cases these groups become very honest and group members gain enough courage to admit that they wrote that secret, while others also disclose that they have had a similar secret. (See Coleman, 2015, p. 106)

REVERSAL TECHNIQUE

This technique is related to the mechanism of compensation whereby participants are asked to act out the opposites that they have repressed in their unconscious. A super kind person is asked to act and say nasty things to the other group members or a shy person is encouraged to act boldly with other group members. This often gets people in touch with feelings they have spent a lifetime trying to avoid.

STAY WITH THE FEELING

When people feel a bad feeling they automatically and reflexively try to avoid the feeling and replace it with a better feeling. In this technique when the therapist tells the client to hold on to the painful feelings, one finds the feelings become less terrifying and that facing painful experiences can integrate the personality.

Sometimes this technique is used differently. For example, if one person is crying and the group is helping with a problem, another person may start crying because of identification with the person's issues. In this situation the therapist might say to the first person, "Stay with that feeling," and then ask person number two to verbalize the feelings being experienced. Later the leader will return to the first person to assure that he or she does not feel abandoned.

PROJECTION GAME

In a group when certain members may criticize others, many times these criticisms are true. The therapist will ask the critical person to look inward and see if the criticism also fits him or herself. Very often the criticisms one has of others also fits ourselves. In other words, "It takes one to know one." Similarly, using this same technique, the group leader may have group members to tell one criticism they have of others. The leader will then ask each member to tell the group how valid that criticism is of his or herself. Examining the criticisms one has of others becomes an important therapeutic technique.

THE DIALOGUE GAME

We have polarities in our personalities that are always waging war with each other. The goal of therapy is not to make these opposites one, but to integrate them so that we can learn to live with the opposites in our personalities, and use the energy to create more productive lives. Both the Dialogue Game and the Empty Chair techniques address the polarities in one's personality and may be used together.

One polarity Gestalt therapists identify is the conflict between <u>top dog</u> and <u>underdog</u>. <u>Top dog</u> is similar to Freud's superego in that it is the interjection of parental injunctions. It may be controlling, bossy, critical, uncompromising, guilt inducing, and constantly overloading the person with <u>should</u>, <u>musts</u> and <u>oughts</u>. Often top dog lords over the person in what is called the <u>self-torture game</u>.

Conversely, <u>underdog</u> is just the opposite. The underdog can be passive, helpless, playful and rebellious. When the alarm clock buzzes in the morning, top dog and underdog start their battle. Top dog demands that you get up and underdog says stay in bed all day.

EMPTY CHAIR TECHNIQUE

In the Empty Chair technique two chairs are placed in the center of the group and a person with the conflict sits in each, one chair at a time, and has a dialogue with the other chair. Top dog might say to under-dog, "You are evil and bad; you don't deserve to live. Why don't you go and kill yourself and get it over with?" The same person would then sit in the other chair and say as underdog, "I just can't help all of the bad things I do. I have no control over them and anyway I hate you for reminding me of them constantly." A person can take any polar conflict within the personality (good boy vs. bad boy, passive self vs. aggressive self) and likewise carry on a dialogue between them. As the person begins to verbalize the real issues and feelings, he or she often increases an awareness of their humanness and can gain control over these individual behaviors.

The Empty Chair technique can also be used in a different way. A person may have feelings about having a father that was abusive and the therapist will pull an empty chair in front of the individual. The client will then pretend that this father is sitting in the chair and express the honest feeling felt toward the father.

SCREAM THERAPY

Gestalt Therapy teaches clients to actively and emotively let "feelings out" and "experience" many of the paradoxes that exist within the personality. This kind of "catharsis" has helped clients free themselves of deeply repressed feelings that have "haunted" them. It takes a courageous and creative therapist to run Gestalt groups and to keep clients in the present tense and to face the traumas and paradoxes in their personalities.

One of the more intense offshoots of Gestalt Therapy is called Scream Therapy founded by Dr Daniel Casriel, and it starts with each group member either hugging a pillow or holding hands in a circle with the other group members, and having everyone scream as loudly as they can in unison. This screaming breaks through much of the "façade" that clients use to hide true feelings. In his book *A Scream Away from Happiness*, Casriel writes, "Americans have found it dangerous to acknowledge their true feelings… scream therapy goes rapidly beyond the symptoms of a disorder to the feelings, attitudes and behaviors of today's emotionally frozen men. In scream therapy people can touch and embrace and confront one another hon-estly-something they cannot do in most instances in our culture." Casriel had much success working with people with addictions and personality disorders. Coleman also found that these "emotive techniques" can be very effective. (See Chapter 13 on Group Therapy.)

A CHRISTIAN PERSPECTIVE OF GESTALT THERAPY

Gestalt Therapy and emotive therapies can be helpful in reducing anxiety, teaching clients to break their images, and getting through hostility and bitterness to the softer emotions of pain, hurt and love. However, they may or may not lead a person to the source of "true love," namely God. Yet, these types of therapies are successful in helping individuals "integrate their personalities" which may make them more open to belief in the "true" God. Unfortunately, the Gestalt therapist usually does not point to the God of the Bible.

References

Casriel, D. (1976). *A scream away from happiness.* New York: Grosset and Dunlap.

Coleman, T. (2015). *How to make group psychotherapy work.* Bloomington, IN: Xlibris.

Fagan, J., and Shepherd, I. (Eds.). (1970). *What is gestalt therapy?* New York: Harper and Row Publishers Inc.

Gestalt and Fritz Perls. http://www.gestalttherapy.org or www.gestalt.org.

Jones, S., and Butman, R. (1991). *Modern psychotherapies.* Downer's Grove, IL: InterVarsity Press.

Latner, J. (1973). *Gestalt therapy book.* New York: Bantam Books.

Passons, W.R. (1975). *Gestalt approaches in counseling.* New York: Holt Rinehart and Winston.

Patterson, C.H. (1986). *Theories of counseling and psychotherapy.* New York: Harper and Row Publishers, Inc.

Perls, F. (1969). *Gestalt therapy verbatim.* Moab, Utah: Real People Press.

Perls, F. (1969). *In and out of the garbage pail.* Moab, Utah: Real People Press.

Perls, F. (1989). *The gestalt approach and eyewitness to therapy.* New York: Bantam Books.

Polster, E., and Polster, M. (1973). *Gestalt therapy integrated.* New York: Brunner/Mazel.

Study Questions

1. Fill in the blanks with the correct answers.

    a. An unexpressed feeling such as anger or hurt is called _____.
    b. The goal of Gestalt Therapy is the _____ of the personality.
    c. The moralistic, parental part of the personality is called _____.
    d. The part of the personality that is passive and irresponsible is called _____ _____.
    e. A Gestalt therapist will ask WHAT and HOW questions but never _____questions.
    f. When a person talks to an empty chair, it is called the _____ _____ technique.
    g. When people are asked to apply the criticisms that they have of others to themselves, this is called the _____ game.
    h. A person is very passive and is requested to act aggressive. This is called the _____ game.
    i. A woman tells her hidden guilt. This game is called _____.
    j. A man goes to each person in the group and tells them how he really feels about them. This is called _____ _____ _____.
    k. A woman acts out her dream in the middle of the floor. This is called _____ _____.
    l. People get "stuck" and don't finish business because they have _____ _____.
    m. People have holes in their personalities because they don't use certain _____.
    n. Gestalt groups are always run in the _____ tense.

2. Explain what Perls means by his equation: Now = experience = awareness = reality.
3. Why are Gestalt groups run only in the present tense?
4. Explain why Gestalt therapists ask HOW and WHAT questions and not WHY questions.
5. What are the goals of Gestalt therapy?
6. Explain which Gestalt games would work best for you as a client.
7. Name some unfinished business that you have.
8. Explain one aspect of Gestalt therapy that you most like.
9. Explain one aspect of Gestalt therapy that you least like.

CHAPTER EIGHT

TRANSACTIONAL ANALYSIS

Transactional Analysis (TA) is a cognitive therapy rather than an emotive therapy like Gestalt Therapy. Cognitive therapy means that its primary purpose is to change a person's thinking about his or herself and not get out deeply repressed emotions. TA was founded by psychiatrist Eric Berne (1910–1970). Like other therapists, Berne started as an aspiring psychoanalyst but was rejected for membership by the Psychoanalytical Institute. This angered Berne so much that he embarked on developing Transactional Analysis. In 1964, Berne published *Games People Play*, a best-selling book that introduced the ideas of Transactional Analysis. Three years later Thomas Harris wrote a TA best seller called *I'm OK—You're OK*. The public was now aware of Transactional Analysis.

Berne teaches that people have choices and that the goal of therapy is awareness, intimacy, and spontaneity. People can make real choices and become responsible and autonomous. Berne explains that because of false early choices in our childhoods, we learn to play games with each other. Game playing is unhealthy; it is a way of manipulating someone so one always comes out of game playing with a bad feeling. The goal of TA is to help a person become free of games.

The TA therapist develops a treatment contract with the client, and the client is urged to take responsibility for working toward those goals. Even though in TA the relationship between therapist and client is one of equals, the therapist is also a teacher who carefully explains the dynamics of Transactional Analysis.

THE FOUR DIVISIONS OF TRANSACTIONAL ANALYSIS

Transactional Analysis has developed into four interrelated parts that attempt to help the person conceptualize and predict human behavior.

1. STRUCTURAL ANALYSIS is helping the person to understand internal functionings.
2. TRANSACTIONAL ANALYSIS is helping the person to understand interpersonal relationships.
3. GAME ANALYSIS is helping the person to understand the unhealthy games people play with each other.
4. SCRIPT ANALYSIS is helping the person to understand the script or preplanned view of life that one is following.

STRUCTURAL ANALYSIS

Transitional Analysis therapists divide the person's personality into three parts. These parts are called ego states and are labeled PARENT, ADULT and CHILD (P-A-C).

The parental ego state is somewhat similar to Freud's superego (even though Berne would vehemently deny this.) It consists of the parental injunctions that are internalized into the personality. Often these injunctions are shoulds, musts, oughts and do's. Usually the parent presents itself in superior acting gestures, i.e. finger pointing, and verbalizations, i.e. "You are bad."

Berne divides the parent into two parts: The <u>Critical Parent</u> and the <u>Nurturing Parent</u>. Even though Berne would again deny it, the Critical Parent is similar to Freud's conscience. It is the critical prejudicial part of the personality. It makes statements like, "I think all young people today are going to the dogs," or "You were absolutely wrong when you did that." The Critical Parent is very active in accusing the person and causing guilt when a person is depressed. The Critical is often rigid and moralistic.

The Nurturing Parent is similar to Freud's ego ideal. It praises, encourages, rewards, and of course, nurtures. The Nurturing Parent says things like, "That was a wonderful thing you did!" or "You did a great job. Keep it up."

Unfortunately, the Critical Parent is stronger in most people than the Nurturing Parent because growing up parents tend to criticize more than compliment and, as a result, the critical internalizations of the Critical Parent are more ingrained than the pleasant internalizations of the Nurturing Parent. When a person feels guilty, depressed, or suicidal, it is the Critical Parent that is working over-time.

The Adult Ego state is the part of our personality with which we most often identify. It is not emotional, but is the information processing part of the personality. It is rational and deals with external reality and is concerned with adapting to reality and finding the best solution; it is similar to Freud's ego.

The Child Ego state is literally the child in our personality. It contains the impulses, feelings and urges we possess. It is similar to Freud's id in some ways.

Berne divides the Child into three parts, the <u>Natural Child</u>, the <u>Adapted Child</u> and the <u>Little Professor</u>. The Natural Child is the infant in our personality. It is amoral, fun loving, spontaneous and pleasure seeking. The Adapted Child is far more compliant than the Natural Child because of experiences with the world and parental figures. The Adapted Child often sends things like, "I must do that." The Little Professor is the unschooled wisdom in the child ego state. It can be quite intelligent, intuitive, manipulative, and creative.

As a person learns about the ego states of Transactional Analysis, one then learns to understand which ego state he or she is using the most. Unlike Jungian analysis, where a goal of therapy is the integration of the personality, Transitional Analysis believes that the ego states should be very distinct from each other and should not overlap.

When one ego state overlaps with another it is called <u>contamination</u>, and one of the goals of TA is to help people overcome this contamination. The Parent, the Child or both ego states can contaminate the Adult ego state. Contamination is demonstrated graphically by:

Figure 1   Figure 2   Figure 3

In Figure 1 the child is contaminating the adult. This type of contamination tends to make the Adult more childish and act more immature. In Figure 2 the parent is contaminating the Adult and this causes the Adult to think rigidly and prejudicially with statements like, "All minority groups are no good." In Figure 3 both the Child and Parent are contaminating the Adult and this strongly prevents the Adult from clear rational thinking.

Exclusion, like contamination, is considered to be a problem in the personality because the person should be able to use any ego state on demand. A person that is a constant Adult is excluding the Child and the Parent states and typically is overly rational, unfeeling, and unable to relax. A person that is Adult is often prejudicial in thinking, moralistic, and unable to stop working to play. The Constant Child, on the contrary, wants to do nothing but play. The child acts irresponsible, impulsive, rebellious and unsocialized. The goal of therapy in this case of exclusion is to help people develop more flow between the ego states.

TRANSACTIONAL ANALYSIS INTERACTIONS

TA therapists analyze interactions between people into three types of transactions: complementary, crossed and ulterior.

Complementary transactions are those interactions that are appropriate and expected and often between the same ego states.

Person 1: "Would you like to come out and play?"
Person 2: "Wheee! Yes I would, we can swing on the swings."

Crossed transactions are painful for one party. They are often unexpected responses and they often cause the person to get angry or withdraw.

Child: "Mommy, can I go out and play?"
Mother: "Shut up and do your homework"

Ulterior transactions are complex, often disguised, transactions where on the surface the person seems to be one way, but, in reality, is really acting like another.

An example of this is occurs when a boy says to a girl, "Would you like to go to the barn and see the horse?" when actually his intentions are sexual. The ulterior transaction is represented by the dotted line.

GAME ANALYSIS

Berne and other TA therapists believe that games are very common in society. Games are transactions where one person tries to manipulate another person. Games always result in someone getting hurt and they can block intimacy and genuineness. An example of one game is what Berne calls <u>Wooden Leg</u>. In this game the person plays the role of a "sick" person in order to get sympathy and concern from others. In that way, a person doesn't have to shoulder his or her share of the responsibilities. Since no one condemns a "sick" person, the person succeeds in manipulating others to get what he or she wants.

Another game is called <u>Seducto</u>. In this game the person flirts with someone and then later rejects the other person. This obviously causes bad feelings for the rejected party. Some games can be very serious such as <u>Cops and Robbers</u> where the robbers invite the cops to try and catch them. This can sometimes end in death. Everyone should examine their lives to identify how much of their life is game playing, and then try to understand why they play these games.

SCRIPT ANALYSIS

Just like an actor acts out a script, by age five all people have internalized a way of looking at themselves and what they can do, according to Berne. Often the scripts that people internalize from others are nonverbal. Nevertheless, they contain beliefs that people can deeply internalize if they don't make themselves aware of them. These scripts can seriously rule lives.

Some of the parental injunctions that a person may internalize include: "You're bad," "You're just like your father," "You don't listen," "Don't be …" In TA it is important to become aware of early scripting in order to become free of them. Eventually "Don't be…" scripts could lead to self-destructive tendencies in some people.

Berne says that people act out scripts to get <u>strokes</u>. Strokes are reinforcers, both verbal and physical. People try to get positive strokes (rewards or green stamps) and avoid negative strokes (punishers called brown stamps). The way it is explained to children is a fuzzy ball is given to the children and the children explain that it feels nice. This ball is called a warm Fuzzy and it represents nice comments that we like from others (positive strokes.) Then the children are given a prickly ball and it is explained that we don't like "prickly" comments (negative strokes.) People collect these strokes or stamps and that eventually effects the way the person looks at others.

A depressed person can collect enough negative strokes to decide to commit suicide. Conversely, a student can study hard, get a good grade and reward him or herself with a night at the movies.

Berne seems to look at life as an ongoing transaction within oneself and with those around. These can be seen within the various games people utilize in their transitions through life. The goal of Transactional Analysis is to help a person become game free, which will lead to more spontaneous, authentic, and fulfilling relationships. One must realize that these ways of behaving stem from the choices one makes, all with various consequences. As you consider your choices as a student of psychology or a practicing professional, may your choices lead to self-growth and willingness to always give your best effort. No one can expect more of you than your best efforts.

A CHRISTIAN PERSPECTIVE OF TRANSACTIONAL ANALYSIS

When Eric Berne used the word "games," he was referring to deceptive, manipulative and sometimes even illegal behaviors. Many people, even Christians, have been guilty of playing destructive psychological games at one time or another. These types of behaviors are clearly frowned on by God. Again, the Bible says in John 8:32 that **"you shall know the truth and the truth will set you free."**

Both biblically and psychologically this Bible tenant makes much sense. If a person lies to a therapist about one thing, the therapist will wonder what else the client has to conceal. A person with antisocial personality disorder may lie about his illegal activities and when prosecuted for the truth will pay for lying by going to jail. Psychologists that work in psychiatric Institutions have found that paranoid individuals, and especially people with paranoid schizophrenia, are full of "false beliefs" or delusions. One psychologist in interviewing a paranoid patient heard him shout, "I am god almighty ruler of the universe." The therapist knew clearly that if he confronted the patient with the "truth," the person would violently attack him as he had done to others before.

In psychotherapy countless therapists have observed that when clients get "totally, completely and brutally honest," they experience a great therapeutic relief and a reduction in anxiety. The truth really does set a person free.

One thing, however, is missing in a therapy that is godless or without a Supreme Being, and that is that the most important truth is God. Jesus said, **"I am the way the truth and the life, no one comes to the father except though me." (John 14:6)**

References

Barnes, G. (Ed.) (1977). *Transactional analysis after Eric Berne.* New York: Harper College Press.

Berne, E. (1961). *Transactional analysis in psychotherapy.* New York: Grove Press.

Berne, E. (1964). *Games people play.* New York: Grove Press.

Bontrager, J. (1974). *Free the child in you.* Philadelphia: Pilgrim/United Church Press.

Goulding, M., and Goulding, R. (1979). *Changing lives though redecision therapy.* New York: Brunner/Mazel.

Haughton, R. (1974). *The liberated heart.* New York: Seabury.

Harris, T. (1967). *I'm ok—you're ok.* New York: Avon.

Jones, S., & Butman, R. (1991). *Modern Psychotherapies: A comprehensive Christian appraisal.* Downer's Grove, IL: InterVarsity Press.

Study Questions

1. Complete the following statements.

    a. Transactional Analysis divides the personality into _____, _____, and _____.

    b. The child ego state is divided into _____, _____, and _____.

    c. The ego state that has to do with rational, objective thinking is called the _____.

    d. The part of the parent ego state that is moralistic and condescending is called the _____ _____.

    e. The part of the child ego state that is full of feelings, spontaneous, and impulsive is called the _____ _____.

    f. Appropriate predictable responses are called _____ transactions.

    g. Inappropriate interactions that cause other persons to feel hurt are called _____ transactions.

    h. Communications that are disguised and actually mean something other than they seem on the surface are called _____ transactions.

    i. When a person gets a bad feeling from something that is done to him or her, it is called a negative _____.

    j. When the child ego state overlaps the adult, the child is said to be _____ the adult.

    k. When a person is "locked" into the parent ego state to the exclusion of the adult and child, the person is said to be a _____.

    l. The three types of transactions are _____, _____ and _____.

    m. You give a child a piece of candy. The child is taught this is a _____ _____.

    n. You yell negative things to a friend. You have given that person a _____ stamp.

2. Explain at least three games that you play or have played with someone else. How did the game make you feel? How did it make the other person feel?

3. Describe at least three games that you have seen others play. What were the consequences?

4. List some early parental injunctions that you can remember (i.e. children are to be seen and not heard.)

5. Explain some should in your life that you may need to examine.

6. Analyze what percentage of time you use your parent, your adult and your child. Explain the significance of these amounts for you.

TRANSACTIONAL ANALYSIS SELF ANALYSIS KIT

See what scripts and feelings have influenced you the most in your life. Do not give each answer a lot of thought; just answer each automatically and see what your responses are.

1. Explain how you see yourself and your identity.
2. What do you think is your strongest asset?
3. What do you think is your weakest point?
4. What do you admire most in others?
5. What do you dislike most in others?
6. What was your mother's main criticism of you?
7. What did your mother compliment you about?
8. What was your father's main criticism of you?
9. What did your father compliment you about?
10. Other than your parents, what person had the greatest influence on you? Why?
11. How did you view yourself as a child?
12. What do you want most out of life?
13. What is your biggest fear in life?
14. If you could change something in you, what would it be?
15. What is your most common criticism of others?
16. When you were small, what advice do you remember most?
17. When you were small, how did you view the world?
18. Identify a traumatic experience in your life. How did you feel?

CHAPTER NINE

BEHAVIOR THERAPY

Behavior Therapy is based on the assumption that most maladaptive behaviors are learned and, because they are learned, they can also be unlearned. Since most of the work in Behaviorism was done by Americans, Behavior Therapy is one of the most influential in American academic institutions. Most American college and university psychology departments are more behaviorally oriented than any other school of psychology. Behavior therapists pride themselves with the idea that they are the most scientific of all the therapies. The sheer volume of empirical research attests to the fact that Behavior therapists are trying to adhere to the Scientific Method. Along with cognitive behavior therapies, studies indicate that Behavior Therapy may be the most effective type of therapy.

Studies with Classical or Respondent Conditioning have helped Behavior therapists develop many effective therapies, especially for emotional problems, such as anxiety and phobic disorders. Behavior therapy has its historical roots in the studies of <u>Classical Conditioning</u> and <u>Operant Conditioning</u>.

CLASSICAL CONDITIONING

The first studies in classical conditioning (also called <u>Respondent Conditioning</u>) were done by a Russian physiologist named Ivan Pavlov who did his work from the 1890's into the next century. Pavlov found that he could get dogs to salivate (<u>conditioned response</u>) to a bell (previously a neutral stimulus and then a conditioned stimulus.) Normally a dog will not salivate to a bell but will salivate (unconditioned or unlearned response) to food (unconditioned stimulus and also a reinforcer.) Pavlov rang the bell (neutral stimulus) and then presented the food (<u>unconditioned stimulus</u>.) The bell became associated with the food and thus the dog started salivating to the bell (conditioned stimulus.)

Classical conditioning is associated with involuntary reflexive behaviors. That is, the organism has no choice in how to respond. Many emotional disorders are classically conditioned. A famous pioneer in Classical Conditioning, John Watson (1920) gave the example of classical emotional conditioning in an infant called Albert. Watson actually created a phobia in Albert by presenting him with a white rat (<u>neutral stimulus</u>) to play with and then making a loud noise (unconditioned stimulus or UCS) behind Albert's back. This caused fear (unconditioned response) in Albert and made him cry. Watson did this several times until finally Albert began to cry whenever he saw the white rat. As a result, the rat became a conditioned stimulus (CS) that was associated with the noise. In fact, later Albert became afraid of anything that was small, fuzzy or white, including a lady's fur coat. (Watson pp.1–14) The reactions to similar stimuli (in this example, anything fuzzy or white) is call <u>stimulus generalization</u>. Being able to differentiate between the whit rate and other white stimuli is call <u>stimulus discrimination.</u>

OPERANT CONDITIONING

This type of conditioning is also called <u>instrumental conditioning</u> and concentrates on the conditioning of people's voluntary behavior. Operant conditioning is associated with the root word to <u>operate</u>. A person that operates a car has a voluntary free choice where that car will go.

Psychologist B.F. Skinner popularized the concept of operant conditioning. He identified an important ingredient in operant conditioning as <u>reinforcement</u>. A reinforcer is a stimulus that increases the probability that a response will occur. Giving money to a child that mows the lawn or the loud noise in the Albert experiment are both reinforcers. Skinner divided reinforcers into <u>positive</u> and <u>negative reinforcers</u>. A positive reinforcer is a reward, something that the organism wants. A negative reinforcer is the removal of a noxious stimulus or the removal of a stimulus that the organism doesn't want. Giving the organism a noxious stimulus is called a <u>punisher</u>.

Positive reinforcers are divided into two types: <u>primary reinforcers</u> and <u>secondary reinforcers</u>. Primary reinforcers are those that are inborn and unlearned, such as food or sleep. Secondary reinforcers are learned and get their power as reinforcers because they have been paired with primary reinforcers or other conditioned reinforcers. Of the stimuli that influence behavior, positive reinforcers have been shown to be the more powerful, while in many ways, punishers have been shown to be less powerful. In Behavior Therapy the therapist manipulates positive reinforcers, negative reinforcers, and punishers attempting to help the client change behaviors. The therapist also can teach the client how to manipulate these reinforcers in one's own life (i.e. how to reward oneself for a positive behavior).

Since a therapist is not a manipulator, he or she must first establish a relationship with the client and gain cooperation, just as in other types of therapy. Also, a Behaviorist believes that it is vital for the client to agree upon clear measurable <u>goals</u> and to work to accomplish these goals. Thus, the motivation of the client is very important. The client who is not goal oriented probably won't be successful in achieving a goal. Behavior Therapists can be versatile in their approach and often use other techniques rather than only relying on learning therapy and behavior therapy.

EXTINCTION

The principle of extinction is also important in the therapeutic process. Extinction is the non-reinforcement of a behavior so that when that behavior is ignored or not rewarded, it will disappear or become extinct. For example, if a parent is taught not to pay attention to a child's whining behavior, the whining may disappear.

TECHNIQUES USED IN BEHAVIOR THERAPY

1. SHAPING

Shaping happens when a person gets successive approximations of the desired behavior. A mother might want to get her daughter to clean her room and set up a reinforcement schedule of hugs and cookies (positive reinforcers.) Mom starts rewarding her daughter for giving a half-hearted attempt at cleaning her room, but the next time Mom will not reinforce until the child does a successively better cleaning.

2. SELF-MONITORING

People have bad habits that are almost automatic, somethings which they may do without thinking (e.g. compulsive eating or smoking.) Self-monitoring is often the first step to understanding and changing a disturbing behavior. In the self-monitoring technique, the person is urged to focus on the behavior that is being emitted and then to record these behaviors in a log. Included is counting the times one automatically performs the undesired behavior. This self-monitoring helps the person become more aware of the behaviors and the reasons behind why these behaviors occur. For example, a person might binge eat right after coming home from a frustrating job. One might find out that the reason for doing this is because of frustration and anger.

3. SYSTEMATIC DESENSITIZATION

This technique, when used successfully, helps people extinguish a large range of disorders, including anxiety, depression, anorexia nervosa, obsessive compulsive problems, phobic disorders and others. It is based on the principle that anxiety and relaxation are incompatible behaviors. When relaxation is taught, then anxious or phobic feelings will become extinct.

In this technique the person is first taught to think of naturally relaxing images, such as sitting on the beach or being in the park. Then the person is taught deep muscle relaxation. Before this, however, the person has talked to the therapist about his or her anxiety arousing fears and has developed a hierarchy of anxiety producing situations. The client and therapist have created a list of situations that go from the most anxiety producing to the least anxiety producing.

For example, a female that needs an operation but is terrified of going to the hospital might have "Being in the operating room with the doctors ready" as number one on her list to "Looking at the outside of a hospital" as the least of her anxiety producing situations. Next the person is instructed to become deeply relaxed and go through the hierarchy from the least anxiety producing image to the most anxiety producing image. The therapist describes the images to the client and if she signals that they are anxiety producing (i.e. by a slight move of the finger) the therapist moves back on the hierarchy for a time. Eventually the client is able to imagine the entire hierarchy of images anxiety free. This technique allows the person, when actually faced with these situations, to feel relaxed.

Some remarkable breakthroughs are happening with this technique lately because of virtual reality. Some therapists have found success using this new technology to bring phobias to extinction.

4. FLOODING AND IMPLOSIVE THERAPY

Flooding is a technique where the subject is exposed to an anxiety producing situation (either real or imagined) and learns to face the situation and ultimately reduce the anxiety. With flooding, the person's mind is literally "flooded" or overloaded with the anxiety producing image. In this technique the person many times relates to feelings and it is not uncommon to cry.

In implosive therapy the therapist discusses the anxiety arousing situation, i.e. the hospital, with the client and the person imagines the scene and experiences the anxiety. Sometimes, the therapist even has the client imagine the dire consequences of something that is feared, i.e. dying in the hospital. Caution, however, must be exercised. These techniques should be used very carefully by an experienced therapist, because if used improperly, they can be quite traumatic for the client.

In both flooding and implosive therapy, relaxation is not always taught.

5. AVERSIVE THERAPY

Even though numerous studies have indicated that punishment is not always effective, sometimes it seems the only alternative, and, in fact, can be used in some situations. Several types of punishment used include:

a.   TIME OUT

Time out is often used with children. Sometimes a student that acts up in class is getting positive reinforcement from the attention (laughing) that other classmates give the child. The teacher will isolate him or her from the class for a short period of time. This punishment is called time out.

b.   OVERCORRECTION

Overcorrection is sometimes used with children or developmentally delayed clients. It requires a disruptive child to not only clean up the mess that she has made, but also clean up the environment to a better than normal state. Even though this is a type of punishment, it has beneficial outcomes.

c.   CHEMICAL AND ELECTRICAL AVERSION

With smoking and alcoholism there are chemicals that a person can ingest so that whenever one smokes or drinks, a chemically induced nausea and ill feeling will occur. This nauseated feeling associated with the compulsive behavior helps the person stop the compulsive behavior.

In electrical aversion an electric shock is paired with images or behaviors that the person wants to eliminate. For example, a man that is bothered by homosexual arousal is shown pictures of naked males and immediately given a mild electrical shock. The person then starts to feel an aversion to the naked males because of the pairing with the noxious stimulus of the shock. This technique has been tried in certain types of sexual deviations. More recently this has been discouraged on legal and ethical grounds.

d.   COVERT SENSITIZATION

This technique is used totally with the imagination and does not have the negative side effects of the chemical or electrical therapies. This is often used with clients that show compulsive behaviors such as over eating, sexual offenses, or smoking. In this technique the client is to imagine direct consequences to the negative behavior. For example, the sexual offender is asked to think about the consequences of getting caught, the shame of family and others knowing, going to jail and its accompanying horrors (Maletzy, 1980). Often sessions are recorded and the person listens to them at home.

6.   MODELING TECHNIQUES

Modeling is a form of learning in which a person learns a behavior by watching someone else. Some psychologists suggest that one learns most behaviors through modeling or imitating others. Modeling is effective in treating in a large variety of problems, from helping autistic children learn to speak to helping children get over phobias. In a classical study by Bandura, Ross and Ross (1971) children watched a model hit a large inflated doll, subsequently throw it up in the air, kick and hit it with a mallet. When the children were put in the room many imitated almost exactly the same destructive behaviors with the doll. Conversely, when the children watched models showing positive behaviors, such as sharing and cooperation, and saw models rewarded for their positive behaviors, the children subsequently tended to show similar constructive behaviors.

Studies have been done with a model demonstrating the handling of a snake or playing with a dog in front of the phobic person. When the person sees that the model is having a good time and is not being harmed, the individual often gains the courage to play with the animal and gets over the phobia for the animal.

With adults that are alcoholic, psychotic, or drug addicted, role modeling and imitating the role model helps them learn more appropriate interpersonal behaviors within the community. For example, a client may watch a role model demonstrate how to handle a job interview. The client will imitate the interview experience through role playing in order to increase one's confidence for a real job interview.

7. TOKEN ECONOMY

People are rewarded with money when they perform the work that the employer has requested. Money is a powerful reinforcer because it can be traded for other primary and secondary reinforcers. Token economy is very much like this in that the client is given some type of token (poker chips, punches in a card) for constructive behaviors (bed making, food preparation, polite behavior, talking honestly in a therapy group.) The client can subsequently "cash in" the token for material things, privileges or similar advantages. It is effective because token economy gives the client a choice of what can be earned. Token economy is used in schools, institutions, rehabilitation programs and similar settings committed to the approach.

Sometimes punishers are introduced into a token economy system. If the client shows negative behavior, a specified number of tokens are taken away. Some have criticized this approach saying, firstly, that it makes a client materialistic, and secondly, if the client does something positive, he or she is looking for a hand out. However, it remains a powerful use of positive reinforcement when helping the client understand the transition between an institutional setting and the real world.

8. SEX THERAPY

Sexual dysfunction in our culture is very high. Sex researchers, Masters and Johnson have concluded that about 50% of married couples suffer from some type of sexual dysfunction. Often people are too embarrassed to talk about their sexual problems, even to their therapist, and, likewise, many psychotherapists are not trained to help with those sexual problems.

a. MISUNDERSTANDING ABOUT SEX

Many people are anxious about the way their bodies look and are afraid that their partner will find them unattractive. Others, even though married, do not embrace that sexual relations are meant to be healthy, pleasurable and celebrated. Often people learn about sex and the sexual response from movies, jokes, internet and tales from others, and as a result become terribly misinformed about the sexual response. People also are afraid of getting pregnant or getting sexually transmitted diseases, and, as a result, are unable to relax sexually.

b. MALE & FEMALE DIFFERENCES

With an over emphasis on sex in our society, there are people with some real misconceptions about sexual functioning. It behooves couples to research sexual impulses and sexual responses.

A wife may feel it is her duty to satisfy her husband even though he may be selfish or misinformed about sexual responses. Since some men are sexually very insecure, a woman might fake orgasms in an attempt not to wound the man's pride. This faking can cause a woman to become more resentful of the man and to block honest communication. One prominent hang-up for a woman is the feeling of being <u>used</u>. <u>Feeling used</u> occurs when a woman perceives that others are looking at her as an object or servant, rather than a person.

Men often dysfunction because they have performance anxiety and are anxious that the woman will blame them if they do not "give her an orgasm." Also, a man cannot hide his sexual arousal like a woman can. It seems clear that men are more lustful when it comes to sex. They are the ones that usually pressure women to have sex. There is a belief that men say "I love you" to get sex and women give sex in an attempt to get love.

The research seems to suggest that women are the ones that are more likely to get hurt (used) in a casual sexual relationship (i.e. they can get pregnant). Today's couples routinely have intercourse before marriage. Recent studies suggest that in the US and Europe more and more couples are "living together" rather than getting married. Some research, however, has found that arranged marriages, marriages where the couples are virgins, and marriages where the couples are older, tend to be more lasting. This contradicts popular beliefs and practices.

Surveys tend to indicate that one reason that a woman consents to a man sexually is because of <u>the need for acceptance</u>. On the other hand, one of the big reasons why a man would have casual sex with a woman is to <u>prove his masculinity</u>. MOST MEN SPEND MOST OF THEIR TIME TRYING TO PROVE SOMETHING THAT IS OBVIOUS. Some studies suggest that if men felt more secure about their manhood, sex addictions would not be as problematic as they are among men.

One thing that men need to understand about women is that they are touch oriented. Women like to be held and caressed to satisfy their <u>skin hunger</u>. One survey of married women found that they would prefer to snuggle rather than have intercourse with their husbands.

Men, on the contrary, are more visually oriented and more quickly aroused than women. Men are more orgasm oriented than most women. Women take longer to be aroused and to cool down. Therefore, a couple should be aware of the biological differences for a more fulfilling sexual encounter for both the man and woman.

c. SENSATE FOCUS

Masters and Johnson, pioneers in the field of sexual functioning, have had success in treating most sexually dysfunctioning couples. First, they require a thorough physical examination because diseases like diabetes, drug abuse and other problems can interfere with sexual functioning. Next, they have the couple remove themselves from distractions (phone, children, etc.) to practice <u>Sensate Focusing</u>. This technique requires the couple to explore and to stimulate each other's body to find what areas give the other person pleasure. In this way a man may learn, for example, how to help the woman naturally lubricate so that coitus is pleasurable upon inserting the penis.

During the sensate focus process, the couple is requested to refrain from having intercourse. This abstaining helps reduce the performance anxiety, especially in the man, and helps the woman get over feelings of being sexually used. The couple learns to give each other feedback. They learn to communicate since a lack of communication is at the base of most sexual dysfunction. Masters and Johnson found that helping couples communicate their needs and feelings, both in and out of bed, helps most to have a healthier sexual relationship.

One example that has improved some women's ability to have an organism is to locate the <u>G-Spot</u>, a gland inside the female vagina. When a woman has an orgasm the G-Spot secretes a semen similar to a man's semen (minus the sperm.) When the G-Spot secretes, the sensation for the woman is indistinguishable from urinating. Because the desire is not to urinate in bed many women hold back and thus do not attain orgasm. Therefore, it is helpful for women to attain orgasms if they urinate before intercourse. When they feel an orgasm coming during intercourse they encouraged to push, instead of hold back. While this leads the woman to secrete a small amount of urine, it also helps the G-Spot to secrete, and for many women to attain orgasm.

9.   VIRTUAL REALITY THERAPY

This newer therapy occurs when a model person demonstrates appropriate behavior for different types of situations. For example, how to appropriately engage another person in conversation is modelled. This therapy often employs goggles which realistically show people using appropriate healthy behaviors. This exposure encourages clients to imitate these behaviors through role modeling. The client will then rehearse or imitate these behaviors for the therapist. In another scenario, a person with PTSD could be gently exposed to a traumatizing event from the past while in a deeply relaxed state. The association of the "safe place" relaxation to this traumatic event could extinguish the intense fear. These techniques are practiced by Applied Behavior Analyst (ABT) therapists who are integrating behavior therapy with other therapies (Psychodynamic, and Cognitive Behavioral) to obtain more observable, constructive client changes. (Anthony, pp.182–223)

People have criticized Behavior Therapy as being deterministic and quick to view people as mechanisms to be manipulated through reinforcers and punishers. In comparison to other therapies, however, there is little question that Behavior Therapy is the most empirical and scientific. Along with Cognitive Behavior Therapy, Behavior Therapy has some of the most effective approaches to helping clients with specific problems. Jones explains it by saying, "Behavior Modification is one of the few approaches to counseling that gives us effective procedures for dealing with children and others for whom verbal discussion is an ineffective impetus for change. It also has produced techniques for many problems which have been documented to be effective." (Jones 1999)

A CHRISTIAN PERSPECTIVE OF BEHAVIOR THERAPY

God does exist and does intervene in "nature." Our "relationship with God makes us qualitatively different from animals." (Bovin 1985) Bovin explains that dogmatic naturalism and determinism are at odds with God's teachings. Naturalism in psychology refers to the belief that "reality consists solely of natural objects and that therefore the methods of natural science offer the only reliable means to knowledge and understanding of reality." (APA 2019) Similarly, determinism is defined as an approach that proposes all behavior has a cause and is thus predictable. B. F. Skinner asserted that free will is an illusion. Human behavior is governed by internal and external forces over which a person has no control. Naturalism and determinism dominate psychology, and as such, overlook the intervention of God. There are supernatural powers such as God, angels, and demons.

Dr. Maxine Bradshaw concludes, "Behavior Therapy discounts the role of one's spiritual connection. It asserts that a stimulus occurs to which one reacts. Christians purport that human beings have a God-given choice before a response is made. When you consider this theory, consider your own actions and reflect on your spontaneous reactions, as well as those which are borne out of deliberate and prayerful considerations."

References

Anthony, M.M. (2003). *Behavior therapy.* New York: Guilford.

Skinner, B. F. http://www.sntp.net/behaviorism/skinner.htm.

Bandura, A. ed. (1971). *Psychological modeling.* Chicago: Aldine-Atherton.

Bovin, M. (1985). Behavior therapy: What does it have to offer the Christian church? *Journal of the American Scientific Affiliation*, 37, 79–85.

Bradshaw, M. (2019). Unpublished comments used by author permission.

Kaplan, J., & Tolin, D. (2015, October 20). Exposure therapy for anxiety disorders. *Psychiatric Times.com.*

Jones, J., & Butman, R. (1991). *Modern psychotherapies: A comprehensive Christian appraisal.* Downer's Grove, IL: Intervarsity Press.

LoPiccolo, J. (1978) Direct treatment of sexual dysfunction. in J. LoPiccolo and L. LoPiccolo (Eds.), *Handbook of sex therapy.* New York: Plenum Press.

Maletsky, B. (1980) Self centered versus court referred sexually deviant patients. *Behavior Therapy.* 11, 306–314.

Masters, W.H. and Johnson, V.E. (1970). *Human sexual response.* Boston: Little, Brown.

Morgan, B. and MacMillian, P. (1999). Helping clients move toward more constructive change. *Journal of Counseling and Development.* 77, (2), 153–159.

Shannan, et al. (2013). Virtual reality exposure therapy for social anxiety disorder. *Journal of Social Psychology and Clinical Psychology,* 81 (5), 751–760.

Skinner, B.F. (1971). *Beyond freedom and dignity.* New York: Knopf.

Stanpfl, T. (1975, February). Implosive therapy. *Psychology Today.*

Stevens J. (2015, October 20). *Body watch: Virtual reality.* LA Times retrieved.

Watson, J.B., and Raynor, R. (1920). Conditioned emotional reactions. *Journal of Experimental Psychology,* 3 (1), 1–14.

Wolpe, J. (1969). *The practice of behavior therapy.* New York: Pergamon Press.

Wolpe, J., and Lazarus, A. (1975). *Behavior therapy techniques.* New York: Wiley.

Study Questions

1. Fill in the following questions correctly.

    a. Classical conditioning was first developed by _____.
    b. Another term used for classical conditioning is _____ conditioning.
    c. Another term used for operant conditioning is called _____ conditioning.
    d. In classical conditioning, the inborn unlearned response is called the _____ response.
    e. In classical conditioning the learned response (i.e. salivating to the bell) is called the _____ response.
    f. In _____ conditioning the organism is considered to have a free choice.
    g. An inborn unlearned reinforcer is called a _____ reinforcer.
    h. A learned reinforcer is called a _____ reinforcer.
    i. A reward is called a _____ reinforcer.
    j. A noxious stimulus that the organism does not want is called a _____.
    k. Getting successive approximations of the desired behavior is called _____.
    l. A technique that teaches a person deep muscle relaxation and then imagines a hierarchy of anxiety producing situations is called _____ _____.
    m. Punishment is used in _____ therapy.
    n. A therapy where a person imitates another is called _____.
    o. _____ _____ is a type of therapy, often used in institutional settings, where a person is given something that can be turned in later for a reward.
    p. In sex therapy the married couple learns to touch each other's body and then communicate how it feels. This is called _____ _____.

2. Reflect on when you were a child. What reinforcers and punishers did your parents use to influence your behavior? What would you do differently with your children?
3. Find an area in your life where you feel most anxious or phobic. Next, practice deep breathing. Then, practice tensing and relaxing all of the large muscle groups in your body (i.e. arms, legs, face.) After you are able to relax fully, write down a hierarchy of anxiety producing stimuli and practice successively relaxing to each level in that hierarchy.
4. Explain at least 10 reinforcers or punishers that you have used in the past. What types of reinforcers were they?

CHAPTER TEN

COGNITIVE BEHAVIORAL THERAPIES

The various cognitive behavioral therapies were developed and adopted by behaviorists who realized that the pure reinforcement or punishment of behavior was not enough to help people with psychological problems. Cognitive behavior therapies attempt to bridge the gap between behavior and the internal processes—thoughts, beliefs and attitudes. These various therapies are in some ways off shoots of behavior therapy.

COGNITIVE THERAPY OF AARON BECK AND DAVID BURNS

Aaron Beck was one of the leaders in cognitive behavior therapy. Beck taught that everyone has cognitive distortions or ways of thinking that are irrational and maladaptive. He explained that anxious, phobic and depressed people have automatic thoughts that are somewhat out of contact with reality and need to be examined rationally. The irrational thoughts, fears and beliefs cause the person to have irrational anxieties. Different irrational beliefs that a person might have include feelings of stupidity, fear of mental illness, or feelings of being bad. Like other cognitive therapists, Beck believes that if you want to change irrational emotions you need to change a person's thinking.

Beck prescribes Cognitive Therapy (CT) for many types of disorders, especially anxiety and depression. Cognitive Therapy is brief and time limited, meaning that the therapist only works on the cognitive distortions. When they are cleared up and the emotional distress subsides, the therapy is terminated. Beck believes that cognitive therapy is a "collaborate effort between therapist and patient" and emphasizes the importance of a "sound therapeutic" relationship between therapist and patient. Cognitive Therapy is based on the Socratic Method, a technique whereby therapist questions in detail the patient's ideas, beliefs and attitudes. This questioning is to help the client find the irrational aspects of one's thinking and then to change this thinking to be more rational.

Cognitive Therapy has been labelled very structured and directive, problem oriented, educational, inductive, and homework oriented. In other words, the CT therapist goes directly to a person's irrational thinking and questions that person about the irrational thoughts, attempting to help the individual to see that it is the irrational thoughts that contribute to the disorder.

To illustrate, a depressed person may say, "I am stupid and no good. I treated my mother horribly and now she is dead and it is too late for me. I just want to die. That is why I tried to take my life." This statement is loaded with irrational statements. Beck would question in minute detail what the person means when she says that she is no good. Beck asks, "Can you be more specific?"

Under a therapist's careful questioning the client begins to understand that she is neither stupid nor no good, and that she does deserve to live. She recognizes that it would do no one any good if she took her life. Beck gets the person to see that her irrational thoughts are causing her to be depressed and if she would change the irrational thinking, she could recover from her depression.

One method that cognitive therapists use is to give the patient homework. This homework can range from telling your brother your real feelings to counting the number of your morbid thoughts. This homework is reality based and designed to change one's thinking to a more rational mode. Once more rational thinking is instituted, then more rational and effective behavior can develop. Cognitive therapy has proven quite effective with people who suffer from depression.

In the preface to his book, *Feeling Good: The New Mood Therapy*, Burns wrote about the positive effects of cognitive therapy for depression. Burns says:

> "The research seemed to reveal that the depressed individual sees himself as a <u>loser</u>—as an inadequate person doomed to frustration, deprivation, humiliation, and failure. Further experiments showed a marked difference between the depressed person's self-evaluation, expectations, his aspirations on the one hand and his actual achievements—often very striking—on the other. My conclusion was that depression must involve a disturbance in thinking: the depressed person thinks in idiosyncratic and negative ways about himself, his environment, and his future. The pessimistic mental set affects his mood, his motivation, and his relationships with others, and leads to the full spectrum of psychological and physical symptoms typical of depression. We now have a large body of research data and clinical experience which suggests that people can learn to control painful mood swings and self-defeating behavior through the application of a few relatively simple principles and techniques. The promising results of this investigation have triggered interest in cognitive theory among psychiatrists, psychologists, and other mental health professionals." (Burns, pp. xi–xii)

In this same book, Burns discusses ten <u>Cognitive Distortions</u> he believes are present in most depressive states. They are:

COMMON COGNITIVE DISTORTIONS

1. ALL-OR-NOTHING THINKING

You see things in black and white categories. If your performance falls short of perfect, you see yourself as a total failure.

2. OVERGENERALIZATION

You see a single negative event as a never-ending pattern of defeat.

3. MENTAL FILTER

You pick out a single negative detail and dwell on it exclusively so that your vision of all reality becomes darkened, like the drop of ink that discolors the entire beaker of water.

4. DISQUALIFYING THE POSITIVE

You reject positive experiences by insisting they "don't count" for some reason or other. In this way you can maintain a negative belief that is contradicted by your everyday experiences.

5. JUMPING TO CONCLUSIONS

You make a negative interpretation even though there are no definite facts to support your conclusion.

a. MIND READING

You arbitrarily conclude that someone is reacting negatively to you, and you don't bother to check this out.

b. THE FORTUNE TELLER ERROR

You anticipate that things will turn out badly, and you feel convinced that your prediction is an already established fact.

6. MAGNIFICATION (CATASTROPHIZING) / MINIMIZATION (DENIAL)

You exaggerate the importance of things (such as your goof-up or someone else's achievement), or you inappropriately shrink things until they appear tiny (your own desirable qualities or the other fellow's imperfections). This is also called the binocular trick.

7. EMOTIONAL REASONING

You assume that your negative emotions necessarily reflect the way things really are: "I feel it and therefore it must be true."

8. SHOULD STATEMENTS

You try to motivate yourself with should and shouldn't, as if you had to be whipped and punished before you could be expected to do anything. Musts and oughts are also offenders. The emotional consequence is guilt. When you direct should statements toward others, you feel anger, frustration, and resentment.

9. LABELING AND MISLABELING

This is an extreme form of overgeneralization. Instead of describing your error, you attach a negative label to yourself: "I'm a loser." When someone else's behavior rubs you the wrong way, you attach a negative label to him: "He's a louse." Mislabeling involves describing an event with language that is highly colored and emotionally loaded.

10. PERSONALIZATION

You see yourself as the cause of some negative external event for which in fact you were not primarily responsible. Not only are these distortions commonly found in depressed individuals, but they are also found in all of us to some degree. They contribute to some of our anxieties and distorted world views. The goal of Cognitive Therapy is not only to help the person identify these cognitive distortions, but also to change this thinking to more realistic, rational modes of thinking.

RATIONAL EMOTIVE THERAPY OF ALBERT ELLIS

Albert Ellis (1913–2007), the founder of Rational Emotive Therapy (RET), like many of his contemporaries, was a frustrated psychoanalyst who strode off in a new direction. Ellis's ideas are quite similar to those of Beck and Burns in that Ellis believes that people are loaded with <u>irrational beliefs</u> and that these beliefs cause unnecessary anxiety and suffering. Ellis's view of human nature is that people have a tremendous capacity to think rationally or to think irrationally. The goal of Rational Emotive Therapy is to help people think in more rational terms.

At the core of emotional problems, Ellis says, is <u>blaming</u>. People blame themselves and others which causes much needless suffering. In RET the person learns to let go of blaming and learn new, healthier <u>self-statements</u>. The term <u>self-statements</u> according to RET therapists are those deeply conditioned comments we make when we talk to ourselves, and which tend to color our view of the world. The person who constantly sees the world in a pessimistic light needs to look at these invalidating negative self-statements and change them to more realistic self-statements.

The relationship between the therapist and the client is one of teacher and learner. The therapist (teacher) is constantly helping the client (learner) to examine his or her belief system and is encouraging the client learner to change negative self-statements to positive ones.

COMMON IRRATIONAL BELIEFS

Ellis lists eleven irrational beliefs that he says make people "crazy" and are associated with a variety of psychological disorders. They are:

1. It is absolutely essential to be loved or approved of by every significant person in one's life.
2. To be worthwhile, a person must be competent, adequate, and achieving in everything attempted.
3. Some people are wicked, bad, and villainous and therefore should be blamed or punished.
4. It is terrible and catastrophic whenever events do not occur as one hopes.
5. Unhappiness is the result of outside events, and therefore a person has no control over such despair.
6. Something potentially dangerous or harmful should be cause for great concern and should always be kept in mind.
7. Running away from difficulties and responsibilities is easier than facing them.
8. A person must depend on others and must have someone stronger on whom to rely.
9. The past determines one's present behavior and thus cannot be changed.
10. A person should be upset by the problems and difficulties of others.
11. There is always a right answer to every problem, and a failure to find this answer is a catastrophe.

THE ABC'S OF RATIONAL EMOTIVE THERAPY

Rational Emotive Therapy teaches that positive thoughts lead to positive feelings and behaviors. Ellis explains that some people believe that certain events in our lives automatically cause certain emotions and Ellis elaborates that this is not true. He says that all events get filtered through our cognitive or belief system before they go on to create emotions. It is what we think or believe about events that affects our emotional lives, more than the events themselves. Often people <u>make awful</u> or <u>catastrophic</u> the events in their lives instead of viewing them in perspective.

For example, Joe might ask Mary out for a date and get rejected. Joe might then start magnifying the event by saying, "She is evil anyway," or "I am so ugly and no good that no girl would ever want to go out with me," or "I feel so bad that I will never ask another girl out again in my life." Rejection can also initiate an irrational belief system which can lead to irrational, inappropriate emotions and consequent irrational behaviors. For example, Joe might get nasty with Mary the next time he sees her. An RET therapist would reason with Joe, teach him to stop blaming himself and others, and to look at the situation logically. MAYBE, Mary already has a boyfriend. NO, she is not evil for rejecting him. YES, Joe is good looking and there are other girls that will accept his request for a date.

In helping clients dispute irrational beliefs, Ellis gives them <u>homework</u> in which they test reality and learn new behaviors. In the case of Joe, the therapist might suggest that his homework be talking to other girls and finally asking others out for dates.

The ABC system in RET explains that A is an *Activating* <u>Event</u> which causes B, a <u>Thought or *Belief*</u> <u>System</u>, which causes C, the <u>Emotional and Behavioral *Consequences*</u> of the thought or belief system. The goal of RET therapy is to intervene at B (the thought or <u>belief</u> system) with the therapist helping the client, by using scientific logic (*Disrupting Intervention*), to change B to a more flexible and realistic mode of thinking. E (*Effect*) then helps the client develop more reasonable ways of looking at interpersonal situations and reality in general F (New *Feeling*).

A (**ACTIVATING** EVENT) → B (THOUGHT or **BELIEF** SYSTEM) → C (EMOTIONAL and BEHAVIORAL **CONSEQUENCE**) → D (**DISPUTING** INTERVENTION) → (**EFFECT**) → (NEW **FEELING**)

In other words, examine the negative belief system and substitute the irrational belief with a more rational and effective one, and a new more positive feeling will flood the mind and change the emotions to more positive ones. (Ellis and Harper)

Ellis cautions people about using terms like "must," "ought," "have to," "need," and "should" because they are absolutes and can have dire emotional consequences. RET therapists help clients to eliminate "must" like statements from their vocabularies. Also similar to Gestalt therapists, RET therapists encourage clients to eliminate "to be" statements from their vocabularies, because terms like "I am," "I was being," "she is," or "he was" do not make the distinction between the person and the behavior. This lack of distinction causes the person to label, and labeling a person is dangerous. Instead of saying, "I was evil," the person is encouraged to change the statement to "I acted inappropriately."

This change in language helps the person from labeling her or himself and keeps the focus on the behaviors. If a person labels oneself as bad, it is harder to convince him or her that improvement is attainable. When the person is encouraged to focus on the behavior, and learns to recognize the irrational behaviors, then one can be more easily persuaded to change these behaviors to more adaptive ones.

EVIDENCE BASED COGNITIVE BEHAVIORAL THERAPIES

Newer Cognitive Therapies have developed a large variety of over lapping and evidence-based techniques that address the disorders that are more difficult to treat, such as Post Traumatic Stress Disorder and Personality

Disorders. These various therapies have been quite effective in treating some of the following disorders: Anxiety and Panic Disorders, Complex Stress Disorders, Addiction Disorders (including Anorexia, Bulimia, Substance Abuse), Dissociative Disorders, Depression and Bipolar Disorders, as well a relationship dysfunctions, anger and hostility issues, social dysfunctioning, stress related issues, and numerous physical problems.

The approaches are becoming eclectic and holistic. For example, cognitive therapists are encouraging exercise and diet as part of a treatment plan.

COMPLEX TRAUMA INTERVENTION

To understand newer cognitive behavioral therapy approaches a review of updated research regarding the nervous system functioning is valid. The nervous system that functions when we are in a resting state, called the Parasympathetic Nervous System (PNS), takes care of our everyday bodily functions (building up and repairing the body, and making sure it is functioning properly.) There is, however, another part of the nervous system that is more primitive and it has to do with protection and fighting off fearful invaders, i.e. a vicious dog. It is called the Sympathetic Nervous System (SNS). When the SNS is turned on, it causes what is called the fight/flight response, which has to do with mobilization of the body. Current research has found that the SNS has company when it is activated. These two partners to the SNS are called the Ventral Vagal Complex (VVC) and the Dorsal Vagal Complex (DVC).

At this time a stimulant is produced by the body called adrenalin. If the adrenalin producing system is turned on for too long and the body is not expending the energy it is stimulating, i.e. through exercise, it can start breaking down the body and causing physical and psychological problems. It can cause anxiety, anger, stomach aches, heart problems and other issues. One of the damaging chemicals produced by the adrenal gland that can build up is cortisol. Under stress cortisol can accumulate and damage the body, especially when it isn't exercised away.

The Polyvagal Nervous System (PNS) is a partner to the Sympathetic Nervous System (SNS). There are three parts to the Polyvagal Nervous System (Porges, 1995).

1. Ventral Vagal Complex (VVC)

It is a signaling system responsible for motion, emotion and communication. This is considered the most developed part of the three parts of the Polyvagal Nervous System. It is the body's social engagement system and it is located both in the brain and above the diaphragm. The VVC is fine-tuned to respond to the environment and helps us create choices in the world. It allows us to work with the nervous system to stimulate (energize) or immobilize our bodies (i.e. to consciously hide and be still if there is a burglar in your house.) It blends the nervous system states to alert the body to a threat, and, yet, to be in control.

2. Sympathetic Nervous System (SNS)

It is the basic Fight-Flight-Freeze system that is turned on when we have a strong fear or anger response. It is mainly located above the diaphragm. The SNS overlaps functioning with the VVC and /or the DVC, depending the pending on the perception of a threat. At one time the flight response dominates and at another threat the freeze response may take over.

3.   Dorsal Vagal Complex (DVC)

This is the most primitive part of the SNS and can cause immobilization. This is a passive defense system (e.g. a woman screams and faints.) It is located below the diaphragm and works with other parts of the nervous system to express <u>Fright, Flag or Faint.</u> This system is more destructive and involuntary. Activation of this nervous system can be caused by trauma and can lead to lasting emotional scars which professionals have spent years trying to understand and treat. For example, in treating PTSD veterans, doctors routinely prescribe drugs, but now therapists have learned to treat PTSD with therapy.

Fright—This is dual activation, abrupt alternations between the SNS and DVC leading to panic, dizziness, and nausea.

Flag—DVC also effects the polyvagal nervous system (PNS) leading to blood pressure drops, collapse, helplessness, loss of speech and vision, numbness (shock).

Faint—DVC causes immobilization, dissociation, and/or loss of bowel/bladder control. This causes an involuntary vagal break on the SNS where it can shut down and cause hopelessness, despair, addiction and dissociation. This has historically been difficult to treat when clients get stuck in this state. People may develop these responses as a result of being abused or neglected as children, battered in a relationship, or soldiers who have suffered from combat or imprisonment.

Learned helplessness becomes a conditioned response that has been recognized for years. "Failure to fight or escape, that is, the physical immobilization becomes a conditioned behavioral response," and new therapies are being developed are being developed to treat these complex disorders. (Gentry, pp. 36–43)

DIALECTICAL BEHAVIOR THERAPY (DBT)

A variety of evidence-based treatments have been found helpful for the myriad of psychological disorders. Following are some of the suggestions that DBT therapists are taught to teach their clients.

One approach, developed by Linehan and Tibbitts (2018), starts with a questionnaire about the problems and possible solutions that the client is experiencing. This is done best if the client takes the questions home and carefully answers them as homework. Another way is to ask each question and to discuss each question in depth.

CHAIN ANALYSIS OF PROBLEM BEHAVIOR WORKSHEET

I. Describe the specific PROBLEM BEHAVIOR.

   A.   Be very specific and detailed. Do not use vague terms.
   B.   Identify exactly what you did, said, thought, or felt.
   C.   Describe the intensity of the behavior and other characteristics of the behavior that are important.
   D.   Describe the problem behavior in enough detail that an actor in a play or movie could recreate the behavior exactly.

II. Describe the specific PRECIPITATION EVENT that started the whole chain of behavior. Start with the environmental event that started the chain. Always start with some event in your environment, even if it doesn't seem to you that the environmental even "caused" the problem behavior. Possible questions to get at this are:

   A.   What exact event precipitated the start of the chain reaction?

    B.   When did the problem start?

    C.   What was going on when the problem started?

    D.   What were you doing, thinking, feeling, imagining at that time?

    E.   Why did the problem behavior happen on that day instead of the day before?

III. Describe in general VULNERABILITY FACTORS happening before the precipitation event. What factors or events made you more vulnerable to a problematic chain? Areas to examine include: physical illness, use of drugs or alcohol, stressful events in the environment, intense emotions felt, your previous behaviors that you found stressful.

IV. Describe in excruciating detail THE CHAIN OF EVENTS that led up to the problem behavior. Imagine that your problem behavior is chained to the precipitating event in the environment. What next? How long is the chain? Where does it go? What are the links? The links can be thoughts, emotions, sensations and behaviors. Write out all links in the chain of events, no matter how small. Be very specific, as if you were writing a script for a play.

    A.   What exact thought (or belief), feeling, or action followed the precipitating event? What thought, feeling, or action followed that? What next?

    B.   Look at each link in the chain after you write it. Was there another thought, feeling, or action that could have occurred? Could someone else have thought, felt, or acted differently at that point? If so, explain how that specific thought, feeling, or action came to be.

    C.   For each link in the chain, is there a smaller link I could describe?

V. What are the CONSEQUENCES of this behavior? Be specific.

    A.   How did other people react immediately and later?

    B.   How did you feel immediately following the behavior? Later?

    C.   What effect did the behavior have on you and your environment?

VI. Describe in detail different SOLUTIONS to the problem.

    A.   Go back to the chain of your behaviors following the prompting event. Circle each point or link indicating that if you had done something different, you would have avoided the problem behavior.

    B.   What could you have done differently at each link in the chain of events to avoid the problem behavior? What coping behaviors or skillful behaviors could you have used?

VII. Describe in detail the PREVENTION STRATEGY for how you could have kept the chain from starting by reducing your vulnerability to the chain.

VIII. Describe what you are going to do to REPAIR important or significant consequences of the problem behavior. (Tibbitts, pp.95–97)

MEANINGFUL ALLIANCE and CLIENT FEEDBACK

    Now that the client has identified the chain of events and experiences he or she has gone through, there are important factors and techniques to keep in mind as the therapist encourages the client toward healing.

Studies have found that the first and most important thing to do is develop and deepen a meaningful therapeutic alliance with the client. (Courtois and Pearlman, 2005) As the counselor walks the client through the Problem Chain Analysis a closer meaningful alliance is building between the therapist and the client. The counselor is constantly gaining feed back from the client on whether the problem is being alleviated and the client believes that the counselor is "allied" with the client to solve the problem.

"In 2013, Feedback Informed Treatment (FIT), formally using measures of progress and the therapeutic alliance to guide care, was deemed an evidence-based practice by the Substance Abuse and Mental Health Service Administration (SAMHSA), and listed on the official National Registry of Evidence-based Programs and Practices (NREPP) website. (On this website a large variety of SAMHSA treatments can be found.) Research to date shows that FIT as much as doubles the effectiveness of behavioral health services, while decreasing costs, deterioration and dropout rates. One example is a video demonstration by Scott D. Miller (www. scottdmiller. com) which shows, "I am a really good therapist, but not with you yet. I need your help. Please teach me. Help me how to do it with you. I want you to tell me how to bring therapy to you." (Gentry, p.84)

Another way the therapeutic process has improved is to have the client evaluate how each therapy session went, on a sliding scale, from "I did not feel heard, understood and respected" to "I felt heard, understood and respected." Another is "The therapist's approach is not a good fit for me" to "The therapist's approach is a good fit for me." While this approach is much harder on the therapist than it is on the client, it has been shown to forge a stronger therapeutic alliance with the client. To study this in more detail research the Institute for the Study of Therapeutic Change. (www.talkingcure.com) (Miller, 2002)

TEACH RELAXATION

Pelvic Floor Relaxation

Fear is a commonly brought up emotion that interferes with therapeutic progress. Fear is usually accompanied by tension in the body. With the pelvic floor relaxation technique, the counselor first asks, "Where is the perceived threat right now. Look around tell me if you see something here that will hurt you."

If the client replies, "I am going to die," the counselor might say, "Dying is something we all will face someday, but right now it is not a perceived threat. Look around. Is there any threat in this room? Fear of death reduces your quality of life. Let's learn to live until we die."

As therapy is a coaching process and developing a strong therapeutic alliance with the client, the therapist will then instruct the client in self-regulation. "When you are afraid, your muscles are tense. Imagine the two bones that you are sitting on and imagine a line going connecting the two bones. Next, imagine that two lines go up at 45-degree angles from each side up to your hips and a line connects your two hips.

This is called the pelvic floor. Most of the major muscles of your body go from your legs up through that pelvic floor between your hips and to your stomach and back muscles. Imagine a square from each of your hips through your pelvic floor. Now, let's learn to relax these pelvic floor muscles and feel your whole body relax. First, tense the muscles in your pelvic floor for as long as you can. Second, relax them."

Porges found that "relaxing the tension of the pelvic floor muscles switches the nervous system from sympathetic to parasympathetic dominance, regaining neocortical functioning in 20–30 seconds. This relieves pressure on the vagal nerve. It is impossible to experience stress when you are comfortable in your own skin. (Gentry, pp. 55–56) (Other relaxation therapies are discussed in the chapter on Group Therapy.)

EYE MOVEMENT DESENSITIZATION AND REPROCESSING (EMDR)

Another evidence-based therapy, that takes extensive training to learn, is Eye Movement and Desensitization and Reprocessing (EMDR.) It is used with people that have been traumatized, such as combat victims or rape survivors. It has proven extremely effective with as many as 80 to 100% of trauma survivors in different studies (Shapiro, 2001). The therapist first interviews the client regarding the flashbacks and/or anxiety suffered from trauma or traumas. Then, using a hand, finger or object the therapist moves this appendage bilaterally (left to right) as the client lets the trauma play out in his or her head. This sustained bilateral movement helps survivors integrate and desensitize these past traumatic experiences with minimal pain. EMDR's effectiveness, like all psychotherapies, is contingent upon the development and maintenance of a good therapeutic relationship. (For more information contact http://www.emdr.com)

VALIDATION

A person who confides in a therapist is more likely to open up if the therapist has a kind, loving, soft way of looking at the client, and a relaxed and friendly demeanor (like Mr. Rogers.) When a client confides, one is usually not looking for advice or problem-solving, unless specifically asked for. Rather, the person is looking for validation. With validation, therapists communicate to clients that their life responses make sense and are understandable within the context or situation. Therapists actively accept clients and do not discount or trivialize the client's responses.

There are six levels of validation that Linehan first outlined in 1997.

LEVEL 1 VALIDATION

Overall show interest in the other person through verbal and nonverbal cues. Show that you are paying attention (nodding, soft expression, eye contact.)

Ask questions. "What then?" Give prompts. "Tell me more," "Uh-huh."

LEVEL 2 VALIDATION

Use accurate reflection. "So, you're frustrated because your son hasn't cleaned up his room." Summarize what the person is saying and then ask, "Is that right?" Take a nonjudgmental stance toward the person; be matter-of-fact, and have an "of course" attitude.

LEVEL 3 VALIDATION

Try to read a person's behavior, imagine what he or she could be feeling, thinking or wishing for. Check for accuracy. "Is that right?" It feels good when someone takes the time to think about our life experiences, but it is best to not make assumptions.

LEVEL 4 VALIDATION

Sometimes the counselor might say, "Given your history and all that you have been through, your behavior make a lot of sense and is understandable."

LEVEL 5 VALIDATION

Communicate that the person's behavior is reasonable, meaningful and effective. For example, "It seems very normal to be nervous before a job interview. That sure make sense to me," or "It sounds like you were very clear and direct with your doctor."

LEVEL 6 VALIDATION

Treat the person as valid; don't patronize or condescend. Recognize the person with strengths and limitations. Give the person equal status and equal respect. Be genuine with the person about your reactions to him or her and about yourself. Believe in the other person while seeing one's individual struggles and pain. (Tibbitts, pp.71–75)

TEACH **IMPROVE** SKILLS

Each letter in the word **IMPROVE** stands for a specific skill that the client is encouraged to learn. (Linehan, 2019)

1. **IMAGERY:** Learn to relax and think about beautiful thoughts and lovely places. Meditate on a "safe place" where you can go in to your mind to feel less anxious.
2. **IMPROVE:** Find or create some purpose, meaning, or value in your pain. Remember and learn about spiritual values.
3. **PRAYER:** Pray to God for strength for what you are going through. Open your heart up to God.
4. **RELAXATION:** Learn how to relax by tensing your large muscles and then letting go of the tension.
5. **ONE THING:** Focus all of your attention on one thing and block all other things out.
6. **VACATION:** Give yourself a brief vacation whether it is just staying in bed for a few hours or a walk in the park.
7. **ENCOURAGEMENT:** Be you own cheerleader. Say to yourself, "This won't last forever," or "I'm doing the best I can do."

RADICAL ACCEPTANCE

Most therapists agree that most psychological problems happen because a person won't accept something. Often people fight accepting an anxiety arousing experience that is staring them in the face. Denial is the opposite of acceptance and denial of a reality can destroy a person. The first thing to changing something is to accept it. Radical acceptance is the capacity to see clearly what is happening in the moment, and to accept what we see with love. Radical acceptance will release clients from the past. In this approach (1) clients agree that they have suffered much in the past. (2) They have decided that suffering once is enough. (3) They accept what happened and develop skills to handle the present. (4) Or they decide to stay the same. (Linehan, 2018)

In concluding, generally cognitive therapies are brief or short-term therapy. Unlike psychoanalysis, cognitive therapies are generally very specific and goal oriented. As soon as the client reaches the goal, the therapy is terminated. As a result, cognitive therapies only last for a period from a few weeks to several months. Rarely does cognitive therapy last for years.

The more recent Cognitive Therapies, such as DBT and therapies for Complex Trauma, have developed a large variety of over lapping and evidence-based techniques that are quite effective with many disorders that are more difficult to treat, such as Personality Disorders (PD) and PTSD. The approaches are becoming more eclectic and holistic. For example, cognitive therapists are encouraging exercise and diet as part of a treatment plan.

The SAMHSA Suicide Prevention lifeline (1-800-273-8255) and the National Helpline for treatment referral and information (1-800-985-5990) are available resources as well as www.aabt.org.

A CHRISTIAN VIEW OF COGNITIVE THERAPIES

Both Behaviorism and, its cousin, Cognitive Therapies are wedded to "the behavioristic presuppositions of materialism, naturalism, atomism, reductionism and scientism which are unacceptable for Christians because they exclude God and supernatural activity and they strip humanity of its God-given rationality and dignity." (Jones, p. 207). However, Cognitive Therapies are ever reaching higher for more effective evidence-based techniques that "really work" to reduce disorders such as anxiety, depression, PTSD and others.

Christian therapists often argue that the "irrational beliefs" that clients hold are often judged more by their "utility" rather than their truthfulness. The Bible says, **"You shall know the truth and the truth will set you free." (John 8:22)** Even though some more contemporary Cognitive Therapists are encouraging prayer, to a Christian, it all depends on to whom you pray.

Increasingly, it seems as if more and more Cognitive Therapists are embracing and encouraging New Age concepts and Eastern religions. For example, DBT integrates its cognitive behaviorism not only with analytic concepts but also with the mindfulness training of Eastern religion and Yoga exercises. Mindfulness, meditation, and other Eastern teachings are even being inadvertently taught from the Christian pulpit.

One woman, a college professor, who professed that she was a Christian proclaimed, "I am God and I am one with the Universe." The woman wasn't psychotic; she was deceived. Perhaps it behooves Christian therapists to develop Christian stretching and exercise classes and ditch yoga and its accompanying mantras, which are calling up Hindu gods. Develop Christian meditation instead of "mindfulness," which ultimately leads down the same road of deception. What some psychologists call "truth" may not be what God calls truth.

Does this mean that a Christian shouldn't study psychology? Many Christian psychologists would disagree. There are many teachings in the "mechanics of psychology" that do help reduce anxiety, depressions and other maladaptive behaviors. Of all the theories presented, the Cognitive Behavior Therapies are more closely aligned to biblical principles. The Bible teaches that we are to be transformed by the renewal of the mind, (Romans 12:2) We need to first know the Scriptures, and then study psychology to try and view it as God would see it.

As you contemplate the connections between the mind, spirit and body, you must determine to what extent or if and when you will help others towards positive mental health by utilizing biblical principles and concepts.

References

Academy of Cognitive Therapy. www.academyofct.org.

Albert Ellis Institute. www.rebt.org or www.albertellisinstitute.org.

Association for Behavioral and Cognitive Therapies. www.aabt.org.

Beck, A.T. (1975). *Depression, causes and treatment*. Philadelphia: University of Pennsylvania Press.

Beck, A.T. (1976). *Cognitive therapy and emotional disorders*. New York: International Universities Press.

Beck, A., Rush, A., Shaw, B., and Emery, G. (1979). *Cognitive therapy of depression*. New York: Guilford Press.

Burns, D. (1981). *Feeling good, the new mood therapy*. New York: New American Library.

Corey, G. (2005). *Theory and practice of counseling and psychotherapy*. Monterey, CA.: Brooks/Cole Publishing Co.

Coleman, T. (2015). *How to make group psychotherapy work*. Bloomington, IN: Xlibris.

Courtois, C., and Pearlman, L. (2005). Clinical applications of the attachment framework: Relational treatment of complex trauma. *Journal of Trauma Stress*.

Ellis, A. (1962). *Reason and emotion in psychotherapy*. New York: Lyle Stuart.

Ellis, A. (1973). *Humanistic psychotherapy: The rational emotive approach*. New York: Julian Press.

Ellis, A. (2001). *Overcoming destructive beliefs, feeling and behaviors*. Amherst, NY: Prometheus Books.

Ellis, A. (2002). *Overcoming resistance*. New York: Springer.

Ellis, A. (1984). Rational emotive therapy and pastoral counseling: A Reply to Richard Wessler. *Personnel and Guidance Journal*, 62.

Ellis, A. (1984). The Essence of RET. *Journal of Rational Emotive Therapy*, 2(1), 19–25.

EMDR Therapy as discussed in www.emdr.com (2019). Gentry, E. (2018). *Complex trauma*. Eau Claire, Wisconsin: PESI.

Linehan, M. in Tibbitts, A. (2018). *Dialectical behavior therapy*. Eau Claire, Wisconsin: PESI.

Miller, S. (2002). *Institute for the study of therapeutic change*. www.talkingcure.com.

Miller, S. (2013). Feedback informed therapy. www.scottdmiller.com.

Porges, S. (2011). *The polyvagal theory*. New York: Norton.

Shapiro, F. (2018). *Eye movement desensitization and reprocessing (EMDMR) therapy*. New York: Guilford Press.

Study Questions

1. Fill in the blanks with the correct answer.

    a. Beck teaches that the people who are anxious, phobic or depressed, need to change the way they _____ or believe.

    b. Cognitive therapy is based on the _____ method.

    c. The goal of cognitive therapy is to help the person to think in a manner that is more _____.

    d. Beck said that the basis of most depression is _____ thinking.

    e. The cognitive therapy of Beck and Burns seems particularly effective with people who have a _____ disorder.

    f. A person has a positive experience but discounts it. Burns calls this cognitive distortion _____ _____ _____.

    g. John thinks Sue is going to reject him even though she gives no evidence of it. Burns calls this cognitive distortion _____ _____.

    h. Bill says, "I am stupid." Burns would say the person is using _____ or _____ as a cognitive distortion.

    i. In RET the person learns healthier _____ _____.

    j. In RET the relationship between the therapist and the client is between _____ and learner.

    k. The goal of RET is to change negative self-statements into _____ self-statements.

    l. In the ABC's of RET, C stands for _____ or _____ _____.

    m. In the mnemonic device IMPROVE, what does each of the letters stand for?

    n. All cognitive behavior therapists tend to give _____ for a client to perform in order for clients to learn to test reality.

    o. When a person relaxes by visualizing a walk on a sandy beach this technique is called _____ _____.

2. Make a list of at least ten words or phrases that cognitive behavior therapists would suggest you eliminate from your vocabulary.
3. Carefully reexamine the list of the 10 cognitive disorders listed by Burns. From your own life, give an example from each of a time you have used this distortion.
4. Make your own list of at least 5 distortions that a depressed person might have.
5. Explain the reason Ellis would discourage a therapist from asking WHY questions.
6. Carefully review the list of common cognitive distortions given by Ellis. Of which are you guilty? Explain.
7. Explain the value of teaching a client to visualize a safe place.
8. What is the role of the sympathetic nervous system?

CHAPTER ELEVEN

REALITY THERAPY

William Glasser (1925–2013) was a psychiatrist who became interested in helping people with conduct disorders, particularly in <u>acting out</u> disorders, when he started to work for the Ventura School for Girls, a school for juvenile delinquents. In this setting he developed Reality Therapy (RT). Even though the ideas of Reality Therapy were developed over fifty years ago, many of the ideas are still relevant.

Psychologist Dr. O. Herbert Mowrer in the forward to Glasser's book (1975) summarizes Glasser's ideas:

> "Reality Therapy outlines a new and positive approach helping the emotionally distressed. Attacking the whole concept of 'mental illness' and orthodox Freudian methods, Dr. Glasser contends that the mentally ill are unable to satisfy their needs realistically and behave irresponsibly because they 'deny the world around them.' As a therapeutic method, Reality Therapy emphasizes moral values. It does not concern itself with the patient's past, but with his present and future. The therapist, says the author, has the task of teaching his patients to acquire the ability to fulfill their needs and to do so in a way that does not deprive others of the ability to fulfill their needs."

Glasser rejects completely the traditional medical model that sees behavioral problems as an "illness" that medicine will cure. He said that the medical model characterized mental illness as pure determinism. Reality Therapy teaches clients that they are no longer a victim, and that they are responsible and have control over their behavior. The therapist works with the client to plan better choices or better goals for the future. Little time is spent talking about the past. Convincing clients that they have control over their future is the key to understanding this therapy.

The basic idea behind RT is that some people have a <u>failure identity</u> and have learned to try to <u>fulfill their needs</u> in an <u>irresponsible manner</u>. Glasser says that while everyone has same basic needs, the most important are:

1. The need for survival
2. The need to love and be loved
3. The need to belong and to have a worthwhile feeling about oneself and others.
4. The need for power. The need to believe you have control over your life.
5. The need for freedom or independence.
6. The need for fun.

Whether individuals fulfill their needs or not, Glasser explains, they do develop an identity. Reality Therapy is a very directive form of therapy in which the therapist attempts to help develop a <u>success identity</u> by helping the client learn to satisfy his or her needs in a <u>responsible manner</u>. Glasser basically equates irresponsibility with mental illness, and responsibility with mental health.

Glasser outlines seven steps in Reality Therapy as follows:

1. ESTABLISH RAPPORT

This step is vital because if the client is not friends with the therapist, then all else will fail. The therapist must act in an empathetic, understanding way toward the client and to try to convey that he or she really cares and believes that the client can develop a success identity. Remember, <u>a client doesn't care how much you know, until he or she knows how much you care</u>. One of the ways to show you care is to listen very closely.

2. FOCUS ON THE CLIENT'S PRESENT BEHAVIORS

After developing a rapport with the client, the RT therapist asks the client about his or her behavior and if these actions are fulfilling the needs that are now present. The therapist helps the person review daily activities and ascertain if the way they are being handled is working. Most of the time is spent on present behaviors and changing them so that the future can be brighter. The therapist tries to work as an advocate and convince the client that they are working together to help the person have a more fulfilling life.

3. HAVE THE CLIENT EVALUATE HIS OR HER BEHAVIOR

Is the client fulfilling his or her needs in a responsible manner? The therapist asks if the behavior that the client is showing is the best approach to fulfilling this individual's needs.

4. DEVELOP A PLAN

Work with the client to find a plan that is reasonable, workable and achievable. Make sure the goals are within the client's reach.

5. GET A COMMITMENT FROM THE CLIENT

If the client is not committed to change, then the plan is doomed to failure. The client must see the value of the plan and want to work toward its goals. The therapist tries to keep the client focused on individual abilities and strengths, and encourages the person to believe that the goals set can be achieved.

6. DO NOT ACCEPT EXCUSES

Even though the RT therapist refuses to punish behavior, the therapist believes that the client will have to accept the <u>reasonable consequences</u> for one's own behaviors. After the client starts to succeed in responsibly fulfilling his or her needs, and starts getting a taste of a success identity, self-esteem improves.

7.   DO NOT GIVE UP

No matter what happens, the therapist should maintain a positive outlook toward the client and be optimistic about the client's ability to attain the goals. Likewise, it is important to distinguish between the person and the person's behaviors. The client is never labeled or put down, but sometimes the person's behaviors are confronted. While the person is never confronted, the irresponsible behaviors are identified and examined. The client is then encouraged to change them to more responsible behaviors.

Finally, Reality Therapy is a very directive type of therapy, quite similar to Adler's approach, and almost as directive as Rational Emotive Therapy. The therapist acts as a role model, teacher and cheerleader. The therapist is always trying to help the client simplify the therapeutic steps in order to experience the success identity as quickly as possible. With the taste of success will come the want for more success. When the plan is not working out in the desired fashion, the plan will be redeveloped to make it more within the client's reach.

A CHRISTIAN VIEW OF REALITY THERAPY

Reality Therapy is in harmony with the basic Judeo-Christian religious belief, according to Young, who listed five principles of Reality Therapy with compatible biblical principles.

1.   Reality Therapy stresses that everyone is responsible for his or her own actions. (Rom. 2:5–8; 1 Cor. 3:8; Ezek. 18:20; Gal. 6:7)
2.   In order to be responsible, a person must have rules or principles to obey and the opportunity to choose to obey. (Gen. 24:15–17, Josh. 24:14–15)
3.   All actions are followed by consequences. (Deut. 24:16)
4.   People are capable of changing behavior. (Ezek. 18:30; Acts 26:20)
5.   Involvement is important in changing people. (Eph. 5:32) (Jones p.247)

While Adler seemed to see Individual Therapy as congruent with biblical teachings, Glasser made no such assumptions. Glasser based his concepts of responsibility from his own ideas and not from any underlying biblical teachings. "Grace" is not an assumption that Glasser entertains. Some authorities have noticed that some counselors have taken the responsibility teachings too far and have created authoritarian programs that were detrimental to a healing atmosphere.

In spite of the criticism, Reality Therapy has been quite useful in working with delinquent youths and in drug rehabilitation programs and more recent studies have shown its effectiveness with teachers and counselors in a school setting. In more recent years the teachings of Reality Therapy have become less stringent and less inflexible.

References

Corey, G. (2009). *Theory and practice of counseling and psychotherapy*. Belmont, CA: Thompson Brooks/ Cole.

Glasser, W. (1998). *Choice therapy*. New York: Harper Collins.

Glasser, W. (1969). *Schools without failure*. New York: Harper Row.

Glasser, W. (1970). *Mental health or mental illness*. New York: Harper Row.

Glasser, W. (1972). *The identity society*. New York: Harper Row.

Glasser, W. (1975). *Reality therapy*. New York: Harper Row.

Glasser, W. (1976). *Positive addiction*. New York: Harper Row.

Glasser, W. (1984). *Take effective control of your life*. New York: Harper Row.

Jones, S., and Butman, R. (1991). *Modern psychotherapies*. Downer's Grove, IL: InterVarsity Press.

Mason, C., and Duba, J. (2009). Using reality therapy in schools. *Internal Journal of Reality Therapy*, 29.

Reality Therapy. http://www.wglasser.com and www.realitytherapywub.com

Young, J. (1982). The morality of reality therapy. *Journal of Reality Therapy*. 1, 8–11.

Study Questions

1. Fill in the blank with the correct answer.

   a. A person that is fulfilling his needs in an irresponsible manner is said to have a _____ identity.

   b. A person that is fulfilling her needs in a responsible manner is said to have a _____ _____.

   c. Basically Glasser equates mental illness with _____ and mental health with _____.

   d. If the person is irresponsible his _____ is confronted.

   e. No matter how irresponsible the client is, the therapist should never _____ the client. But sometimes the client will have to cope with _____ consequences.

2. In your own words explain what Glasser means by Success Identity.

3. Why do you think Glasser tells the therapist to only confront the client's behavior and not the client as a person?

4. Do you believe that it is reasonable to almost totally ignore the client's history?

5. What are some of the strengths of Reality Therapy?

6. What are some of the weaknesses of Reality Therapy?

CHAPTER TWELVE

GROUP COUNSELING AND PSYCHOTHERAPY

People are gregarious creatures and they spend much of the day in formal or informal groups. They have a need to relate to and be accepted by others. As a result, group pressure has a strong pull on the individual. Often people do things, both good and bad, in groups that they would never do alone. Some sociologists suggest that because of the breakdown of family and society, many people are looking for groups to which they can belong, whether it is in the church, bar, street corner, community organization or family reunion.

In previous centuries the United States was more of an agrarian society with more than 50% of the population working on farms. The families were larger and more extended. It was common for the grandparents and relatives to live together; the women cooked together and had babies together and the men helped build each other's houses and barns. Today less than 3% of the people work in agriculture and cities have proliferated. Much of that community feeling has been lost; today a large proportion of families are headed by single parents. The above may be a reason why there is a resurgence of interest in groups of all kinds, including political groups, self-help groups, therapy groups and advocacy groups.

TYPES OF GROUPS

Therapy and counseling groups tend to come in various forms. Understand that these groups may overlap in their functioning. Certainly, a self-actualization group could have a therapeutic value or a prevention group could also meet a remediation function.

1. PREVENTATIVE GROUPS: These are often educational or discussion groups to give facts and to help people make wise choices in society (i.e. drugs or AIDS prevention groups).
2. SELF-ACTUALIZATION GROUPS or TRANSFORMATIONAL GROUPS: These transformational groups are meant to go beyond psychotherapy and to help seeking people find fulfillment and meaning in life. Examples of these types include marriage enrichment, marriage encounter, and sensitivity groups. These groups can be large group experiences where average people come together for a short time, or one session, and work on improving the quality of their life. For example, Marriage Enrichment is for married couples to meet in large groups and also as couples to help enhance their experiences as a married couple.
3. REMEDIATION GROUPS: These are most likely to be counseling groups, especially therapy groups, to help people resolve problems and conflicts. They include self-help groups, marathon groups, psychodrama, and group psychotherapy.

SELF HELP GROUPS

The most commonly known self-help group is Alcoholics Anonymous (AA), yet there are numerous types of self-help groups, sometimes called crisis groups, covering a variety of societal problems. There is Narcotics Anonymous (NA) for those who are narcotics addicted. NA and AA also hold separate groups for family members. Overeaters Anonymous, Tough Love, Celebrate Recovery, Grief Share, and groups for people with cancer, sexual disorders, etc. are available. Self-help groups do not have a professional running them; they are simply a collection of individuals with similar problems coming together for mutual support and a feeling that they are not alone. These groups generally have little cost.

Concerning these groups' acceptance by professionals in the field, Sundberg et al. says, "Although professionals sometimes look askance at self-help groups because of the quasi-religious nature of some, they deserve our deepest respect. One-to-one therapies or even therapy groups may have better research and perhaps higher social acceptability, but in terms of the numbers served and the practical durable nature of the help, self-help groups, are a powerful force indeed. In recent years many psychologists have realized their value and have come to understand them not as competitors in treating people but as valuable community resources with unique capabilities." (1983, 359)

To find out more about self-help groups, to do a referral, or to join such a group, the number of the New Jersey Self-Help Clearinghouse is 1-800-FOR-MASH. Other states have similar resources.

MARATHON GROUPS

Marathon groups are therapy groups that are usually run for 24 hours or more. It is believed that when people are tired their defenses wear down and they are more likely to be honest and open about their issues. Many different techniques are used in these groups. In many of these groups each person tells his or her life story.

PSYCHODRAMA

Moreno developed this type of role playing, where the members of the group act out their life, fears, fantasies, etc. as an actor would on the stage. The director of the psychodrama is the therapist, and the member role plays a variety of people or auxiliary egos (auxiliary egos are different points of view or aspects in the person's head) as the director suggests. For example, if a male client has a difficult relationship with his father, the clinician has the client choose someone to role play his father, and he would interact with this role-playing father, saying the things that he would like to tell his father. Later the therapist might suggest that the client do a role reversal, where the client plays his father and the role-playing father plays the client. This gives the person unique insight into his father's point of view.

The psychodrama is an extremely powerful technique and with therapist and audience participation, the client can gain a great amount of insight, catharsis, and self-understanding.

GROUP PSYCHOTHERAPY

In group psychotherapy, members discuss the problems that they have to gain feedback and insight from other members. Group psychotherapy is helpful in encouraging the client to ventilate long repressed feelings, gain more effective social skills, and become more functioning in society. Listed below are some of the positive results gained by attendance in therapy groups.

HELPFUL EFFECTS of GROUP THERAPY

Yalom lists below some of the "curative factors" that a group presents to its members. (1975)

1.   IMPARTING INFORMATION

Group members share knowledge with each other and the group leader also shares information and guidance with the group participants.

2.   CATHARSIS

Catharsis means to get feelings out. Group members learn to let out their feelings in a safe environment. This expression of feeling builds honesty, trust, relief and understanding.

3.   INSTILLING HOPE

As the members watch and use the group, they put the insights gained into action. They become more hopeful and develop more faith in the therapeutic process. Hope is very important to develop. Hope means that the person sees a brighter tomorrow with something to live for. Depressed clients especially have little or no hope, and if the group process can help instill hope in the depressed person, it has been very beneficial.

4.   UNIVERSALITY

As the clients share with each other they learn that everyone is more the same than different, and generally have similar feelings, hopes and fears. In other words, feelings are universal. The feeling of "I am not alone" can be very anxiety reducing for a troubled client.

5.   ALTRUISM

In the beginning of the group a member often feels inadequate and demoralized. As the member continues in the group, he or she realizes that each person can help others and that one's ideas and suggestions have value in helping others.

6.   INTERPERSONAL LEARNING

As the member interacts with others they learn about the world and how to improve their social skills and their problem-solving behaviors in relation to understanding others better.

7.   IMITATIVE BEHAVIOR

As the members watch each other they learn to model more effective behaviors. They learn from each other.

8.   CORRECTIVE RECAPITULATION OF THE PRIMARY FAMILY

Everyone has unresolved family problems. The group can take on the role of a family in which the member can resolve many of the issues that were not overcome as a child. When group members come from dysfunctional families, the group can demonstrate how a functional family operates.

9.   GROUP COHESIVENESS

As the group members become more involved the closeness of the group improves each one's self-acceptance and esteem, and the members become bonded together.

GROUP LOGISTICS

GROUP PARTICIPANTS

The research suggests that the groups that work best are usually <u>heterogeneous</u>, meaning that they have a variety of different members. Obviously, a group with only people that were severely depressed might talk each other into deeper depressions.

There are times, however, when homogeneous groupings are advantageous. For example, women who might feel hindered to discuss their problems if men are present, benefit from all women's groups. Bach (1954) suggested that it is not helpful to mix young with older adults or senior citizens if the topic is sexual experiences. Homogeneous groups with people with certain types of problems (drug, alcohol, sex addictions) have also proven quite effective. Both Hobbs and Bach suggest that there are certain people that do not fit in well with groups and often should be excluded. They are as follows:

1.   People that have psychological sophistication but they use it to treat others cruelly.
2.   Severely aggressive or hostile people because they can destroy the freedom and acceptance among the members of the group.
3.   People who know each other well outside of the group.
4.   People who are psychotic or have an insufficient contact with reality.
5.   People who talk too much and monopolize the group.
6.   Those who are psychopathic or highly impulsive.
7.   Paranoid individuals
8.   Severely depressed or schizophrenic individuals
9.   Extremely critical individuals
10. Narcissistic people
11. People who destroy the group trust by taking information out of the group, or use information learned in group against the person.

This is not an exhaustive list and obviously there are other types of individuals who cannot do well in groups. The group leader can start the person in the group, but if he or she doesn't cooperate, the leader can offer to give private therapy. In reality, however, agencies often dictate that everyone should be in a group. Many agencies have found that if you have "advanced" groups for the highly motivated client, they can still keep the destructive client in a "remedial" group or individual counseling, with the more productive and motivated client in a more dynamic group.

SIZE OF A GROUP

Generally, the ideal group size for adults is between 6 and 12 (Gazda, 1970). In too large a group the person can get bored and feel ignored. Corey (2015), suggests that children's groups be smaller in size with 3 or 4 members because of the children's greater needs for attention. Realistically, however, because of the tremendous need for groups and the lack of trained counselors to run them, groups can become enormous. Agencies find larger groups more cost effective and are often above the optimal size. If you hold larger groups employ more interns, or co-leaders to help run the group. If that is not possible, the counselor can train motivated clients to help run the group.

ADDING NEW MEMBERS

The issue of open versus closed groups is a controversial one. Open groups allow new members to join after the group is formed and closed groups do not admit new members after the group is formed. The best way is to start a group, and then close it to new members for a few weeks. Closed groups tend to build a family atmosphere where there is trust and intimacy. Reality, however, dictates that most groups be open to new members which impacts somewhat on the trust in the group. The solution to open groups is having graduated groups where the more open and honest individuals "earn" the right to enter a more "advanced" group.

FREQUENCY AND LENGTH OF A GROUP

Usually the longer (in weeks) the group runs the more trust and cohesiveness the group develops, especially if the members hold to the concept of confidentiality and the members are supportive of each other. Generally, most outpatient groups occur about once per week and some agencies have some clients seeing counselors privately once or more per week, depending on the person's issue. The length of time a group is run is usually between one and one-half hours to two hours. If the group is larger, the group is often run longer.

RULES OF A GROUP

Rules vary from group to group but generally CONFIDENTIALITY is stressed because if confidentiality is not kept the trust of the group is sacrificed. If a person is caught gossiping about someone else's problem outside of the group he/she is confronted by the group and if the behavior persists, that person is voted out of the group. Many groups also prohibit socializing outside of the group session begins and especially having sexual relations with another group member. Other rules of groups are often no smoking, sleeping, eating, chewing gum and talking to a person on the side. People are told to go to the bathroom before the group and then (unless there is an emergency) wait until after the group session ends to use the bathroom. If the groups are unusually long, the members are given a bathroom break in the middle. It is important to stress, that there should be no walking in and out of the group once it is in progress. Finally, the members are to remember that there is to be <u>No Judging</u>. A client is not to make moral judgments on another client's behavior. Clients are encouraged to talk about what they "did," not what they "would never do." Members are also encouraged to "share the time" so that everyone is able to participate and share in the outcome of the group's success.

GROUP LEADERS AND CO-LEADERS

It is ideal for there to be a least one leader and one co-leader in the group. One leader can run the group and the other can observe what is happening in the group. Two leaders can offer continuity and step in if the other is late, sick, or on vacation, etc. If some group member has an (i.e. panic attack) one group leader can take him or her outside of the group and minister to this member's needs without disrupting the group. Often it is helpful to have co-leaders that are in training; this is an excellent way to train future leaders.

When it is not feasible to have a co-leader, a group leader may train a participant in the group to help and to encourage others in the group process. It is best to have co-leaders sit opposite each other so that they can have a complete view of the group. It does not seem to matter what gender the group leader is, it is the leader's skills that count.

Finally, group leaders have to be very careful and cooperate and back up each other when they are with the group members. A group member will often gravitate toward one of the co-leaders. This can split group loyalties. It is important for the group leaders to show a "unified front" to the group.

LEADERSHIP STYLES

In studying a large number of leadership styles, Yalom found that authoritarian leaders (those that were highly confrontational), and laissez-faire leaders (those that let the group control itself), had the least effectiveness and the highest number of group "casualties." A good group leader should find a middle ground between control of the group and no control. Yalom also explained that expressing anger in group can be productive if it is not directed at someone in the group. Love, warmth and support are most important to the group process. A balance between feelings and thinking is important to a productive group. Corey and Corey (1987 & 2015) identified at least 13 characteristics of an effective group leader. They are as follows:

1. Courage
2. Willingness to model
3. Alive and have a presence
4. Sincere, goodwill and caring
5. Belief in the group process
6. Honesty and openness
7. Non defensiveness in coping with attacks, make mistakes and are willing to admit them.
8. Personal power
9. Stamina
10. Willingness to seek new experiences
11. Self-awareness
12. Sense of humor
13. Inventiveness

It is obviously a tall order to have all of these characteristics; however, it is good to have this list to challenge us to grow and be more effective and flexible.

The poem below depicts an attitude that a good group leader should manifest:

THE SHIP THAT SAILS

I'd rather be the ship that sails
And rides the billows wild and free;
Than to be the ship that always fails
To leave its port and go to sea.

I'd rather feel the sting of strife,
Where gales are born and tempests roar;
Than to settle down to useless life
And rot in dry dock on the shore.

I'd rather fight some mighty wave
With honor in supreme command;
And fill at least a well-earned grave,
Than die in ease upon the sand.

I'd rather drive where sea storms blow,
And be the ship that always failed
To make the ports where it would go,
Than be the ship that never sailed.

Unknown

GOALS OF A GROUP

In addition to the helpful strategies for running a group as presented above, significant group goals include:

a. HONESTY

In groups the members are told to be "Totally, brutally and completely honest." It is explained that honesty is the most important ingredient to healing. Psychologically speaking it is the surgeon's scalpel that does the heart surgery to heal a broken heart. Many clients have to be taught what honesty is, because members erroneously believe that blaming games and projection is honesty. Clients are told to focus on their own issues and talk about their own problems and secrets. One saying repeated in group is "You are only as sick as your secrets." Often it is explained that fungus grows profusely in the darkness but if you bring it to the light, it dies. Just so, secrets need to be brought to the light so that they lose their control on the person's life. Confession is good for the soul.

b. GROUP TRUST

Trust is important if the members are open about feelings and secrets. In trying to create a "functional family" in therapy, group trust must be stressed. Members who take confidential material out of group have to be dealt with.

c.   FOCUS ON FEELINGS

It is explained that there are no right or wrong feelings. All feelings are valid. Speak from the heart, not from the mind. It may be said by a group leader, "I want to know how you feel, not what you think," because often the thinking a member presents to the group is the individual's persona or one's rationalizations. When persons are given the message "don't feel," they have no idea how to identify and express feelings. It is often repeated in groups "NO PAIN, NO GAIN." Therapy can be painful and the more painful it is, the more therapeutic; although it is often difficult to convince members of this fact. Just like surgery, clients usually want therapy to be pain free, but that is impossible. People may have a phobia for pain and then wonder why therapy is not benefitting them. Many members just want a pill to reduce the anxiety and don't want to go through with the painful operation to get to the root of the problem. The more painful the issue, the more gainful the healing. When the client can be taught to dive into the pain, the quicker one can recover from it, and put the anxiety and depression behind, and start feeling joy and love again. (Coleman, 2015)

d.   TEACH EFFECTIVE RELATIONSHIPS IN LOVE

One objective of the group is to teach social and emotional intelligence. Another is to demonstrate what a functional family looks like so the participants can learn to use these skills outside of the group. The members learn how to build functional families and relationships in their everyday lives.

HELPFUL HINTS, SAYINGS and GROUP RULES

Groups are difficult to run, especially if the clients are resistant to being there (i.e., some clients can be forced to attend group by judges or by family, etc.), or the client takes information out of group, which is a violation of the Federal HIPAA rules. If a client is extremely resistant to treatment it is better that he or she be seen privately rather than jeopardizing the group trust or disrupting the openness of the group. It is good to give group members a careful orientation of what is expected in group because clients can become confused and don't understand the value of self-disclosure. It is important for the group leader to get an agreement from each group member, as a matter of honor, to follow all of the rules.

One person should not monopolize the group or hold the group captive. In order to minimize or restrict this from occurring, the group must institute the share the time concept. Some call this step up and step down, in which the individual is encouraged to be sensitive to the needs of the others in the group. Everyone has an equal right to share their feelings. When the leader finds that a member is unwilling to share the time or oblivious of monopolizing the group, the group leader may say "Land the plane." This means the client needs to get to the point so that others can participate in the group also.

Groups are primarily structured to help clients talk about and express their feelings. At first clients are resistant to expressing feelings but as they begin to see the relief that others get from expressing feelings, they begin to open up themselves. One slogan often repeated in group is: "When you think you are looking bad, you are looking good, and when you think you are looking good, you are looking bad."

Explain that groups are not for talking about the weather, bragging about achievements or other innocuous subjects; they are for talking about guilt, shame, conflicts, secrets, and other significant issues. Sometimes a resistant client will take the group on a trip, and talk about what happened in the news instead of what happened to himself and how he feels about it. Then the therapist says, "I want to know how you feel, not what you think." For example, one woman said her father never told her he loved her or expressed any warm feelings toward her. "How did that make you feel?" the therapist inquired. "It was OK, that is the way he was," she said, shaking her head dejectedly. "That's your thinking, I want to know your feelings about him," the therapist replied. "I felt rejected! I hated it! I HATED IT! I HATED IT!" she screamed, as tears began to stream from her eyes.

New clients in group may need to be taught the difference between feeling and thinking. When clients first come to a group, they experience distrust, because they are afraid that group members will gossip about them outside of the group. A group leader may reinforce, "You came alone and you will leave alone," meaning that the client does not see group members socially and will probably never see the person again after the group. Additionally, group leaders strongly discourage any sexual contact between clients.

Therapy strongly discourages blaming games. Often clients will take the focus off themselves by telling how others are totally to blame for their problems. Blaming takes the responsibility off the client and puts it on the person blamed. When this occurs, the important slogan that is taught states "The only person you can change is yourself." Not only is this to get across the point that we can learn to adapt, but also the more we attempt to change others, the more they may resist change. We can only change ourselves. We can learn to adapt.

Another way to get the group involved happens when one member is talking about a particularly painful experience (i.e., being rejected by a loved one), and the leader asks the other group members, "Who here can identify with what he is feeling? Raise your hand if you can." This helps the client know that he or she is not alone. Others also share the same feelings.

EFFECTIVE GROUP TECHNIQUES

A group is divided into three parts, with a different purpose for each section. Presented below are the three parts and effective techniques for each section.

1. Getting the group involved
2. What to do during the group
3. Ending the group

GETTING THE GROUP INVOLVED

This refers to the beginning of the group and creating an atmosphere where the clients can get involved in the group process. Start the group by having a member tell the group the rules, especially stressing **CONFIDENTIALITY**. The member might have the group repeat, "Whatever is said in this group, stays in this group." Emphasize that strict confidentiality will be adhered to and anyone who is caught talking about anything that happened in the group will be confronted and the group has the option to vote that person out of the group. Often this rule makes the members more trusting about opening up about their secrets. Trust is vital to a well-functioning group. People will not self-disclose if they distrust.

Once ground rules are established and reinforced, the leader chooses techniques to actively engage the group members. Listed below are many "ice breaking techniques."

1. TELL THE GROUP HOW YOU FEEL

This is a very simple activity all participants are asked to tell how they are feeling right now. If there are 10 people, each one starts the group by telling how he or she feels. This gives the leader an idea of who needs to use the group that day. Also, a good group leader learns to get every member to talk in every group. This helps each member to feel included and feel valued in the group.

2.   MAKING THE ROUNDS AND LET ME FEED YOU A SENTENCE

In making the rounds a member (number one) is asked to rise and face the person next to him or her (member number two). As both members stand and face each other, they hold hands and make eye contact. The group leader then feeds member number one a sentence. Looking into the partner's eyes number one repeats what the leader said and then finishes the sentence. For example, the leader might feed the sentence, "Right now I feel…" Number one might say, "Right now I feel angry at my wife for leaving me." Number two would repeat, "Right now I feel good because I am here in group with my friends." Number two would then face member number three (both standing) and each one would finish again the "Right now I feel…" sentence until the whole group has finished the sentence.

A therapist can feed the member any kind of sentence. A few popular sentences: "Right now I wish… I love… Right now I want… I like… My mother… Do you know how I feel about you? Do you know how I feel about myself? These sentence starters fed to members are a good way to get everyone in the group involved and participating.

3.   DO SOMETHING OR MAKE A NOISE

This is another simple ice breaker for the group. The leader asks each member to make a noise or do something that expresses how one feels right now. One person might jump up and down for joy while another might moan and mope.

4.   BACK MASSAGE

In this group you have the members count off by twos and the twos stand in back of the number ones and massage their shoulders. The number one switches and massages number two. Since everyone has <u>skin hunger</u> this can involve the entire group. It is important for a trained group leader to demonstrate a gentle shoulder and neck message and then to carefully monitor this activity.

5.   SING SONGS, PAINT BRUSH DANCE or WALK TO MUSIC

Frequently the group opens with music. The members with the group leaders choose songs that are uplifting and socially redeeming and the group sings the song. In choosing songs the leaders need to be aware of the cultural background of the group members. It helps to have a music hookup and some preselected songs to use in the groups. Usually, during all groups, soft music is played in the background. This really wakes up the group. Groups can also end with songs and music

In the PAINT BRUSH DANCE, members pretend that they are surrounded by a canvass. The canvas is even over their heads and on the floor. Have them pretend to feel the canvas and then have them pretend that their right hand is a paint brush and by their right foot is a can of red paint. The leader then plays some fast music without words and asks the participants to dip their hand in the paint and to paint in rhythm to the music on the canvas in front of them. Then the leader tells them to use the left hand as the brush and continue to paint, for example on the canvas behind them. Then one might suggest another part of the body as the paint brush, such as the right foot, belly button, left shoulder, nose, etc. It becomes amusing to see the members contorting their bodies to paint with that part of their body. Members can paint on imaginary canvases in front of them, behind them, to the side and on their neighbor's canvas. The goal is to enjoy, engage and feel relaxed.

WALKING TO THE MUSIC is just what it says; walk around to the rhythm of the music. This livens up the group. Sometimes you can get the group motivated to do a soul train. This use of movement and singing helps the group members learn to cooperate and get in touch with the right hemisphere of their brain (the feeling intuitive side.)

6.   IMAGE BREAKER

In an image breaker the group writes many funny chores on a sheet of paper and puts them in a box. Each member (including the leader) has to draw one out, read it and enact what it says. Examples of image breakers are: act like a chicken, pretend you have to use the toilet but the stall is occupied, ask a member of the opposite sex out on a date and be refused. See how many funny image breakers you can think up. They can be used over again in future groups.

7.   TRUST EXERCISE

To build trust, several exercises are physical in nature. In one you ask one group member to close his or her eyes and stand in the middle of the group. The volunteer is then asked to walk in a straight line, with eyes still closed, until a group member stops this person, turns him or her around and directs the walk ahead again until another member stops and turns the person around. This is a trust exercise, so don't let anyone walk into the wall.

Another exercise is where the person lies on the floor and the group members crowd around him or her and then they put both hands underneath the person and lift the individual slowly over their heads and then set the person back down. After each person has taken a turn, ask the group members how it made them feel.

8.   TENSE BODY AND MAKE SOUND TO PAIN

This exercise is used to create feelings. Group members are asked to tense every muscle in their bodies as hard as they can and make a sound to the pain. Sometimes the song *I Want to Know What Love Is* by the group Foreigner is played, and members are asked to sing along. Then ask them what made them feel. This powerful technique can be used to start the second portion of the group.

9.   RELAXATION TECHNIQUES

There are many relaxation techniques. People are asked to tense their whole bodies as above and then relax and breathe the tension out of their bodies. One suggestion often accompanies this exercise is to imagine one is in a "safe place" (i.e., your bedroom or at the beach). The members are then told to use this image of a safe place whenever they need to reduce stress.

10. GUIDED IMAGERY

With this technique, the leader first relaxes the group, and then in their minds takes them on a trip to the beach or to the house where they lived as a child. This often creates feelings and gives the members something to talk about. The Photo Album also uses this technique. This is where the members are told to imagine that they are looking through a photograph album of their life. "Look at a picture of your mother" and whisper words that you would like to say to your mother.

11. PAIR UP AND DISCUSS TOPIC

This is a simple procedure where after the members find a partner, each pair is given a topic to discuss. Stress that the discussion is totally confidential. Some suggested topics include:

My earliest memory
My mother or father
A secret I have never told anyone
My worst experience
My best experience
The people I have loved and what happened

12. BLOW FAULTS INTO A BALLOON

In this process each member is given a balloon and one by one they are asked to tell the group a personal fault. For each fault confessed, the participant is told to blow that fault into the balloon. After the balloon is fully inflated, members let it go into the air. This technique can be used to release hurt, anger, pain, failures and grief through the same process as you would release personal faults.

13. IMITATE SOMEONE IN THE GROUP

In this group a volunteer is asked to act like someone else in the group. The other members guess who that person is. The one who guesses right can then act like another person in the group. Realistically, this only works when the group members have been together for some weeks and know each other quite well.

14. "WITH THESE HANDS I HAVE"

Members around the group are asked to look at their own hands and repeat and finish this sentence: "With these hands I have…" They may keep going for 10 to 15 minutes and each person successively will have responded several times before this icebreaker is finished. If there is trust in the group, members often reveal guilt and shame that they have been hiding. This activity may also end with a positive message. Allow each member to complete this statement: "With these hands, I will…"

WHAT TO DO DURING THE GROUP

1.   HOT SEAT

In this group a member is asked to sit in the middle of the group in chair and the other members are asked to give affirmations or constructive criticism to the person. This helps the member understand how others view him or her.

2.   COIN GROUP

One technique used after the group members have been together for several weeks is to give three coins (for example, a penny, dime and quarter.) One member at a time must then give another group member the penny and explain why that person is liked. Next the person goes to a member he or she likes a little better and gives the dime and explains. Lastly, the person gives the quarter with explanation. The leader then takes back the coins and has another member do the same thing again. This group indirectly teaches social skills. Some members will get more coins than others. The members should be encouraged to discuss how they felt when they received, or didn't receive, the coins. Always end this technique by validating each member and their importance to the group.

3. AFFIRMATION GROUP OR WOUNDED CHILD GROUP

This powerful group can be run in a variety of ways. One member sits in the middle of the group holding a pillow or teddy bear and one by one each other member touches him or her and says things that one would have liked a mother or father to have said to him or her (i.e., "I love you, you are beautiful, I will protect you") When the members are done the leader asks the person holding the teddy bear how it felt when receiving the comments from the group members.

4. PSYCHODRAMAS

In psychodramas the person actually is asked to act out his or her life, wishes, dreams, etc. on stage with the group leader as director. There are a variety of powerful psychodramas, including:

a. Role playing: In this technique the person plays himself or herself and has other members play significant "others" in his or her life. Someone may play his father and another person her mother. The therapist might stand in back of the role player and act as an "alter ego" by helping find the words that one needs to express. Sometimes a person will be asked to do the whole "family sculpture" where group members are chosen to play members of one's family and then interact with each, expressing true feelings toward each member. The role-playing members of the "family" stand like silent statues.

b. Role reversal: In this technique the person is asked to role play a "significant" person in one's life, (i.e., his or her father) and a member of the group is asked to play him. This gives the person a chance to understand why this father said and did what he did.

c. The double technique: In this process a member will ask two or more members of the group to play the conflicting aspects of his or her personality. For example, a male ex-addict might choose a person to play his addiction, and another to play his desire to be drug free and he will express his feelings in a dialog to each of these two roles. The person might also be asked to express top dog and underdog in his personality. The person will tell the "role players" basically what to feel and say.

d. Empty chair technique: In this process the client imagines someone (i.e. her mother) is sitting in an empty chair and she expresses her feelings to this imaginary person. See chapter on Gestalt Therapy.

e. Family sculpture: In this process group members are each asked to choose other group members to play significant people in their family and their life. One person is then instructed to make the "family" into a sculpture (i.e., mom doing dishes, dad watching television.) After the person has molded the family sculpture, this person is instructed to talk to each "piece of sculpture" and express one's feelings. The "sculpture pieces" do not respond. This group helps the participant express many repressed feelings toward family members.

5. GESTALT DREAM OR FANTASY WORK

This is a type of psychodrama where the person actually becomes the very elements in his or her dream or fantasy and does a dialog about what the symbol in this fantasy or dream really feels or means. For further details on this see the chapter on Gestalt Therapy.

6. DREAM TABLE

Dream Table is a technique to unlock the complexities of the unconscious as revealed through dreams without diagnosis, judging, shaming, blaming, snickering, making wrong, making right or fixing. As with most therapeutic processes, the warm security blanket is Confidentiality! What is said in the room, stays in the room. There are <u>no experts</u> at the Dream Table, but each participant is a co-equal in the sharing of dreams, "If this were my dream…"

"If this were my dream …" was a Dream Model created by Montague Ullman to examine dreams. Dr. Ullman did not believe anyone could or should interpret a dream or that dream dictionaries were necessarily accurate. It is an area that may have troubled Freudian dream analysis. While Freud was brilliant, not everyone viewed dreams the same as Freud.

Dream Table is best run with not more than twelve members and one leader. The dreamer tells his or her dream, and the group members ask a couple of questions: "When did you have the dream? Have you had it more than once? How did you feel when you woke up?" Then, one person repeats the dream so that the dreamer can confirm that that was the dream.

For example, "I dreamed of the color blue." Someone in the Dream Table begins, "If this were my dream …" and without overthinking, just says what pops up in their thought. There is no right or wrong response, just what appears in one's mind's eye.

"If this were my dream, blue is Paul Newman's eyes, the ocean, the sky, I feel chilly—blue is cold. Blue is sad. Blue Mondays. I feel blue. Water is blue, water represents the unconscious, the unconscious is vast, the unknown, the unknown is exciting, I want to explore, I feel like Lewis and Clark on a great adventure! Blue was the name of my dog when I was a kid."

Depending on the allotted time, each person around the Dream Table takes the dreamer's dream and repeats, "If this were my dream …" and states what comes up for him or her. Is any of this correct? Only the dreamer knows!

One can tell what is relevant or close to meaning by observing and checking in with the dreamer. There could be great joy or there could be some tears as something is revealed.

There are two terms in Dreamwork. One term is manifest—what we actually dream—as in the example "Blue." The other, the latent content, is the unconscious meaning of the dream, as in the example on "Blue." If we went around the Dream Table, many more meanings of a dream of Blue would appear.

According to examples from Professor Roger Cunningham, one student was "very distressed and asked if I would help him with his dream. We found a quiet corner and he told me his dream, 'I was riding in a cab with my parents. The cab got into an accident and my parents were killed and I walked away, injury free.' (The Manifest Content) He started crying, 'I love my parents, I don't want them dead!'

Wow, I thought, what a dream to start with, but trusting the process, I repeated the dream to the student and said, 'If this were my dream … I am a college freshman, I am beginning to make my own decisions, I am no longer five years old, my parents are no longer parents of a five-year-old. As I have changed, my parents need to change. I don't want them dead, I want them to grow, to shed their skin, like a snake or a lobster, to be parents of a college student who can choose and buy his own clothes, date who he wants, even out of his culture, to stay out late, choose a career. I need to be allowed to cut the apron strings.' (The Latent Content)

Was I close to a meaning? Who knows? When I looked at the student's face, I could almost see the stress melt away. I could sense his chest expand as he took possession of his new sense of self. I knew that I had hit upon a meaning for this student.

Another student came to the Dream Table. She appeared to be depressed, with unkempt hair and no make-up. She wore drab, un-ironed clothes and was very quiet. She told the group about a recurring nightmare of being stabbed 17 times. I asked how long she had been having this dream. She replied, 'Since it happened!' It seems her boyfriend, in a jealous rage, attacked her. Her mother, who lived in another part of town, had a dream while she was being attacked, woke up, hopped a cab and saved her. So, this entire saga, which she had never shared, poured out of her... I didn't see her for a couple of weeks. When I did see her next, I didn't recognize her. She had allowed all those memories to leave her at the Dream Table, and now she was made up, hair styled, new dress, nails done, the works."

7.   SECRETS GROUP OR PROBLEM GROUP

This very powerful group builds trust. The objective of a secrets group is to help a person reduce anxiety by anonymously revealing one's deepest secrets in a group where people are accepting and non-judgmental. There is an important saying: **"YOU ARE ONLY AS SICK AS YOUR SECRETS**!" Many people have secrets that are deeply hidden from others and even themselves. By creating an accepting atmosphere where participants can hear someone else role play their secret, real trust is established. The group also becomes a confidence builder and generally contributes to the participants' self-esteem.

HOW TO RUN A SECRETS GROUP

A.   MATERIALS NEEDED

The group leader should arm his or herself with pencils, 3x5 cards, tissues, a large empty cup [in which the members tear up and deposit the 3x5 cards after they are used], and a flashlight [if the group leader chooses to dim the lights]. The leader should always use pencils because if a member uses a pen and the others use a pencil, the group members will quickly spot who wrote the penned card.

B.   CHOOSING THE GROUP MEMBERS

The leaders should choose the group members. The optimal group is between 8 and 15 people. If the group is usually run for an hour and a half. Put people who come in late into a new group. It is good if the members of the group are strangers.

C.   THE RULES OF THE GROUP

The leader gathers the group in a circle and carefully explains that whatever is said in the group <u>stays in the group</u> and is not to be repeated outside the group. If the member speaks about a secret that is shared outside of the group, this person will be confronted by the group members. This explanation is vital because if a group member hears his or her secret being judged outside of the group, it will greatly reduce the member's trust and make future groups more difficult because of the distrust.

The members are also to be told that they are <u>not to judge</u> or laugh at a person's secret. This is vital for building trust. Group participants are also told that the card that they write on <u>will be destroyed</u> after their secret is presented. Make sure this is done and that nobody keeps a secrets card.

D. HOW THE GROUP IS INITIATED

The leader passes out the cards and asks the members to print their <u>worst</u> secret on the card. This secret is to be one that they have never told anyone and/or one that has bothered them. Sometimes, if the group is scheduled to run longer, the leader might ask the members to write more than one secret on the card. The leader should also privately offer to write a member's secret for them if they do not know how to write.

E. AFTER THE SECRET IS WRITTEN

The group leader collects all the cards, shuffles them carefully, and passes them back out to the members. The leader tells the members that if they get back their own secret, they are to pretend that it is someone else's secret.

At this time <u>each group member reads the secret</u> on the card he or she has received. It is helpful if everyone reads the secret card aloud, because the group can then help the persons with the most serious secrets first. When a member cannot do the secret, the group leader presents the card.

The leader then selects a member's card and has the member re-read it and <u>pretend that he or she is the one with the secret</u>. If the secret is "I have had five abortions," and the reader is a male, he pretends he is that female and tries to answer questions like she might have responded. Without judging, the other members of the group are then to give advice and support to this role player. Some group leaders may have the person read the card and simply give helpful advice and encouragement. Again, emphasize that no member is to judge that secret. As the group progresses, the members have given some thought to the secrets presented.

During this portion of the secrets group the leader may choose to dim the lights and have the members recite the secret by memory or by flashlight. Often soft music is played in the background.

F. CONCLUDING THE GROUP

To conclude the members are asked to give feedback on the group, and if someone wants to reveal that a particular secret was his or hers, they are encouraged to do so. Do not have the members guess whose secret a particular one was. In many cases if the person has a serious secret the members might urge the person to get future counseling for that problem.

Finally, the members can end the group with a prayer or slogan, such as the serenity prayer, and before leaving the room hug every other member, say "I love you," or give some form of encouragement.

To reiterate the serious nature of the Secret's Group, among the secrets in the past that have been revealed included:

I have had several abortions.
I ran over a child with my car and left the scene.
I was raped.
I killed my cousin.
I am afraid I am homosexual.
I had sex with my mother.

Some members may not initially be very honest in this group but later will discover the level of honesty that the group brings out. Often, as trust builds in the group, people start admitting to their secrets and discussing them openly.

8.   SELF ANALYSIS QUESTIONS

Often group members are given questions to discuss before the group. Some sample self-analysis questions are listed at the end of the chapter on Transactional Analysis. Sometimes they are asked to write the answers to the questions down in the beginning of the group and later asked to discuss them in the group.

9.   SENSITIVITY OR SHARE GROUP

This group is complicated but if done right, with the correct music, is very emotive and therapeutic. On a scale of 0 to 10, (10 meaning outstanding) most participants in past groups have given the group a 9+. In the group, the members sit on a blanket on the floor hugging a stuffed animal or holding a picture or anything of comfort. The lights are dimmed and participants are asked to imagine a photo album with pictures in it. The members are asked to focus on different photos (i.e. someone they loved that rejected them). They are then asked to talk to and to tell that person how they feel, while music is being played in the background. If there are 200 people in the room, 200 people are talking at the same time to that person that rejected him or her. Before the group ends, people are asked to talk to a variety of images as they hug their comfort item. Some of the images evoked are:

See your mother.
See your father.
Someone you loved that died.
See yourself as a baby.
Confront yourself.
See a funeral of someone you loved.
See yourself getting sick, dying and meeting God.
Imagine your house when you were a child.
Hold a child in your arms. Talk to that child.

10. ART THERAPY

There are many things one can do with a pencil and paper. Each member can draw a picture of his or her family of origin, show it to the group and then talk to each person in the picture. Draw a star technique involves group members drawing a picture that represents a significant person in his or her life, or the image of a person who evokes a strong emotion. Members then take turns talking about their picture.

You can make clay figures (i.e. of yourself) and put them on a table with the figures made by other group members. Each group can then discuss why they made their clay that particular shape and why they placed it where they did.

Another group can draw a line (called a life line) that symbolizes your life and the milestones in your life. You then talk to the group about the significant times in your life and how you felt.

11. LETTER OR JOURNAL WRITING GROUP

Each group member is asked to write a letter to a significant person in his or her life and then read it to the group. Significant mental and physical health benefits are attributed to journaling and letter writing. Claudia Kalb (1999) states:

> "Confessional writing has been around at least since the Renaissance, but new research suggests that it's far more therapeutic than anyone ever knew. Since the mid 1980's, studies have found that people who write about their most upsetting experiences not only feel better but visit doctors less often and even have stronger immune responses. Last week, scientists reported findings that make the link even clearer. A study published in *the Journal of the American Medical Association (JAMA)* showed that writing exercises can help alleviate symptoms of asthma and rheumatoid arthritis.
>
> 'It's hard to believe,' says James Pennebaker, a psychology professor at the University of Texas and a pioneer in the field of expressive writing, 'but being able to put experiences into words is good for your physical health. The letters don't even have to be sent and you can always write to yourself in a journal. Psychotherapists say journal keeping can be a powerful adjunct to traditional talk therapy.'"

12. TALK TO PICTURE

In this process the group members are asked to bring the photograph of a significant person in their life, someone that they have feelings toward. Each client is then asked to talk to that picture. This group is especially effective in a grieving group. The person can also hold a picture of himself and do a self-confrontation.

13. RECOVERY WALK

This group is especially effective with recovering clients. The group leader boldly writes certain titles on a sheet of paper, including some of the following.

ADDICTION
SELF
RECOVERY
MOTHER
FATHER
GRANDMOTHER
GRANDFATHER
LOVED ONE
CHILD OR CHILDREN
ABUSER
DECEASED
RECOVERY
GOD

The sheets of paper with one or more of these words written on them are placed in a line on the floor and each member is asked one at a time to step up to the first one and talk to it. If the first step is SELF, then the person is encouraged to do a self-confrontation, and so on. If the person does not have children, he or she could talk to him or herself as a child, or skip that step. This technique helps clients confront a variety of significant issues in their life. Many other words can be added to the list above; it is not inclusive.

14. PROBLEM GROUP

A therapeutic issue is defined as <u>something I refuse to accept.</u> In the Problem Group, each group member is given a paper and pencil and told to write down a serious problem (a therapeutic issue) that keeps reoccurring and that needs work, for example an addiction. The group members are asked to write responses to these reoccurring problems. The members are then asked to discuss each of these answers within the larger group.

1. The theme or problem
2. My first memory of the problem.
3. The feelings that the problem evokes.
4. The body sensation that the problem evokes and where I feel it in my body.
5. The advantage or good feelings I get from this problem (<u>secondary gain.</u>)
6. The price or consequences I pay for with this problem.
7. What I can do to overcome this problem.

ENDING THE GROUP

1. FEEDBACK

At the end of a group members are asked to talk about they got out of the group or what their feelings were about the group. Feedback is important for the group leaders because they can use this feedback to adjust the future groups to better fulfill the members' needs. It is also advisable to pass out anonymous evaluation sheets.

2. WHAT ARE YOU GOING TO DO?

This is an important question to ask at the end of a therapy group, or at the end of an individual session because it helps to focus on the future, which often gives hope. This also requires individuals to think about a plan of action.

3. WHAT WAS THE MOST HELPFUL or LEAST HELPFUL?

This question gives the leaders helpful information on how to construct future groups.

4. SLOGAN or SONG

Often a group can be ended with a saying or inspiring poem or even a song. In groups with alcoholics or drug addicts the serenity prayer is often cited.

5. PRAYER

Ending groups this way offers participants to tell God what they are thankful for or asking God for what they are still in need of. Often the Lord's Prayer or the Serenity Prayer can be used.

6. "WITH THESE HANDS I WILL"

The members are asked to repeat this sentence and therefore share a plan about what they will do in the future to make a better life for themselves. You may also utilize this procedure with varying statements: With these Hands I have; With these feet I will.

7. HUG OTHER MEMBERS WITH FEEDBACK

Finally, ask the group members to give other group members a hug, or say "I love you," or give the member some feedback or encouragement.

References

Bach, G.R. (1954). *Intensive group psychotherapy.* New York: Ronald Press.

Coleman, T. (2015). *How to make group psychotherapy work.* Bloomington, IN: Xlibris.

Corey, G. (2015). *Theory and practice of group counseling.* Monterey, CA: Brooks/Cole.

Cunningham, Roger. (2019). *Dream table.* Unpublished educational paper used by permission of author.

Gadza, G.M. (1984). *Group counseling: a developmental approach* 2nd ed. Boston: Allyn & Bacon.

Hobbs, N. (1951). Group centered psychotherapy. In C.R. Rogers, (Ed.) *Client centered therapy.* Boston: Houghton Mifflin.

Kalb, Claudia. (1999, April 26). Pen, paper, power! *Newsweek.* [75].

Krippner, S., Bogzaran, F., & Percia de Caralho, A. (2002). *Extraordinary dreams and how to work with them.* Albany, NY: SUNY Press.

Magden, S. & Shostrom, E. (1974). Unpublished paper presented to annual meeting of American Psychological Association, New Orleans.

Moreno, J.L. (1959). Psychodrama. In S. Arieti, (Ed.) *American handbook of psychiatry* [Vol. 2]. New York: Basic Books.

Pietrofesa, J., Hoffman, A., & Splete, H. (1984). *Counseling: An introduction* 2nd ed. Boston: Houghton Mifflin.

Ritter, K.Y. (1982). Training group counselors: A total curriculum perspective. *Journal for Specialists in Group Work,* 7, 226–274.

Slavson, S.R. (1947). *The practice of group psychotherapy.* New York: International University Press.

Sundberg, N. (1981). *Introduction to clinical psychology.* Englewood Cliffs, NJ: Prentice Hall Inc.

Ullman, M. (2006). *Appreciating dreams—a group approach.* New York: Cosimo Books.

Yalom, I.D. (1975). *The theory and practice of group psychotherapy* 2nd ed. New York: Basic Books.

Study Questions

1. 1. Find the answer that best fills the blank.

    a. Groups that go beyond therapy to help people live the most fulfilled life possible are called _____ or _____ groups.
    b. Groups that are run for 24 hours or more are called _____ groups.
    c. Groups like NA and AA are called _____ groups.
    d. The group where a person acts his feelings out as if in a play is called a _____.
    e. The group where a member chooses members to be members of his family and then talks to them is called Family _____.
    f. The group where the person sits in the middle of the group and the other members give them affirmations is called _____.
    g. When a person uses projection excessively in the group, they are said to be playing a _____ game.

2. Which of the groups would you like to participate in? Why?
3. Which of the groups or techniques do you feel competent to run?
4. Explain which of the groups or techniques you think is the most therapeutic.
5. Which qualities do you believe are most important for a good group leader to have?
6. What qualities do you think you need to work on to be a better group leader?
7. What do you think are the greatest benefits to the members that are attending a group?

CHAPTER THIRTEEN

FAMILY COUNSELING

Families with problems are complex and challenging. About 50% of all people that enter therapy relate their issue to a couple or family problem (Gladding, 1988). A common situation occurs where there is an identified client (the client who takes on the symptoms of the dysfunction within the family). Maybe the client has a mental illness, an addiction problem, is a rebellious adolescent, or a couple experiencing conflict in their relationship.

In recent years the United States has experienced a breakup within the extended or nuclear family, and a redefinition of family. Today it is common for a family to be headed by one parent, or to be a blended family, or an unwed family. Researchers say that single parent and blended families have more difficulties than nuclear families. Wilcox explains that the family is coming apart because of the reduction in mores (morals) which leads to addiction and lowering of educational levels and income levels. (2014)

One of the results of the breakdown of society are the teens that are brought to family therapy as the identified client. An Associated Press release expressed the problems of teens with the following article:

PANEL SAYS MANY AMERICANS ARE DOOMED TO FAILURE

WASHINGTON—America is raising a generation of adolescents plagued by pregnancies, illegal drug use, suicide and violence, a panel that included medical and educational leaders said Friday. "We are absolutely convinced that if we don't take action immediately, we're going to find ourselves with a failing economy and social unrest," said Roseann Bentley of the National Association of State Boards of Education. The commission's report concluded that "young people are less healthy and less prepared to take their places in society than were their parents." (Mandel, 2017)

Among the findings include: About 30–40% of Americans confess to smoking marijuana every year. Thirty percent of those who use marijuana regularly have marijuana use disorder.

In 2016, there were almost 45,000 suicides according to the CDC's National Center for Health Statistics. They reported that the suicide rate has increased over 24% from 1999 to 2014. This was the highest rate increase in 21 years. Another source, the National Institute for Mental Health (2019) states, "Suicide is a leading cause of death in the United States. It is the second leading cause of death in young people from ages 10 to 35." Additionally, 2.1 million Americans have an opioid use disorder and Americans between the ages of 18–25 are the most likely to use addictive drugs. More facts: Teenage arrests are up over 30-fold since 1950. Homicide is the leading cause of death among 15 to 19 year old minority youths. (www.addictioncenter.com., 2019)

When pondering reasons for the above statistics, the following letter, reprinted in 1995, still holds true.

DEAR ANN LANDERS: I am sending you one of your columns that has yellowed with age, but I think it is very timely. Would you reprint it? Signed: Retired School Teacher from Texas

DEAR TEXAS: I like it better than I did when I first ran it, thanks.

START WITH ONE CHILD.

ADD A LITTLE HOT AIR—Two hours of "when I was your age."

STIR WITH SOME SARCASM—I will bring out the bitter flavor.

FILL WITH BAD EXAMPLES—Preferably your own... Instruct the child how to lie about his age so you can sneak him into the movie at half price. Take "souvenirs" from restaurants and hotels. Towels are nice. Pillow cases are even better.

SEASON WITH INDIFFERENCE—Most families have a lot of "I don't give a damn what you do so long as you don't bother me" lying around.

SIFT IN SOME INDECISION—Not being able to decide what you stand for will give your child that subtle, no-texture, no-substance look.

ADD A DASH OF ALCOHOL—Drink in front of them, behind them and all around them. They will then get the impression that it's a normal and natural part of life. And be sure they see you take a belt when the going gets tough. In a crisis say, "Jeez I need a drink." They will then get the idea that the way to deal with a problem is by getting bombed.

TOSS IN A FEW PILLS—This will teach your children there are chemical solutions to all problems. They should get the idea early in life that nobody has to suffer because there is a capsule or tablet made to order that can protect them against any kind of disappointment, failure or discomfort.

LET SIMMER UNTIL READY TO BOIL—Ignore all symptoms of your child's anger, anxiety or fears. If you pretend they don't exist, they will disappear.

BEAT REGULARLY—It's your job to see the children shape up. Reasoning takes too long, and sometimes, they don't know what you're talking about. [Too young or too stupid.] A crack across the mouth is easily understood.

BAKE IN THE HEAT OF YOUR OWN TEMPER—Being screamed at will give your child that "fresh" quality. It also will make him a screamer, which will make him very popular with his peers, teachers, colleagues and bosses.

OMIT GOD—Teach your kid early that sleeping, golf or tennis is more important than going to a place of worship. On special occasions [severe illness or death], you may have to mention God, but don't overdo it. God is to be used only in case of an emergency. (Landers, 1995)

Using this recipe for raising their children, parents have young people that are often doomed to failure, which for many, will be a precursor to a life of crime, unemployment or dependency, according to research studies.

While some things have stayed the same since Ann Landers' column, we are also living in a different culture. Dr. Ron Toffel (2005) aptly explains that we are in a less innocent and more dangerous society. Today there are many paradoxes built into society. Toffel says, "I cannot tolerate the arrogance of clinicians who think they have all the answers... Let's face it: Kids talk to each other all the time—online, through text-messages, using call-waiting, chilling, sharing the pop culture or TV, and adults do not. Compared to the intensity of teen communication, it is surprising how little the important adults in teens lives speak to each other. We ought not be part of this collective grown-up ignorance."

Toffel explains that parents are often too busy to raise kids, so their children are raised by teachers, media and peers who may have very differing values. How often does another child teach a friend about spiritual and moral values? Notice how the values and morals of our schools and television programs have plummeted. The media is loaded with drug advertisements. Consider this statistic: Americans, who are less than 5% of the world's population, take most of the world's legal and illegal drugs. Toffel explains that parents are often ignorant of the bewildering choice of influences that our children are presented with.

Counselors have a vital role in helping the family get back on track and in helping people reverse these destructive trends in society, but one must be aware of what values the counselor is teaching your child. While reviewing recent literature on family counseling, Toffel and others were confounded by how theoretical most books were without concrete ways to work with families. Rather than review the various theories, such as Co-Joint Family Therapy, Psycho-dynamic Therapy, Systems Theory, Social-Learning Theory, etc., this chapter will discuss issues and techniques taken from these schools. In addition, ideas and techniques this counselor has found useful in over forty years of working with families will be examined. To begin, it is helpful to identify some of the conflicts that challenge both marriages and families.

COMMON PROBLEMS WITHIN THE FAMILY

1.   POOR COMMUNICATION

Most authorities agree that healthy communication is the most important ingredient in a well-functioning family. Often family members resort to anger and violence when frustrated in the family and it is vital that a family therapist teach good communication skills, and healthy ways of resolving conflict.

One recent study suggested that 40 percent of American females have been physically and/or sexually assaulted. Today boys are four times more likely to commit suicide. Many indicators suggest that the American home is becoming less and less a <u>safe haven,</u> and becoming more and more one of the most dangerous places in society. Studies suggest that <u>loving people</u> are the strongest people in society, while some people believe that loving people are weak, and that hostile people are strong. With the recent rash of school shootings, it seems as if young males are increasingly believing that instead of communicating their hurt and pain with someone, the solution to their problems is acting violently.

Some studies suggest that more people today are rebelling against authority. Police and others in authority don't seem to be as respected as in previous generations. If children can't get their pain out, by talking and/or crying, it has been succinctly said that they will "rain bullets on themselves and others." Isn't that what our violence-oriented media has been teaching our young since they were little?

When today's children reach age eighteen, they will have witnessed more than ten thousand violent deaths in the movies and on television. That does not count video games. Advocates agree that violent video games should be banned as some studies suggest they are often the stepping off point from which a vulnerable person will start acting out video fantasies in real life, as seen in Columbine High School, Sandy Hook, El Paso, Las Vegas and more, with the shooters being obsessed with violent video games.

2.   FINANCIAL PRESSURES

Finance is one of the more common reasons for family conflict. One financial expert said that 50% of Americans are within two paychecks of the street. With the increase in gambling and the misuse of credit cards, bankruptcies are increasing. Sometimes a family member is too free with the charge cards or irresponsible with the finances and this causes problems. One study said that one adult in three is afraid of "maxing out" the credit cards. With families living at or beyond their budget, the differences in opinion regarding the allocation of funds can cause intense feelings.

3. SEXUAL PROBLEMS

One study suggests that slightly over 50% of all wives look at a sexual relationship with their husbands as more of a chore than a pleasure. Likewise, about 50% of males complain that they have had a severe bout with sexual dysfunction. If these statistics are true, couple therapy is vital because sexual problems and incompatibility can be a major cause of divorce. Some authorities suggest that couples argue about other subjects because they are too embarrassed to admit that they are having sexual problems. Some wives may fake orgasms because they are afraid to threaten their husband's masculinity. Others may use sex as a manipulative tool; they use it for reward and punishment for the spouse's behavior. (For discussion of sex therapy see the chapter on Behavior Therapy.)

4. DIFFERENT RELIGIOUS AND CULTURAL VALUES

If a Muslin man from Pakistan marries a Christian woman from England there could be a clash of cultures and religions if the individuals choose to adhere to their own religion. In some cultures, the man is more dominant than in others and this can cause problems if the woman is more liberated.

5. IMMATURITY OR DYSFUNCTIONING

Sometimes a person is brought to therapy because he or she has acted irrationally, which has caused a negative impact on the functioning of the family. For example, an adolescent may be failing in school and disrupting the home and the family wants to understand and cope with this disruptive influence. Or a child might be mentally disturbed, intellectually impaired, or have other learning problems. Having a child with special needs puts an extraordinary amount of pressure on the family system; to save the family from disintegrating, therapy is often sought.

6. OCCUPATIONAL PRESSURES

Sometimes a spouse can become overly absorbed in his or her job in an attempt to escape responsibilities at home. A wife could be jealous of the husband's job because she feels stagnated staying home with the children and keeping house. In families where both parents work, conflicts arise in scheduling who will take responsibility for child care needs and household chores: dishes, shopping, laundry, cooking, etc.

7. RELATIVES

Some people after they marry still maintain as strong a relationship with their parents as they did when they were living at home and dependent on their families. Sometimes these loyalties create serious conflicts in the marital relationship. This can happen especially when the married couple lives with the in-laws.

8. UNHEALTHY TIES

When a bond between two people is too strong, it can become possessive and not allow one individual to grow and mature. For example, a mother may favor a child over her husband and may do everything for this child, not allowing him or her to develop the independence needed. This type of bonding is sometimes called triangulation.

9. INFIDELITY

When a person is being unfaithful to a spouse, a serious conflict exists and must be resolved or divorce may result. In this triangle, some persons are more motivated to seek therapy than others. Often the unfaithful spouse is less motivated to seek the therapy. Also, with the spread of sexually transmitted diseases, infidelity is not only a threat to marriage, but a threat to a family's health.

TERMINOLOGY USED IN FAMILY COUNSELING

To familiarize the family counselor with the vocabulary of the family counseling field, this section draws from the major therapies. A therapist must understand how the family is presently functioning in order to help the family mature.

1. FAMILY OF ORIGIN

The family of origin is the family into which the person was born. This family can have a tremendous influence on the person's view of the world and interactions with other family members. For example, if a boy had a father who only worked and when he came home expected to be waited upon by his wife, this young boy might grow up and expect his wife to wait upon him when he comes home from work. This could cause marital conflict, especially if his wife works also. By studying the person's family of origin, the counselor can gain insight into how the person will act when he or she begins a family.

2. ACQUIRED FAMILY

This is the family that the person formulates later in life. This family usually consists of a husband and a wife. Often children are involved as well as relatives adopted into the family. It can take on many configurations. In our modern society "marriage counseling" is sometimes instituted with couples with children, even though the couple is not formally married and the children may have different parents.

3. NUCLEAR FAMILY

This family consists of only the mother, father (parents) and children.

4. EXTENDED FAMILY

This is a nuclear family plus any and all relatives living in the household or nearby.

5. ENMESHED FAMILY

When healthy boundaries fail to develop, the family can become enmeshed and unhealthy interactions can develop which interfere with normal growth and individuation of the family members. For example, a mother may still do the thinking for her married daughter to the detriment of her daughter's relationship with her new husband.

Enmeshment within a family breaks down the roles that a family member should normally master, and can interfere with the normal functioning of the family. One example of enmeshment occurs when a mother and father do their son's school work so that he can get good grades in school. Obviously, the student should be responsible for his own work. In this case, a family counselor teaches the parents to not enable the child. This means adding healthy responsibility to the child and building boundaries where appropriate.

Enmeshment can also interfere with a child's normal psycho-social development and some researchers suggest that it can contribute to mental illness (Minuchin, p. 54). For example, a son who doesn't develop healthy boundaries could depend on his parents for everything and not become a responsible adult. This can contribute to illnesses such as schizophrenia or drug addiction. Often this over dependence or unhealthy dependence is called co-dependency.

6. DISENGAGED FAMILY

Disengagement within a family is the extreme opposite from enmeshment. It is also unhealthy and does not lead to a harmonious home. In disengagement there are too many walls or boundaries and members are getting their own way, regardless of the needs of the family. As a child grows older it becomes healthy to disengage more and more from his or her family, but extreme disengagement is never appropriate because family members do have some responsibility for each other; a balance is needed within a family. A disengaged family is also called a disjointed family.

7. BLENDED FAMILY

Divorce is very common today. When divorced couples remarry, they often bring with them children, and these two families "blend" together to make a new family. Simply having an adopted child in the family can qualify the family as a blended family. Many researchers have found that blended families have more problems and conflicts than an original nuclear family.

8. SYSTEMS AND SUBSYSTEMS

Family Counseling is based on the principle that what happens to one member affects all members of that family because they are all interrelated. As such, the family is viewed as a system. "All complex systems are divided into subsystems. Such subsystems may contain any number of people within the family, and subsystem groupings may be determined by age, generation, gender, interests, and so forth. There is usually a parent subsystem and a children subsystem, as well as less obvious ones. For example, the mother aligns with the male children, and the father forms another subsystem with the female child. Subsystems may be fluid in the sense that any individual within the family may belong to more than one subsystem. The mother may be part of the spousal subsystem in certain ways, of the female subsystem in other ways, and another subsystem, such as athletics or women's group, in still other ways.

The following concepts of boundaries, power, triangles and homeostasis are important in Systems Theory, one of the more comprehensive concepts in family therapy. Several basic assumptions of Systems Theory applied to families include:

(a) Systems are organized wholes with interdependent parts.
(b) Causality is circular rather than linear and one can effectively intervene at any point in the system.
(c) Systems seek to maintain homeostasis, but effective systems do change when needed.

(d) Systems contain subsystems, of which a major example is the triangle, and all systems have boundaries, rules, and patterns." (Gelso, pp. 434–444)

9. BOUNDARIES

Boundaries are limits or walls that separate various aspects of a relationship between two people. Boundaries may be detrimental if they impede a person's growth or individuality. For example, a mother may still give her 25 year old daughter who is living at home an early curfew. A therapist could help the mother and daughter work out boundaries to allow the daughter more independence. In this way a boundary will be built so that the mother shows more respect and gives her daughter more freedom.

In the case of a family that is disjointed, where there are too many walls, the people do whatever they like without regard for the others. The therapist will help the family tear down some boundaries so that in specific areas the family members are responsible and accountable for each other. For example, instead of everyone messing up the house and no one cleaning it up, the therapist might encourage the members to assign specific chores and help each other clean the house.

A healthy family has flexible and reasonable boundaries. While an infant must be clothed every morning by its parents, boundaries develop in the area of dressing so that as the child is developing and maturing there is a clear boundary and respect for the person's ability to dress his or herself.

10. POWER

The family counselor must be able to identify who are the power brokers in the family. While everyone has some power within a family, there generally is a hierarchy of power. One spouse may be the most powerful member of the family structure but through alignment (see below), the other may gain greater power within the family. In a family, possibly because of her nurturing abilities, the mother could be the most powerful person, or because the mother backs the father's wishes, the father gains power through this alignment.

11. ALIGNMENT

There are many alignments within a family. An alignment happens when two or more family members share a similar interest, goal or opinion. For example, two brothers may share a common interest in basketball and spend hours daily on the basketball court. A mother might share a mutual goal with her daughter stemming from her daughter's interest in dancing. The whole family might be aligned by a common interest in camping. These alignments often can draw the aligned people together.

12. TRIANGLES

Triangles are subsystems that arise within the family system. The triangles often develop because of tension or conflict among two or three members of the family. For example, a wife that is not getting her needs met by her husband might become overly attached to her son and in this way a triangle could develop. This can sometimes lead to emotional illness in the son. Another example is when a husband that is not getting his needs met by the wife might become an alcoholic or engages in an extramarital affair.

13. HOMEOSTASIS

Homeostasis is another word for balance. Family therapists explain that healthy functioning families attempt to maintain a balance so that the family's different members each has responsibility around the house. Homeostasis occurs when each member performs a fair share of the chores and each pulls his or her weight.

14. FAMILY LEGACY

All families have expectations and traditions that are held sacred. These add up to a family legacy which become family norms to which the members believe they must adhere. For example, a woman may grow up in a family that demands that the family gather together during certain holidays. This woman might marry a husband who has no such expectations and this could create conflict between the couple. Bicultural families often have many of these types of problems, including different expectations for holidays, family events and every day traditions, such as prayer at mealtimes. The therapist must understand the family legacy.

15. MUTUALITY

Burke explains mutuality as "the ideal way of relating, in which the different self-interests of family members are harmonized, and the individual's needs and family's needs are balanced. With mutuality, the family boundaries are permeable enough to allow individual members to try out different roles but defined enough so that appropriate roles do not become ambiguous." As a result, a family system that shows mutuality does have its division of labor and boundaries, but it is also very flexible. (1989, p.298)

16. NON MUTUALITY

Non mutuality is a destructive situation where the individual and the family are not relating and they are not sharing common interests. In this case the individual may be alienated from the family and the family is not meeting his or her needs. (Wynne, 1958)

17. PSEUDO MUTUALITY

The word "pseudo" means false. In the case of the pseudo mutual family, there is an appearance of mutuality or family harmony, but it is only superficial and the members are only play acting. There seems to be a lack of real meaningful communication. This type of interaction tends to block the child's emotional and social growth. Wynne identifies that this type of communication common in the families of schizophrenics. (Wynne, 1958)

18. MARITAL SKEWNESS

Marital skewness refers to a marriage where most of the power is in the hands of one spouse and that spouse dominates the other. There tends to be a lack of mutuality in this relationship and this type of family is viewed as unhealthy for the children. Often children with schizophrenia also can come from this type of family.

19. CODEPENDENCY

This is an unhealthy dependence that individuals have on each other or on a family system. A wife and children with their alcoholic husband/father may show codependent behaviors by covering up the father's drinking and performing tasks that the father would normally be expected to do. In other words, they have an unhealthy system of codependency. This is also called <u>enabling</u>.

20. DOUBLE BIND

Double bind communications are those that are contradictory or opposite in meaning. For example, the parent may chastise the child for not talking to them but when the child does start communicating with the parent the parent tells him or her to shut up. These types of communications confuse a person and lower one's self confidence. Carson (1988) explains that this type of communication happens also in families where there is a schizophrenic.

21. SCAPEGOATING

Scapegoating happens when one person is singled out as the cause of the family's problems. In one family the youngest female may be looked upon as the trouble maker and is unduly punished, whereas her sisters and brothers can do no wrong in her parents' eyes.

GOALS AND INTERVENTIONS IN FAMILY THERAPY

Different therapists treat families differently. Some therapists include the extended family and/or the family's friends, clergy or neighbors. Other therapists see the family together at times and on other occasions meet only with individuals within the family. For this discussion twelve goals with accompanying interventions have been gleaned from major family therapy theories.

1. IMPROVE COMMUNICATION

Good communication skills are vital to a healthy family. Numerous faults found in relationships impede successful communications. <u>Mind reading,</u> assuming you know another's thoughts and feelings, is one. For example, a husband may assume that he knows what makes his wife sexually satisfied, when, in fact, he has been too embarrassed to ask her. Using the Socratic Method, a method in which the therapist asks questions and allows the clients to derive their own solutions, the therapist can help the couple develop communication skills. Therapists ask questions such as, "Mary, what do you want most from your husband?" or "Joe, what upsets you most about your wife?" By asking these questions, the family may learn more about each other's hopes, fears, needs, likes and dislikes.

Often family members don't really listen to each other. For some families one message is "Don't talk!" Remember the adage, "Children are to be seen and not heard?" To amend this lack of communicating, some therapists will ask questions like, "George, what do you think Mary means by what she just said?" In other words, an important function of a family therapist is to teach communication and listening skills.

Another common fault in communication is that people interrupt the communicator before he or she is finished. This often makes a person feel angry and frustrated. Also, family members may need to learn to be clearer and more concise in their communications. A person must learn to express his or her needs, "I am hungry," before these needs can be met. Good communication skills create better mutuality and respect in a relationship and, consequently, lead to a more harmonious family.

The therapist may assign homework for clients to develop communication skills. The clients might be given a list of questions or sentence completions to discuss with each other. Communication starters may include:

What do you wish most about your family?
My most pleasant memory with you has been…
The things I like the most are…
What upsets me most is…
My biggest faults are…
I can improve the quality of life in this family by…

An effective way to help family members learn to take turns in listening and communicating is the pen technique. When family members tend to interrupt each other and fail to listen, the therapist will give one member a pen. While that member has the pen only he or she can talk, and everyone else must remain silent. After the pen holder has spoken about what was on his or her mind, the therapist will ask each family member to rephrase what they heard the person say. If the pen holder felt understood by a family member, he or she will give the pen to the person who most correctly interpreted the sentiments. Hopefully by the end of the session each member will have held the pen, expressed their feelings, and felt understood.

In healthy family communication it is imperative to instruct each family member to use I statements and to avoid you statements. A person is instructed to talk about how the behavior of another family member made him or her feel. For example, the wife might say to the husband, "When you come home angry, I get very upset and fearful. I don't think clearly when you are angry." The husband might respond, "I didn't realize that my anger upset you so much. I am really angry at my demanding boss; I don't mean to take it out on you."

When members learn to use the I statement technique, they start to realize that only they can change themselves, and that arguing and making you statements only makes others defensive.

Therapists try to show family members that arguing make matters worse. Escalating a conflict only hurts the feelings of other family members and makes for more hard feelings. Members are encouraged to tell the angry person how badly they hurt when the person is angry at them and hopefully help the person realize how destructive this anger is to the family.

Studies confirm that the more a person expresses rage or anger, the angrier he or she becomes. It is sometimes appropriate to talk about what makes one angry, but rarely appropriate to unload this anger on someone else. This behavior shows poor social skills and alienates the person from the others. Jails and mental hospitals are full of angry, hostile people.

A DEAR ABBY reader (Feb. 1, 1996) sent the list her parents used in their fifty-year happy marriage.

Rules for a Happy Marriage

1. Never both be angry at the same time.
2. Never yell at each other unless the house is on fire.
3. If one of you has to win an argument, let it be your mate.
4. If you must criticize, do it lovingly.
5. Never bring up mistakes of the past.

6. Neglect the whole world rather than each other.
7. Never go to sleep with an argument unsettled.
8. At least once every day say a kind or complimentary word to your life partner.
9. When you do something wrong, admit it and ask for forgiveness.
10. It takes two to make a quarrel, and the one in the wrong is usually the one that does the most talking.

2. DEVELOP MORE FLEXIBLE BOUNDARIES

In family therapy help the family find the middle ground between an enmeshed family (where there are no boundaries) and a disengaged family (where there are too many boundaries.) The therapist acts as a catalyst to help reorganize the family.

In some marriages the husband may view his role as the protector and provider of the family and the wife might complement this by seeing her role as housekeeper and primary caretaker of the children. In a healthy family these boundaries between functions are not rigid. For example, if the wife is tired or ill, the husband might cooperate by fixing dinner, changing diapers and vacuuming the house. Conversely, if the husband becomes ill, the wife might show flexibility by going to work or by mowing the lawn.

In the enmeshed family when certain members are co-dependent (too dependent) upon other members, one or more persons can become an enabler and do too much for the person. Co-dependency often occurs in a family where an adolescent is addicted to alcohol or drugs. In one extreme example the addict may manipulate his co-dependent mother to such a degree that the mother will give her son money so that "he won't have to steal it." In this case, boundaries need to be built between mother and addict. The addict son needs to learn responsibility and the natural consequences of his behavior without his mother "bailing him out."

Often these co-dependencies can be viewed as triangles. If a husband becomes overly attached to his son, to the exclusion of the wife and mother, a triangle is formed and can be an unhealthy bond for the child. It is important for the child to see that the father loves and supports the mother. A family therapist will do boundary work to encourage the strengthening of the husband-wife bond and develop an appropriate boundary between the father and son.

3. MAKE ADJUSTMENTS FOR LIFE CYCLE PASSAGES

Evelyn Duvall's model (1977) identifies the following life cycle periods, and tends to center on an ideal family. New and different problems arise within broken homes, mother and children homes, and blended families. It takes the empathetic and astute therapist to adjust when working within the different family systems and life cycles. The family counselor needs to be familiar with the various dimensions that can occur at each life stages and must learn techniques to work with each new stage and subsystem of the family. This is depicted in the pages following.

STAGE OF FAMILY LIFE CYCLE	POSITIONS IN FAMILY	STAGE-CRITICAL FAMILY DEVELOPMENTAL TASKS
1. Married Couple	Husband Wife	Satisfying marriage. Adjusting to pregnancy, and the promise of parenthood. Fitting into the kin network.
2. Childbearing	Wife-mother Husband-father infant daughter or son or both	Having, adjusting to, and encouraging development of infants.
3. Preschool Age	Wife-mother Husband-father Daughter-sister Son-brother	Adapting to critical needs and interests of preschool children in stimulating growth-promoting ways. Coping with energy depletion and lack of privacy as parents.
4. School Age	Wife-mother Husband-father Daughter-sister Son-brother	Fitting into the community of school age families in constructive ways. Encouraging children's educational achievement.
5. Teenage	Wife-mother Husband-father Daughter-sister Son-brother	Balancing freedom with responsibility as teenagers mature and emancipate themselves. Establishing post-parental interests and careers as growing parents
6. Launching	Wife-mother/grandmother Husband/father/grandfather Daughter-sister/aunt Son-brother/uncle	Releasing young adults to work, military, college, marriage, etc. with appropriate rituals and assistance. Maintaining a supportive home base.
7. Middle-aged	Wife-mother/grandmother Husband-father/ grandfather	Rebuilding the marriage relationship. Maintaining kin ties with older and younger generations.
8. Aging family members	Widow/widower Wife-mother/grandmother Husband-father/ grandfather	Coping with bereavement and living alone. Closing the family home and adapting to aging. Adjusting to retirement.

4.   DEVELOP FAMILY INSIGHT

Family members cannot make the necessary changes in the family structure if they don't understand what is going wrong. The therapist needs to help set the stage for the family to develop insight into its behavior. For example, a young adult may graduate from high school and not be interested in either going to college or going on job interviews. The parents of this young person might not understand the role they are playing in the young adult's lack of motivation by continuing to feed, clothe, shelter and support him or her. In other words, they are enabling this child to stay around the home. By developing insight into their co-dependent behavior, the parents learn to take appropriate action by giving their child deadlines, such as getting a job, or finding housing elsewhere.

It has been said that <u>parents should give their children both wings and roots</u>. Young adults must be prepared to fly like an eagle but they also should feel loved and secure about their home. Raising healthy children is a delicate balance that must lead to independence if the child is to succeed.

Although many family therapists are directive, it is often more helpful if the therapist uses carefully asked questions (Socratic Method) to facilitate the family members to develop their own best solutions. If is often difficult to provide insights to some families when certain members may be defensive. However, when the family members come up with their own insights and solutions, they are more likely to value them and thus more likely to implement them. Also, when the family comes up with its own solution, if something goes wrong, they are less likely to blame the therapist.

One technique the therapist can use to help the family gain insight into its workings is a <u>Family Sculpturing</u> process. First, the therapist asks the family to stand together like an "ideal family." In this process the family might hold hands facing each other in a circle. This may be interpreted as equality among the group members. Next, the therapist asks the family members to arrange themselves as they really are in the family structure. In one case a young daughter stood apart from the other family members with her back to them. She explained that it symbolized that she felt rejected from them and also felt ashamed of her parents' excessive drinking. This sculpting technique often opens up discussions and helps the family communicate feelings and perceptions. It is also excellent in identifying any unhealthy <u>triangles</u> within the family.

Learning how to use <u>genograms</u> in understanding family structures has proven very helpful to families in developing insights. A genogram is a family genealogy, including the ancestors, parents and children of a family, and is drawn up by the therapist. Introduced into the diagram are divorces, substance abuse, mental illness, etc. The genograms allow the family to be aware of and understand reoccurring family problems. For example, if a genogram showed that one's ancestors had alcohol problems, it could give offspring an incentive not to drink, as certain drug problems and mental illnesses are partially genetically linked.

Blaming is a very destructive game that is played in families. Insight into these blaming games is helpful for the family to see the role of hostility and to learn more helpful empathetic techniques in reaching out and helping each other. The therapist can help the family identify blaming games by understanding that approaches, such as scapegoating (blaming a family member) is destructive to the family structure.

PARENTING YOUNG ADULTS

One of the most challenging age groups with which to counsel is teenagers. Parents often need insights into how a teen thinks. Discussing with parents the 27 statements below written by a teenager may be effective. This article was printed in the Huntington Penny Saver, Inc. (Coleman 1999)

A Memorandum from Your Child

RE: Me

1. Don't spoil me. I know quite well that I ought not to have all I ask for. I'm only testing you.
2. Don't be afraid to be firm with me. I prefer it. It lets me know where I stand.
3. Don't use force with me. It teaches me that power is all that counts. I will respond more readily to being led.
4. Don't be inconsistent. That confuses me and makes me try to get away with everything that I can.
5. Don't make promises; you might not be able to keep them. That will discourage my trust in you.
6. Don't fall for my provocations when I say and do things to upset you. Then I will try for other such "victories."
7. Don't be too upset when I say "I hate you." I don't mean it, but I want you to feel sorry for what you have done to me.
8. Don't make me feel smaller than I am. I will make up for it by behaving like a "big shot."
9. Don't do things for me that I can do for myself. It makes me feel like a baby, and I may continue to put you in my service.
10. Don't let my "bad habits" get me a lot of your attention. It only encourages me to continue them.
11. Don't correct me in front of people. I'll take much more notice if you talk quietly with me in private.
12. Don't try to discuss my behavior in the heat of a conflict. For some reason my hearing is not very good at this time and my cooperation is even worse. It is all right to take the action required, but let's not talk about it until later.
13. Don't preach to me. You'd be surprised how well I know what's right and wrong.
14. Don't make me feel like my mistakes are sins. I have to learn to make mistakes without feeling that I am no good.
15. Don't nag. If you do, I shall have to protect myself by appearing deaf.
16. Don't demand explanations for my wrong behavior. I really don't know why I did that.
17. Don't tax my honesty too much. I am easily frightened into telling lies.
18. Don't forget that I love to use experimenting. I learn from it, so please put up with it.
19. Don't protect me from consequences. I need to learn from experience.
20. Don't take too much notice of my ailments. I may learn to enjoy poor health if it gets me too much attention.
21. Don't put me off when I ask <u>honest</u> questions. If you do, I might stop asking and seek information elsewhere.
22. Don't answer "silly" or meaningless questions. I just want to keep you busy with me.
23. Don't ever think that it is beneath your dignity to apologize to me. An honest apology makes me feel surprisingly warm toward you.
24. Don't ever suggest that you are perfect or infallible. It gives me too much to live up to.
25. Don't worry about the little amount of time we spend together. It is how we spend it that counts.
26. Don't let my fears arouse your anxiety. Then I will become more afraid. Show me courage.
27. Don't forget that I can't thrive without lots of understanding and encouragement, but I don't need to tell you that, do I?

Likewise, from an educator's point of view, Dr. Hilde Dyer identifies stressors, classroom rigors and resiliency as significant in healthy child development. She advocates that parents and educators align to support rigorous classroom environments rather than discourage academic excellence. Children need to learn to deal with stress, disappointments, overcome obstacles and accept failure as part of the growing process. This includes family commitments to provide home environments where homework and assignments are approached with a positive attitude, and accurate family communication.

Dr. Dyer writes, "Parents and educators need to be cautious in evaluating stress. Certainly, stress-inducing situations exist. Divorce, chronic illness, financial concerns, etc. create stress for children. But words have a life of their own. For example, a teacher is *mean* because she gave a child a zero for an assignment that was not turned in. Is the teacher actually being mean? A parent is *really strict and cruel* because bedtime is at a fixed hour? Is a fixed bedtime cruel and inhuman? When children use words to describe situations (such as calling the teacher mean or the parent cruel), parents and educators must separate themselves emotionally from the situation and realistically evaluate the state-of-affairs. Such is the case with the term *stress*. It is more prudent to put scenarios into perspective, using other terms such as angry, scared, offended. I have had numerous conversations with students and parents where *rightly dividing words* (accurately determining intent of words) leads to better understanding stress-related situations. By being more specific, adults can help children navigate perceived stress more realistically thereby more accurately responding to felt emotions. This is an important step for self-awareness and integral in the process of maturing as a student."

We need to help build resilience into each student. Dr. Dyer quotes Peter Gray, Ph.D. when he says:

I have described the dramatic decline, over the past few decades, in children's opportunities to play, explore and pursue their own interests away from adults. Among the consequences are well-documented increases in anxiety and depression, and decreases in the sense of control of their own lives. We have raised a generation of young people who have not been given the opportunity to learn how to solve their own problems. They have not been given the opportunity to get into trouble and find a way out on their own, to experience failure and realize they can survive it, to be called bad names by others and learn how to respond without adult intervention. So now here is what we have: Young people, 18 years and older, going to college still unable or unwilling to take responsibility for themselves, still feeling that if a problem arises, they need an adult to solve it.

In other words, we need to teach our children to master their own tasks, including reworking their efforts until they achieve success and develop the resilience to fall down and get back up. She concludes, "Resiliency in the classroom translates to resilience in relationships, the workplace and life in general."

5. USE POSITIVE REINFORCEMENT AND TRUST BUILDING

Psychologists have shown conclusively that we all live for things that fulfill our needs and wants. Ideally a functional family is loving and responsible. In as many ways as possible the family members are taught to be kinder and more thoughtful to each other (positive reinforcement) even when the feeling is not always there. These positive reinforcements may be lacking in a dysfunctional family. Because there is often much hostility and rejection in a dysfunctional family, the members of the family have to be taught to "catch more flies with honey than with vinegar." One of the ways to achieve positive change is through negotiation, as taught by Stuart (1980). Stuart explains the four steps in the negotiation process.

1. Each member of the family is asked to list specific changes that one wants to see in another family member. For example, a working wife might request the husband to wash the dishes and help with the housework. To help develop more mutuality, the husband also makes his requests known.

2. To make sure the request is clearly understood, the other members of the family are asked to rephrase the request as understood. For example, the husband says, "What I hear you saying, honey, is that you want me to do the dishes every evening and run the vacuum cleaner once a week." They are asked to be as specific as possible to prevent any misunderstanding.

3. A <u>contract</u> is written up for each family member and signed so that every member is clear that they are committed to the change.

4. The contract is put into action and the family members discuss how they are doing with it in future family sessions. Often the contract is re-written in later sessions to make it more equitable.

Another effective way that Stuart teaches how to positively reinforce each other is called <u>caring days</u>. In the process of caring days, the therapist gives the family an assignment. On certain days family members are to show at least five caring behaviors to the other family members, even if they don't feel like it. Sample caring activities might include that the couple get together to <u>listen</u> to each other and tell about their day, or that one parent will give each family member at least three hugs that day. Caring days are designed for family members to practice how the family can become more fulfilled and happier when they think about each other. The goal is that those caring days would later become a part of daily behavior.

To help build trust for the family it is especially important for the husband and wife to find time to talk about their day; this is called <u>day review</u>. Another way in which a busy couple can be brought together is for the therapist to request that this pair have at least one date per week. Often the husband and wife after marriage get so busy with the activities of family living that they forget to nurture each other. This weekly dating process has been shown to be very effective when the demands of children consume so much time.

Trust is one of the important foundations in a relationship, and if distrust occurs, the relationship will suffer. Discussing one's day builds trust because it is positively reinforcing the need to be listened to and to be heard. Additionally, if the spouse has a secret life (i.e. an affair on the side) a review of the day wouldn't ring true and one would have to get honest more quickly. When a person chooses to have an affair, it may be because his or her needs are not being met at home, or because outside temptations (being complimented and admired by another person), are eroding the relationship's commitments.

In summary many therapists require the following:

1. <u>Day Review</u> for at least 15 minutes per spouse per day.
2. <u>One date per week</u>.
3. <u>At least one honeymoon per year</u>.

It is also important to give the children in the family a time to review their own day with the adult listening. In addition to trust, this helps build closeness between parent and child. Additionally, since positive reinforcement and trust building are essential in a healthy child's development, it is advised that the parent should not do for the child what the child can do for one's self. Doing this is called a <u>double bind</u> and can seriously reinforce resentment or undermine the child's self-confidence. The child needs as much responsibility as can be handled to learn mastery of his or her own world.

6. FACILITATE POWER SHIFTS

If you have ever studied chickens you will quickly notice that they are constantly fighting for power and that there is a pecking order, where the top chicken or rooster gains the most power in the hen house. If you watch children in a playground you will also see that they develop a pecking order, and some children have more power than others. Also, in a family there is a power structure. Sometimes the power is not distributed appropriately causing the other family members to become resentful because of their lack of freedom or place in the pecking order.

A common family structure is the <u>authoritarian</u> family. Usually the father is the power broker and the other family members have little say. McClelland (1965) has shown that this dictatorial type of family structure undermines confidence and causes resentment. Often power struggles between couples can split a family and cause a schism into which the children are forced to take sides.

At times the therapist will enter the family structure and use authority as a therapist to <u>unbalance</u> (Minuchin and Fishman 1981) the family structure and cause the family to share the power more evenly. For example in a family where the father yields his power over the family because of his control of the finances and the mother has the children on her side because of her nurturing abilities, the therapist will urge the father to let the mother pay the bills and make financial decisions and will urge the father to get more involved with the raising of the children. When a chauvinistic husband can see that his becoming more nurturing and equitable can create greater happiness within the family, he can be persuaded to become more flexible.

7. ALTER DESTRUCTIVE HABITS

Often families can become dysfunctional when one or more family members have an addiction or some other disorder that seriously disrupts the family. For example, one family had an adolescent son who was addicted to narcotics and had stolen money and valuables from his family. The mother was co-dependent because she was convinced that it was somehow her fault the child was addicted. The father also blamed the mother for the son's addiction and escaped by staying long hours at work to avoid the tension in the family. The remaining son and daughter felt torn and neglected and the family was in turmoil.

In cases such as the above, the therapist may intervene and educate the family as to its alternatives. (For example, they can try to get the son into a treatment center, and if he refuses, to change the locks on their house and let him fend for himself.) Sometimes when a substance abuser realizes the harsh realities of the world and "hits bottom" he comes to his senses and gets help.

The therapist also may employ the help of Narcotics Anonymous, ALANON, ALATEEN, or other self-help groups in which the family could get additional support or understanding. The therapist will educate and work with the family concerning any destructive tendencies such as co-dependencies, triangles, and blaming games. This is done to help the family cope and bring its members closer together in a crisis because often one dysfunctional family member can tear the family apart.

8. INCREASE FAMILY'S EMOTIONAL MATURITY

"Have no feelings" is the message a dysfunctional family usually gives to its members. As a result, the dysfunctional family members learn to close the door to their feelings. John Bradshaw explains in his book, *Homecoming,* that a person who has closed the door to his or her feelings can express only two feelings. The first is <u>hostility</u> and the second <u>lust</u>. It is easy to see the role of anger, blaming, and rejection in a dysfunctional family. Lust, however, can be expressed as an addiction to anything: sex, drugs, or relationships. Here it is vital that the therapist help this person open the door to feelings and learn to love again.

In her article "Have a Good Cry," Gini Kopecky cites leading authorities on the importance, even the necessity, of people opening the door to their emotions and having a good cry. This is especially important for boys. She quotes psychologist Ronald Levant, Ed.D., clinical supervisor of the Couples and Family Center at Harvard Medical School's Cambridge Hospital: "Boys learn early on to deaden their awareness to different types of emotions. They shut off both vulnerable feelings—such as hurt, disappointment, sadness, and fear, and tender ones, such as compassion, warmth and affection…. What this leaves is only <u>anger</u> and <u>lust</u>…. As a result, when painful emotions arise many men explode in rage, others run from these feelings and squelch them."

Families must be taught to take healthy risks and to be vulnerable again. While the various therapies presented in this book each have a different approach to helping the family, the overall goal is to help people get in touch with their natural affections. The main method used is simply to help the family members express how they feel about themselves and each other with honesty. For example, families need to learn to communicate their feelings without playing games, including blaming. A therapist must learn to facilitate this identification and expression of emotions through processes that touch deeply hidden feelings to help people express them honestly. Honest communication, releasing hurt, and tears, brings the person back in touch with long-repressed love feelings.

9.   EDUCATE

It is not only vital that the professional keeps up with the latest theories and techniques, a family therapist should also encourage clients to attend seminars, read books, and be familiar with the latest in family therapy. The therapist should also be familiar with child raising techniques, and methods to improve communication skills.

A danger occurs when counselors believe that they have all the answers and stop educating themselves. A good counselor should also recognize his or her limitations. For example, if the therapist has clients with sexual problems and is not a sex therapist, then the clinician should make an appropriate referral to a sex therapist.

10.   DEVELOP HEALTHY SPIRITUAL AND MORAL VALUES

America is going through a spiritual and moral decline. Divorce is at an all-time high. Many of the Judeo-Christian principles have become lost as people increasingly become more selfish. These two appear to be related. Trust, loyalty, and integrity are less important in today's generation.

The saying that the "Family that prays together, stays together" has scientific verification. Generally, a strong belief in God tends to keep a family together and build greater trust and loyalty than is found in families that do not believe in God. One study found that couples that pray together daily have less than 1% divorce rate. Belief in a higher power gives family members hope in times of crisis and sickness, dying and death.

Some marriage counselors have been too eager to agree with spouses that want divorces. Recent studies, however, show that divorce can have catastrophic effects on children and that there are no easy divorces. It is very difficult for a divorced couple to remain friends after a divorce, especially if there is a court battle over custody and alimony.

One of the ways that a counselor can help the family to think about higher values is by asking questions such as, "What would you do if your spouse became terminally ill?" or "What do you believe will happen after you die?"

11.   INITIATE PREMARITAL COUNSELING

Often overlooked by people that plan to marry is premarital counseling. In premarital counseling the couple are asked to discuss and make decisions about what they want for the future. Some of the questions asked may include:

1.   What would you like to do on your vacations?
2.   What relatives will you visit on what holidays?
3.   How many children do you want?
4.   If and when you have children, who will be responsible for childcare?

5. Who will do which household chores?
6. How frequently do you plan to have sex?
7. What religious institution will you attend?
8. How will financial decisions be handled?
9. What will you do if your spouse is mortally ill?

Many people have very unrealistic notions about what a marriage is. Some marriage counselors explain that everyone is somewhat incompatible. When you have low expectations of your spouse's role, you will have better success in your relationship with him or her. Research studies suggest that couples that have more similar interests tend to have stronger marriages. If the couple has serious disagreements on important issues it is vital to find this out before they marry. It is important for the couple to agree about the answers to the above questions before they marry. Some couples draw up premarital contracts. This contract can head off many disagreements after marriage.

12. HELP FAMILY FOCUS ON POSITIVE BEHAVIORS

In every dysfunctional family there are not only things that the family is doing wrong, but also things that they are doing right. Minuchin (1981) and other structural family counselors help the family focus on what they are doing, or have done right in the past. They help reformat the family's perceptions to identify past successes so that it can expand those positives to become a more functional family. For example, the therapist might help a family reformat its perceptions of a family member as "crazy," to less pathological proportions, by labeling the behavior as acting out. This reframing technique helps the family feel more confident when helping other family members. It also helps the family members to realize that they are responsible for changing themselves, and that this is not the responsibility of the therapist.

A CHRISTIAN PERSPECTIVE OF FAMILY THERAPY

Approaches to family therapy is as diverse as the number of family therapists, and not all therapists are Christian. This can be a conflict in counseling for a nonbeliever when working with Christian clients, or a Christian therapist working with someone uninterested in biblical guidance. Clients before initiating a therapeutic relationship may inquire if the therapeutic approach points to the God of the Bible. Conversely, some Christian couples may feel labeled by a therapist as "inflexible and rigid" in their beliefs. **Mathew 10:36** says, **"A man's enemies will be the members of his own household."**

Beverly La Haye (1990) said, "Marriage and the family are institutions founded by God. They are considered his highest priority for individuals next to personal salvation. They are worth defending in battle." The Bible clearly shows how God sees healthy families as a priority. It is incumbent on Christian counselors to do everything we can to try to keep marriage partners and families together.

Here are a few of God's edicts:

- **Honor your father and mother that it may go well with you and you may live long on the earth. (One of the 10 commandments and found in Exodus 20:12)**
- **Children, obey your parent in the Lord, for it is right. (Eph. 6:1)**
- **Fathers, do not exasperate your children: instead bring them up in the training and instruction of the Lord. (Eph. 6:4)**
- **Wives, submit to your husbands as to the Lord …Husbands, love your wives just as Christ loved the church and gave himself up for her. (Eph. 5:22–26)**

References

Aponte, H.J., & Van Drusen, J.M. (1981). Structural family therapy. In A.S. Gurman and D.P. Kniskern (eds.), *Handbook of Family Therapy*. New York: Brunner/Mazel.

Bowen, M. (1976). Theory in the practice of psychology. In P. Guerin (ed.) *Family therapy*. New York: Gardner Press.

Bradshaw, John. (1992). *Homecoming: reclaiming and healing your inner child*. New York: Bantam Books.

Burke, J. (1989). *Contemporary approaches to psychotherapy and counseling*. Belmont, CA: Broooks/Cole Publishing.

Carson, R. (1988). *Abnormal psychology and modern Life*. Glenview, Illinois: Scott, Foresman.

Coleman, T. R. (2015). *How to make group psychotherapy work*. Bloomington, IN: Xlibris.

Duvall, E. (1977). *Marriage and family development* (5th ed.). New York: J.B. Lippincott.

Dyer, Hilde. (2019). *Resilience in the classroom*. Unpublished educational paper used by permission of author.

Dyer, Hilde. (2019). *Rigor and Its implications*. Unpublished educational paper used by permission of author.

Dyer, Hilde. (2019). *The role stress plays in motivation*. Unpublished educational paper used by permission of author.

Gelso, Charles. (1992). *Counseling psychology*. New York: Holt, Reinhart & Winston.

Gladding, S. (1988). *Counseling*. Columbus, OH: Merrill Publishers.

Gray, Peter. (2015, September). Declining student resilience: a serious problem for colleges. *Psychology Today*.

Greenberg, Melanie. (2016, December 18). Why some stress is good for you. *Psychology Today*.

Kopecky, Gini. (1999). Have a good cry. In Coleman *Understanding counseling and psychotherapy, 3rd Ed*. Acton, MA: Copley Publishing Co.

La Haye, Beverly. (1990). *Marriage and the family*. NIV Bible: Zondervan. 1304.

Landers, Ann. (1995, December 9). Follow the surefire recipe to 'cook up' a troubled child. *Daily Record*, Morris County, NJ.

Mandel, Peter. (2017, January 29). Panel says many Americans are doomed to failure. *Pittsburgh Post-Gazette*.

Marriage and family therapy. *www.aamft.org/faqs/index/nm.asp*.

McClelland, D.C. (1965). Achievement and entrepreneurship. *Journal of Personality and Social Psychology.* 10, 389–392.

Minuchin, S. (1974). *Families and family therapy.* Cambridge, MA: Harvard University Press.

Minuchin, S., & Fishman, H.C. (1981). *Family therapy techniques.* Cambridge, MA: Harvard University Press.

Papp, P. (1973). Family sculpting in preventive work with 'well' families. *Family Process.* 12, 197–212.

Stuart, R.B. (1980). *Helping couples change.* New York: Guilford Press.

Satir, V.M. (1967). *Cojoint family therapy.* Palo Alto, CA: Science & Behavior Books.

Taffel, Ron. (2005). *Breaking through to teens.* New York: Guilford Press.

Wilcox, Bradford. (2014, December 21). Why the working class family is coming apart. *Desert News*.

Wynne, L.C. (1958). Pseudomutuality in the family relations of schizophrenics. *Psychiatry.* 21, 205–220.

Study Questions

1. Fill in the blank with the answer that is most correct.

   a. A child hides her alcoholic father's bottles for him to keep her mother from knowing that the father is drinking. The child is demonstrating a _____ toward the father.

   b. A family has many secrets that they do not share with anyone outside of the family system. They are always enabling each other by lying and covering for each other to the police and school authorities. This is an example of an _____ family.

   c. A husband is having an affair with a woman other than his wife. This is an example of a _____.

   d. A chart that a therapist makes of the family history and family tree is called a _____.

   e. A husband, wife, and children combination is called a _____ family.

   f. A husband, wife, children and any relative that live nearby is called an _____ _____.

   g. A therapist helps build walls in a family system. These walls are called _____.

   h. A mother gives her son money to buy his drugs so he will not have to steal the money. She is _____ the son.

   i. A family blames one member for all of the troubles in the family. This is called _____.

   j. The mother asks her son why he never talks to her and share his feelings with her. Whenever the son tries to tell her his feelings, she tells him to "shut up." This is an example of _____.

   k. A family is harmonious with an equality in the family chores. This family demonstrates both _____ and _____.

   l. A divorced woman with children and a divorced man with children marry. They have just formed a _____ _____.

   m. A family has a long list of expectations and traditions which they closely follow. This is called a family _____.

   n. A son and his father are both fiercely interested in fishing and go fishing every time they can. They demonstrate an _____.

   o. A family is alienated and they come and go at all times of the day and night with no accountability to each other. This is called a _____ family.

   p. In this family the mother rules the father and children. This family demonstrates _____ _____.

   q. This family appears to be happily functional on the surface but underneath there is conflict and strife. This is an example of _____.

   r. When a family is said to be in balance it is said to show _____.

2. What is the most important function of a family therapist?
3. What is the most effective tool in family therapy?
4. What is the most important goal in family therapy?
5. Why is a genogram important?
6. How would you get an enmeshed family to reveal its secrets?
7. Why does a therapist work with the family as well with the "identified client"?
8. What do you identify as the most important problem facing the American family today?
9. In one family the members constantly argue and scream at each other. How would you handle this situation?
10. What are the reasons that a family member or members will not seek therapy?

CHAPTER FOURTEEN

ADDICTIONS AND RECOVERY

Nobody needs to be convinced that the United States has a serious problem with substance abuse, but most people are really shocked when they view the statistics of the problem. These numbers speak for themselves.

The July 29, 2019, report from www.addictioncenter.com states:

- 14.5 Million Americans have an alcohol abuse disorder.
- Drug overdose deaths have more than tripled since 1990.
- From 1999–2017 at least 700,000 Americans have died from overdosing on drugs.
- Americans between the ages of 18–25 are the most likely to use drugs.
- 88,000 people die every year in the US as a result of alcohol abuse.
- In 2019, about 130 Americans a day died of opioid abuse.
- 43% of Americans confess to having smoked marijuana.
- About 30 to 40 million Americans smoke marijuana every year.
- 30% of people who regularly smoke marijuana have "marijuana use disorder."
- From 1990 to 2019 the amount of THC in marijuana has gone from 4% to 12%.
- Heavy marijuana use has been found to lower IQ and motivation to work and learn.

Anyone can become addicted and addictions are wide-ranged; there are addictions to sex, drugs, food, cigarettes, gambling, money, etc. Often addictions come in clusters, so that if the person has one addiction, he or she is likely to have others. Most addictive substances are anxiolytics (they reduce anxiety) and/or analgesics (they reduce pain). People also become addicted to hormones that their bodies secrete. One type of hormone is called endorphins, a narcotic manufactured by the body. When the body experiences physical and emotional pain, the body secretes endorphins to help reduce the stress the body is feeling from external pain or even to reduce too much adrenalin, a stimulant the body produces.

People use addictive substances to attempt to reduce anxiety and reduce pain. Studies show that people in high stressed jobs, including medical doctors, nurses, and police officers, tend to have above average addiction rates.

GENETIC INFLUENCES

Since genetics play a factor in alcohol abuse, studies suggest a link between ancestral usage of alcohol and a person's abuse of alcohol. Cotton (1979) said that in the United States "the familial transmission of alcohol abuse was found to be six times that of the general population…one third of all alcohol abusers have at least one parent who has experienced a problem with alcohol." Similar studies suggest that other drugs also may have strong genetic influences.

In the United States 2.6% of the population have been diagnosed with Bipolar Disorder. Bipolar Disorder has been found to be genetically transmitted. Several studies suggest that over 60% of this population use addictive substances, i.e. drugs or alcohol. Many of these people, who are unaware they are bipolar, use these substances in an attempt to manage their mood swings. Bipolar persons tend to collect at a much higher percentage in drug programs because they are far more susceptible to abusing drugs.

Super drinkers are people who do not suffer from many of the detrimental aspects of hangovers. They can bounce out of bed the next day, after drinking a case of beer, with no hangover. Irish, Eastern European and American Indian populations historically have greater numbers of super drinkers than other ethnic groups. Research suggests that these people are far more prone to alcoholism.

In contrast, Asian populations experience among the lowest rates of alcohol abuse. Japanese, Chinese and Korean populations often experience an unpleasant physiological reaction to ethanol. This response is characterized by a rapid increase in the flow of blood to the face, neck and chest, elevated heart rate, decreased blood pressure, headaches and nausea. These symptoms are similar to those experienced when persons on Antabuse (A substance often given to serious alcoholics so that when they drink, they get very ill.) consume alcohol.

OTHER BIOLOGICAL INFLUENCES

One chemical in the brain is serotonin. When person's level of serotonin is normal, a person feels good, alert, and maintains a sense of well-being. When serotonin levels are low, the person is clinically depressed. There are two well-documented drugs that destroy serotonin in the brain and can lead to a clinical depression. One is alcohol and the other is cocaine. Another serotonin destroyer is anger. Often a person who is clinically depressed (low in serotonin) will increase his or her drug intake in order to feel better, which lowers the serotonin level even more, and slides the person lower into depression. Many substance abusers attempt or commit suicide because they are so depressed. Persons who are clinically depressed will explain that it is one of the most painful experiences that they have ever had, and that the reason that they obsess about suicide is that they want the pain to stop. A severely serotonin depleted individual might overdose or commit suicide simply because of the pain that is felt. As a result, many addicts are not afraid of death. (Bardi, 2019)

THE FIRST BIG HIGH

One commonality that often arises from every addiction is that big emotional blast that most addicts get on their way to getting hooked. Most heroin or cocaine addicts relate the vivid memory they have of their first big high. This kicks off a career of trying to replicate that high. This is also true of a gambler who remembers the euphoria of the first big jackpot. Even some alcoholics recall that first big drunk.

TOLERANCE

Addictions are progressive. A heroin addict must increase his or her dosage to get the same amount of euphoria, or a sex addict needs to watch more and more explicit videos for the same amount of arousal. In other words, addicts build up a tolerance to their addiction of choice. As tolerance builds up, other addictions can be introduced into it, i.e. a cigarette smoker tries pot, then heroin, then cocaine as the addicted descends into the search for the better high. Too often the addictions do not let go until the person is incarcerated or dead.

WITHDRAWAL

When addicts stop using their drug, they develop various types of uncomfortable symptoms that make them crave the drug even more. Withdrawal could simply be restlessness and irritability, as is seen with the sex addict or gambler, or could produce serious biological withdrawal complications, such as delirium tremens (DTs) in the alcoholic. Therefore, addicts shuffle between getting high and being sick, which is an ever-descending spiral into loss of self.

SOCIOLOGICAL PROFILE

One of the personality traits that surfaces as a central structure of the addictive personality is hostility. Other factors associated with alcohol and drug abuse are listed below by Sarason. (1999)

1. Extreme economic deprivation
2. Neighborhood disorganization
3. Early and persistent behavior problems, including aggressive behavior and hyperactivity
4. Poor family management practices
5. Family conflict
6. Lack of cohesion within the family
7. Academic failure
8. Social pressure to use drugs
9. Alienation and rebelliousness
10. Rejection by peers

Luthar (2013) relates that even culturally advantaged youth are giving in to the temptations of various addictions because of the increasing pressure that parents and society put on them to have higher GPA's and achieve the same economic level that their parent have attained. Luthar explains that this is leading also to increased levels of "self-blame, shame, depression" and consequently overdose deaths from drugs.

Americans are increasingly becoming a more addictive society. Gusovshy (2016) notes that people in the USA make up less than 5% of the world's population but take more than 80% of the world's drugs. Americans tend to emphasize the external ways of satisfying our needs, rather than developing personality traits and resilience to cope with life's problems.

Gambling is presently proliferating in America. One study suggests that there are more than 10 million gambling addicts (North American Foundation for Gambling Addiction, 2016) and that most people that gamble or buy lottery tickets make $20,000 a year or less. The ones that support the gambling industry are the ones who can least afford it. In Mississippi, people spend more on gambling than on all retail buying, including groceries, in the entire state. Younger people tend to gamble more than older people. It is much more common among males than females.

ADDICTIVE PERSONALITY PROFILE

Psychological studies have found that most clients that enter rehabilitation programs have an external locus of control view of the world. In other words, they use the defense mechanism of projection, or they look outside themselves for happiness. They tend to think that joy comes in the form of clothes, money, sex, cars, and other material things. The opposite are persons who have an internal locus of control. These take more responsibility for their behavior, are more caring, and more successful. The goal of therapy is to help clients develop an internal locus of control.

Severely addicted clients have a broken heart. One study strongly suggested that over 50% of the female clients in substance abuse programs suffer from Post Traumatic Stress Disorder. Many clients have suffered emotional trauma and other types of rejection and abuse. Of Sarason's characteristics listed above, the failure, social alienation, rejection, and abuse that most clients have suffered as a result of family conflict have broken their hearts.

How does someone heal a broken heart? One can heal by communicating the trauma in an accepting environment and through receiving social support. A person can also get rid of stress chemicals from the body, not only by talking about the issues, but also by letting the hurt feelings out and by receiving emotional support.

Some clients, however, look upon love, crying, caring, and accepting as signs of weakness. As a result, they cover up their broken hearts with hostility. The prime defense mechanisms in hostility are projection and displacement. These defenses, however, help the client take the focus off of how badly he or she is hurting inside and put it on the external environment. That is why clients play blaming games. It is, therefore, very difficult to get an addictive personality to look at the hurt and pain, because he or she is angry at society and taking these feelings out on others. (Coleman 1999)

HOSTILITY

Studies show that <u>the more a person acts hostile, the more hostile one becomes</u>. (Coleman 2015) Some authorities suggest that one of the first, if not the first, addiction of an addict is hostility. Yes, it does feel good to get the revenge, but it does not solve the problem. Not only does getting revenge and acting out on hostility make a person feel good, but also by temporarily reducing anxiety, hostility can make one <u>psychologically ill</u>.

Hostility artificially raises a person's self-esteem and increases pride. In other words, when a person starts to think better of him or herself, the more hostile one becomes. One study compared prison inmates with college students on their outward levels of self-esteem. Surprisingly, the prisoners reported much higher self-esteem and were more prideful than the college students. Perhaps empty self-esteem (as opposed to self-confidence) is counterproductive.

The way hostility works is that it increases pride. In this manner the person is actually looking down on humanity, and instead of seeing people as equals, looks at people as objects to keep at bay and manipulate. This increased self-esteem makes the client increasingly more difficult to treat. The more bitter and hostile a person becomes, the more anti-social he or she also becomes, which in turn increases the guilt and shame. Sometimes, the addict will eventually break down, humble him or herself and admit to an experience of guilt and shame.

Hostility also shows very poor social skills. Society reacts negatively to the person with a high level of external locus of control, which enrages the person more. Therefore, the addictive personality will attempt to reduce the anxiety and pain by increasing their addictive behavior. <u>The angrier they are, the more they lose control. The more they lose control, the angrier they become and the worse their addictions get</u>.

Physical health is also affected. Smith states, "Research findings indicate a clear pattern—being an angry or hostile person is bad for your heart. For example: People most prone to anger were almost three times more likely to have a heart attack than those with low anger in a recent study of 12,986 participants." (p. 46)

For a ferocious client, it is very difficult to get him or her to admit to a broken heart, to cry and to receive social support. When a person is hostile, this hostility deeply represses the love feelings and makes one become incapable of natural affection. Because the person cannot make heart to heart connections with others, manipulative behaviors occur. He or she uses others as objects. For example, sex no longer is an expression of affection; it is a selfish way of getting release.

When the person is out of touch with love feelings, lust is often interpreted as love. If you ask men in prison if they know what love is, they will say yes and point to the picture of the naked woman next to their bed and tell you how they would like to make love to that woman, confusing lust with love. (Coleman 2015, pp. 29–39) Finally, addicts will explain that their drug became their lover and was the sole pre-occupation of their life.

REACHING THE ADDICTIVE PERSONALITY

If the engine that drives the addictive personality disorder is hostility and distrust, many clients also suffer from various levels of anti-social personality disorders. Since many come from dysfunctional families, if the client is in group therapy, the group should be set up as a functional family. The group leaders need to teach natural affection to the members and develop trust and support among family members. Members can be encouraged to go underneath the hostility, which is an image, and genuinely discuss what broke their heart.

HONESTY

Therapy is where broken heart surgery takes place. It takes much courage for a client to undergo heart surgery and to mend a broken heart, but the surgeon's scalpel is honesty. A client is encouraged to be totally, brutally and completely honest in a confidential environment. When clients are completely honest and open, they are able to get at the pain that is hiding behind the hostility and rejection. When individuals succeed in getting out their hurt feelings and in mending their broken hearts, they learn to love again.

One highly effective way to help people reduce guilt and shame is to run Secrets Groups where clients are able to get their deepest secrets out anonymously. Secret Groups can be very emotive and cleansing sessions and the group can turn into a functional family. The client may be able to take what is learned in the group and hopefully create more functional relationships outside the group. The goals of therapy are to teach love, trust, morality, honesty, humbleness and spiritual values. (Coleman, 2015)

THE TWELVE STEP PROGRAM

A counselor must be fully aware of the Twelve Step Programs, initially started by Alcoholics Anonymous. These programs are advocated for two reasons. One, they work. Two, they are free!

Bill W. in *The Big Book of Alcoholics Anonymous* states that alcoholism is a three-part disease: mental, physical and spiritual. All of the Twelve Step literature can be condensed into six words. Trust God, Clean House, Help Others. These six simple words need to be performed in the order given. It is primary that the addict comes in touch with his or her own sense of a higher power. Reading *The Big Book of Alcoholics Anonymous* will provide the counselor with the Twelve Step concept of higher power. Higher Power, for a beginner in the recovery process, can simply be the group. A realization that others have gained recovery can be enough stimulus to pull the client forward.

In moving from an external locus to an internal locus, one needs to Clean House. This is where the real work of the Twelve Steps begins. To highlight, the Fourth Step is divided into four parts and the *Big Book* suggests that the client write out the Fourth Step. The four parts are Character Defects, Fears, Resentments and How I Hurt Others. Clients take their own inventories, listing what they believe are their character defects, fears (or therapeutic resistances), resentments (anger), and lastly, How I Hurt Others.

In the Fifth Step, the client chooses a trusted member of the group as his or her sponsor to share the results of the Fourth Step. This session should be scheduled to take 4 to 5 hours. While this is an extremely challenging step, the results are hopefully now being able to work with a changed individual.

Each step has promises and a prayer, so that the client can be encouraged to continue to the next step. The promises of the Tenth Step state that when you see alcohol "you will recoil as if from a hot flame." To someone seeking recovery, this is quite a promise! Helping Others is the domain of the Twelfth Step and when one has cleaned house, he or she may be ready to help others.

In accepting the diseased model of addiction, one learns the individual will always be an addict, but that a person can move into Recovery. For the client early in Recovery, it seems that the cravings will never leave. They are asked to examine the question: What good is not using, if that craving is always there?

THE TWELVE STEPS OF ALCOHOLICS ANONYMOUS

1. We admitted we were powerless over alcohol—that our lives had become unmanageable.
2. Came to believe that a Power greater than ourselves could restore us to sanity.
3. Made a decision to turn our will and our lives over the care of God as we understood Him.
4. Made a searching and fearless moral inventory of ourselves.
5. Admitted to God, to ourselves, and to another human being the exact nature of our wrongs.
6. Were entirely ready to have God remove all these defects of character.
7. Humbly asked Him to remove our shortcomings.
8. Made a list of all persons we had harmed, and became willing to make amends to them all.
9. Made direct amends to such people wherever possible, except when to do so would injure them or others.
10. Continued to take personal inventory, and when we were wrong, promptly admitted it.
11. Sought through prayer and meditation to improve our conscious contact with God as we understood Him, praying only for knowledge of His will for us and the power to carry that out.
12. Having had a spiritual awakening as a result of these steps, we tried to carry this message to alcoholics, and to practice these principles in all our affairs.

The steps of AA came from biblical principles. However, in the development of the program, in order to appeal to people of all spiritual beliefs, God was changed to a Higher Power. A book that Christian believers find even more powerful and therapeutic is *The Twelve Steps for Christians* (1994). This book gives a biblical grounding, step by step, for each of the twelve steps and how a person can pattern one's life and gain recovery through practicing these principles.

RECOMMENDATIONS FOR RUNNING A RECOVERY PROGRAM

Much work needs to be done to run effective substance abuse treatment programs. At times government rules interfere with running the best program. On the other hand, the criminal justice system is realizing that very little rehabilitation happens in prison and is starting to release prisoners into therapeutic communities. The bad news is many of these therapeutic communities are becoming like the institutions of old and are simply warehouses for warm bodies.

We should look at the research and find out what really works and seek the most effective techniques to run programs. One study found that while Christian-based recovery programs, i.e. Teen Challenge, and Youth Challenge, have an up to 80% recovery rate, many therapeutic communities do not allow the clients to seek a Higher Power. Chuck Colson, former director of Prison Ministries started a very radical treatment program for offenders. George Will (1999) writes in his article "Believers Truly Setting Prisoners Free" the following:

Sugar Land, Texas—It is commencement season across the country, including here under a tent in a corner framed by a high fence topped with razor wire. A handful of convicts at the prison are receiving certificates of graduation from Inner Change Freedom Initiative, a voluntary 18-month, predawn to past-sundown daily immersion in basic Christianity, leavened by lessons in basic life skills.

Five are being baptized this day—full immersion in a tub of water—as the waving of fans, inscribed 'You have been set free from sin and have become slaves of righteousness' (Romans 6:18), gives way to clapping to the rhythm of *Take Me to The Water*. Few of the graduates have ever graduated from anything else.

Prisons just don't seem to work in rehabilitating people. "An estimated 68% of released prisoners were arrested after 3 years, 79% within 6 years, and 83% within 9 years." (National Institute of Justice May 21, 2019) When faith-based rehabilitation programs were established, statistics showed that the recidivism rate was only 8%.

Many therapeutic communities simply lecture their members. However, it is evident that when more effective therapeutic interventions are provided to clients, more healing occurs. Also, when clients are given positive learning experiences, instead of punitive consequences, there could be growth. Therapeutic communities would ideally be set up in environments where there are less temptations to cop drugs a block away. Research also shows that if clients were to plant gardens, learn animal husbandry, chop wood, and exercise daily, they could be taught greater responsibility and give more meaning to their lives.

Therapeutic communities could be set up in ways similar a college. There is no social promotion in a college. A member is required to clearly earn the levels that are achieved within the program. Often clients in a rehabilitation facility see themselves as simply doing the time and are waiting to get out after their time is up.

Additionally, every client should be given a *Recovery Workbook* the day he or she enters a rehabilitation program. This workbook should include the rules of the program, the purpose of the program, the purpose and rules of groups, why feelings are important, how to work out a therapeutic issue, etc.

Clients also should be required to complete the following in their workbooks, and when appropriate discuss or read parts of their workbooks to peers and counselors:

1. Do a complete and detailed biography, which should include all the traumatic as well as good experiences, of one's life.
2. Write down the relationship with his or her mother, and be required to complete a detailed letter to her, with true feelings and memories. This letter may or may not be sent, depending on the client's desire.
3. Follow the same procedures from number 2 above, but this time the subject is father.
4. Follow the same procedure from number 2, but this time for other significant people in one's life, i.e. grandfather, grandmother.
5. Write in detail what one remembers about loneliness, pain, anger, love, abuse, guilt and shame.
6. Understand what caused this addiction.
7. Write a detailed letter to oneself and read it to the family.
8. Initiate a recovery plan, including life's goals.

Finally, the client should be kept busy. All too often, therapeutic communities keep the clients sitting around. Exercise and sports should be integrated into the program. Meditation, including prayer and stress reduction should be a daily requirement. There also should be regular therapy groups (Coleman 2015) and family therapy for the client. Lastly, alumnae should be integrated into the program, having them come back to give talks and seminars.

MOTIVATIONAL INTERVIEWING

A popular therapeutic system, called Motivational Interviewing (MI), developed by Miller and Rollnick (2002) has been quite effective with substance abusing clients and also clients with co-occurring disorders. This motivational strategy is employed to help both clinician and client working together toward the common goal of helping the client. MI does make a distinction between agreeing with a client's denial system (which is counterproductive) and sidestepping it in order to make some progress. With practice and experience, the clinician will come to recognize when to sidestep disagreements and pursue MI and when to move forward with traditional methods with clients who are motivated sufficiently and ready for change. (US Department of Health and Human Services, 2008, pp. 115–120).

The developers of MI have identified six possible stages of change and possible "motivational enhancement approaches" that can be used for substance abusing clients.

1. PRECONTEMPLATION—The client is unaware of the problem or has no intention of changing. Presented are some suggestions a therapist might explore in a nonjudgmental way.

    a. Talk about concerns about the client's substance abuse.
    b. Ask the client to try a "trial abstinence."
    c. Ask about the client's perception of use of various substances.

2. CONTEMPLATION—The client is admitting a problem exists but has not made a commitment to do something about it.

    a. Discuss positive and negative aspects of using substances.
    b. Ask the client if he or she might try a trial abstinence.

3. PREPARATION—Ask about client's positive and negative views about his or her substance use and abstinence and what effective action the person might take.

    a. Acknowledge the importance of the decision to seek treatment.
    b. Support the client's self-efficacy.
    c. Discuss that the work ahead will be very difficult.
    d. Explain that a relapse should not disrupt the client.

4. ACTION—Explore behaviors and experiences that can and possibly be changed over the next few weeks to overcome the problem.

    a. Have the client talk about the difficulties of withdrawal from substances and the temptations of relapse.
    b. Support the client's determination to stay positive.
    c. Reinforce the client's benefits to stay in recovery.

5. MAINTENANCE—Client agrees to stay in abstinence.

    a. Discuss with client the difficulties and temptations that will arise in the future.
    b. Recognize the client's struggle ahead and explain that relapse should not disrupt the therapeutic relationship.

6. RELAPSE—Several studies suggest that most addicts relapse about six times. Therefore, each client is urged to persist.

    a. Discuss the relapse triggers and how they can be overcome.
    b. Support the client's confidence that he or she can overcome the problem.

A CHRISTIAN PERSPECTIVE OF SUBSTANCE ABUSE TREATMENT

Recovery is a commitment to a lifelong process of self-improvement. It does not end when the final therapeutic session ends. Recovery entails treatment of the whole person—spirit, soul, and body and may involve therapy for years. Building a network of support around the individual, which many churches can do, that hold the individual accountable for his or her action or inaction, is a great help towards maintaining sobriety and positive recovery. Every Christian needs to stand up for Christ in the recovery community because it is a fertile field for Jesus to bring "the sick and suffering" to Himself.

To repeat, if you work in this field you need the book *The Twelve Steps for Christians.* Seek or develop inpatient and outpatient programs based on Biblical principles. For the recovering person, biblical truths will continue to address one's dependency on God. Everyone needs these.

Let us examine our ways and test them, and let us return to the Lord. (Lam. 3:40)

Confess your sins to each other and pray for each other so that you may be healed. (James 4:10)

So, you think you are standing firm, be careful that you don't fall. (1 Cor. 10:12)

Brothers, if someone is caught in a sin, you who are spiritual should restore him gently. But watch yourself, or you also may be tempted. (Gal. 6:1)

References

Alcoholics Anonymous. (1953). *Twelve steps and twelve traditions*. New York: Alcoholics Anonymous World Services, Inc.

Bardi, Jason. (2019). Serotonin receptors and drug abuse. www.scripps.edu.

Chueng, Y.W. (1993). Beyond lives and culture. A review of theories and research in drinking among Chinese in North America. *International Journal of the Addictions*, 28, 1497–1513.

Coleman, T.R. (2015). *How to make group psychotherapy work*. Bloomington, IN.: Xlibris.

Coleman, T.R. (1999). *Understanding counseling and psychotherapy*. Acton, MA: Copley Publishing Group.

Cotton, N.S. (1979). The familial incidence of alcoholism: A review. *Journal of Studies on Alcohol*, 40, 89–116.

Gusovsky, Dina. (2016). Americans consume the vast majority of the world opioids, CNBC.com.

Kalb, C. & Rogers, A. (1999, June 14). STRESS, *Newsweek*.

North American Foundation for Gambling Addiction. 2016.

Luthar, S. (2013). The problem with rich kids. *Psychology Today*, Vol. 46. 6.

Miller, W.R., & Rollnick, S. (2002). *Motivational interviewing*. New York: Guilford.

Sarason, J.G., & Sarason, B.R. (1999). *Abnormal psychology, the problem of maladaptive behavior*. Upper Saddle River, NJ: Prentice Hall.

Smith, Deborah. (March 2013, Vol.34. No.3 p.46). Angry thoughts, at-risk hearts. *APA Monitor on Psychology*.

Friends in Recovery. (1994). *The twelve steps for Christians*. Scotts Valley, CA: RPI Publishing Inc.

National Institute of Justice. May 2019.

Will, George. (1999, June 3). Believers truly setting prisoners free. *Newark Star Ledger*.

www.addictioncenter.com. 2019.

Study Questions

1. The substance that reduces anxiety is called an _____.
2. The substance that reduces pain is called a _____.
3. People that are excessive drinkers but don't feel the detrimental effect on their body until years later are called _____.
4. A person is very depressed when his or her brain level of _____ is low.
5. Two addictive substances that contribute greatly to depression are _____ and _____.
6. When a person needs greater and greater amounts of a drug to get the same euphoria, this is called _____.
7. A person who first enters a drug program is more likely to have a _____ _____ of _____.
8. One study found that a large percentage of females suffer from _____ _____ _____ disorder.
9. Clients that project their feelings are playing _____ games.
10. One of the core feelings that increases pride and contributes to an addictive personality is _____.
11. The most important concept in a therapy group is to be completely _____.
12. One of the goals of a group is to create a _____ family.
13. Write down each step of the Twelve Steps and explain why it is important to recovery.

CHAPTER FIFTEEN

CHRISTIAN COUNSELING

<u>The Bustle in the House</u>

The bustle in the house
The morning after death
Is solemnest of industries
Enacted upon the earth
The sweeping up the heart
And putting love away
We shall not want to use again
Until eternity.

Emily Dickinson

IS THERE A GOD?

Have you ever wondered if God exists, and if so, why doesn't He make the earth a nicer place to live? We all wonder what will happen to us after we die. Dr. Maurice Rawlings, a specialist in cardiovascular diseases, in his powerful book *To Hell and Back* (1993) speaks to the future after death. As personal physician at the Pentagon for the Joint Chiefs of Staff, including Generals Marshall, Bradley, Patton, and President Dwight Eisenhower, he was no friend of religion and was even cynical about the idea of God until he had a startling experience. He relates it as follows:

"The whole thing occurred late one day in 1977 when the other doctors had left the Diagnostic Center to finish rounds elsewhere. Pam Charlesworth was finishing an EKG on a patient with chest pains.

'It's normal,' she said.

I shook my head. 'Hook him up again and this time exercise him enough to reproduce the pain. A smoldering heart attack could still be there.'

The treadmill rumbled to life, moving Charlie McKaig, a forty-eight year old mail carrier from Lafayette, Georgia, at a progressively rapid rate. Pain reappeared along with sweating and breathlessness. An unusual humming from the monitor caused us to look up to see an unexpected run of ventricular tachycardia (rapid, dangerous heartbeat.) This was followed by a very long pause in the beat and then followed by slow, widened beats and then by a flat line.

Surprisingly, Charlie continued to talk for a while, unaware that his heart had stopped. Four or five seconds later, he looked suddenly dumbfounded. It was as if he were about to ask a question. Then his eyes rolled up in his head and he fell, the treadmill sweeping the body away like too much trash.

This reminded me of similar problems occurring in the heart lab where the heartbeat stops for some reason but amazingly, the patient continues to talk for a while. Hitting them on the chest or making them cough repeatedly usually starts them up again so the procedure can be completed as if nothing happened.

With Charlie's head sharply extended, chin toward the ceiling, one of the nurses breathed the 'kiss of life.' Another nurse started the IV for medicines. By then an underlying block in the heartbeat had appeared on the monitor. That means the heart was not conducting the beat properly and a temporary pacemaker would be needed for the heart to respond to the CPR.

Using a large-bore needle, I entered the big vein under the collarbone, then threaded the pacemaker wire in the right side of the heart and attached the wire to a pulse generator box to initiate every beat, not missing a stroke.

But blood was spurting everywhere. Whenever I stopped pushing on his chest in order to adjust the pacemaker, the heart would stop, and Charlie's eyes would roll up, he again would sputter, turn blue, and begin to convulse.

With bare hands, I would reach over and start him up again. But this time he was screaming the words, 'Don't stop! I'm in hell! I'm in hell!'

Hallucination, I thought. Most victims say, 'Take your big hands off me, you're breaking my ribs, but he was saying the opposite: 'For God's sake, don't stop! Don't you understand? Every time you let go, I'm back in hell!'

When he asked me to pray for him, I felt downright insulted. In fact, I told him to shut up. I said I was a doctor, not a minister and not a psychiatrist. But the nurses gave me that expectant look. What would you do? That's when I composed a make-believe prayer.

I made him repeat the make-believe prayer word for word to keep him off my back. Meanwhile, I resuscitated with one hand and adjusted the pacemaker with the other. 'Say it! Jesus Christ is the Son of God, go on and say it!' I said. 'Keep me out of hell and if I live, I'm on the hook, I'm yours. Go on, say it!' He said it.

And then a very strange thing happened that changed <u>our</u> lives. A religious conversion experience took place. I had never witnessed one before. He was no longer the wild-eyed screaming, combative lunatic who had been fighting me for his life. He was relaxed and calm and cooperative. It frightened me. I was shaken by the events. <u>Not only had that make-believe prayer blown out the soul of Charlie McKaig, but backfired and got me too. It was a conviction I cannot express even to this day</u>.

Since then, Charlie has out lived three pacemakers, and it has been difficult to believe that this miserable prayer of mine had opened the road to my own salvation. A spiritual bonus for the simpleminded. The lesson? Don't say make-believe prayers. They can work. And they can dissect your soul like a surgeon's scalpel." (pp. 24–26)

Maurice Rawlings became a committed Christian as a result of Charlie McKaig's hellish, and then heavenly experiences. For those of us have seen people die and have pondered their fate after death, we have wondered what we could have said to comfort them about death.

There are hundreds of documented near death experiences but another recommended book is *My Journey to Heaven* by Marvin Besteman. Like Rawlings and Besteman, I have studied a large variety of religions and found only Christianity to be fulfilling and satisfying. This chapter is in large part of my personal experiences, beliefs and convictions. All of what I believe is biblically grounded. Combining Christian principles with psychotherapy has been effective for many years in my practice.

Victor Frankel, the founder of Logo-therapy, was in a Nazi concentration camp and saw thousands die. He found that one of the main reasons that many died was because they gave up <u>hope</u>. They saw life as meaningless and empty. Likewise, psychologists have always known that humans are purposeful creatures and that goals make life worth living. Psychologists also know that a goalless person is often anxious, depressed, or even drug addicted. Mental institution patients, especially the more regressed ones, live meaningless, aimless existences. To help a depressed person someone needs to show him or her that life is meaningful and worth living.

Additionally, some people may erroneously view God as a cruel punisher. They may think that He created an awful earth, full of diseases, wars, and personal sufferings. If it is this evil, why did He create it? Human nature neglects to understand that God does not intend evil for His creation, but God intends for us to feel good about ourselves and to do good for others. The Bible says, **"Each of us should please his neighbor for his good, to build him up." (Rom. 15:2) "Therefore encourage one another and build each other up, just as in fact you were doing." (Thes. 5:11)** These sayings seem like good psychology.

Carl Jung saw the importance of a future when he explained the teleological approach (See the chapter on Analytic Psychology.) Jung believed that we are spiritual as well as material beings, and that dream analysis emits rich spiritual meaning.

Christian clinicians find that the Bible is the greatest psychological document written. Many empirical findings in psychology agree closely with Biblical teaching. Christians seem to have a far easier time experiencing death because they can look ahead with hope and excitement. Since many people in the United States are affiliated with Christian denominations, it is important to relate the effectiveness of Christian counseling to the field of psychology in helping people live more <u>responsible, loving, longer, healthier and hopeful lives</u>.

CAN YOU TRUST THE BIBLE'S PSYCHOLOGY?

Can you always trust psychology? If it is true that many psychologists are not believing Christians, can you trust that their findings are religiously sound? Well, can you trust an auto mechanic's manual? Of course, you can trust the manuals on cars. Probably they aren't perfect, but they are helpful if you want to fix a car. Likewise, psychology is the study of human behavior. It isn't perfect, but it can be helpful.

William Kirwan says:

> "Biblical Christianity and psychology, when rightly understood do not conflict, but represent functionally cooperative positions. By taking both spheres into account, a mental health professional can help Christians avoid the inevitable results of violating psychological laws structured in the human personality by God ... Therefore, it seems incumbent on psychologists in the evangelical camp to integrate their counseling theories and methods with the word of God. At present only a few counselors seem able to do the two.... Although their philosophical conclusions are doubtless anti-Christian, their empirical findings are not." (1984 pp.21–25)

Many psychological principles are biblically sound and complement biblical teachings. If the psychological principle disagrees with the Bible, then that area of psychology hasn't caught up with the Bible. If the principle agrees with the Bible, then use it. For example, for years many psychologists believed that children should be indulged and rarely punished. Today the child raising techniques are swinging to more biblical techniques because of the selfishness shown by the undisciplined "Dr. Spock" generation, currently referred to as the snowflake generation. However, the Bible likewise cautions about being too strict with children when it says, **"Provoke not your children to anger, lest they be discouraged." (Col. 3:21)**

Many have embraced the value of faith and hope in therapeutic treatment. Among the faith-based or religious communities, there are some debates concerning God and psychology. Specifically, some

Christians have said that a "good" Christian doesn't need counseling; he or she just needs good preaching. **ENCOURAGEMENT:** Be your own cheerleader. Say to yourself, "This won't last forever," or "I'm doing the best I can." Yet, both Jesus and Paul spent much of their time listening to the problems of those around them. Weren't they, in their own way, therapists with sound advice?

Another goal for writing this chapter is to encourage more Christians to go into the field of counseling and psychotherapy. There is an obvious need. Many clergy express difficulty with finding good Christian psychotherapists and psychologists for members of their congregations. With Christian trained therapists more churches could open up their own counseling centers and rehabilitation programs. At present, government funded programs are not as effective as the Christian programs. One study suggested that the average government funded programs are less than 25 percent effective while some Christ-based programs, such as Teen Challenge and Youth Challenge, are up to 85 percent effective for recovery of clients. Celebrate Recovery is another Christian based program that focuses on recovery.

CHRIST'S EXAMPLE

In his best-selling book, *The Art of Loving*, Eric Fromm equates a loving person with being a psychologically healthy person. Both psychology and the Bible agree that humans are selfish creatures. On the backwards of mental hospitals clients are in their own little worlds and not at all interested in another person unless he or she has cigarettes or candy. In fact, if a patient falls down with a heart attack, most of the clients would simply ignore it or even take the person's cigarettes. There is no caring of the patients for each other. Conversely, love seems to be the emotion that lifts people above their self-centered state. The Bible states that **God is love. (1 John 4:8–9)**

Kirwan explains, "Christians have a strong basis for self-confidence in the unconditional love, acceptance and positive regard for them which Christ demonstrated in dying on the cross… In his atoning death Christ looked at us sinners and said, 'I love you as you are.' He attached no conditions to our acceptance of us except our faith… He even experienced hell for us." (p. 107) **"For God hath not given us the spirit of fear; but of power, and of love, and of a sound mind." (2 Tim. 1:7)**

Rogerian therapists know the power of rejection and criticism in breaking down a person's self-confidence, which is why they strongly promote unconditional acceptance by the therapist. The Bible also promotes building a strong self-worth through acceptance when it says, **"Him that cometh to me I will in no wise cast out." (John 6:37)** In the story of the Prodigal son, God shows how He will accept his children back if only they ask. God also reassures the believer when He says in **Hebrews 13:5, "I will never leave you or forsake you."**

Numerous years ago, Charlotte had recently found out she was dying from a brain tumor. She offered this letter from an unknown author. Charlotte said the letter moved and comforted her. When shared with others, they too are moved by God's Love. Even though not from the Bible, it communicates God's deep caring for us.

A LOVE LETTER FROM JESUS

How are you? I just had to send you this letter to tell you how much I care about you and love you. I saw you yesterday as you were walking with your friends. I waited all day hoping you would walk and talk with me also. As evening drew near, I gave you a sunset to close your day and a cool breeze to soothe you. Did you like it? I then waited but you did not come. Oh, yes, it hurt me, but I still love you because I am your friend.

I watched you fall asleep last night. I longed to touch your brow, so I spilled moonlight upon your pillow and your face. Did you feel it? Again, I waited wanting to rush down so we could talk. I have so many gifts for you.

You awakened late this morning and rushed off into the day. My tears were in the rain. Today you looked so sad and alone. It makes my heart ache because I understand. My friends let me down and hurt me many times, but I still love you and I try to tell you in the quietness of the grass. I whisper my love to you in the quivering of the leaves of the trees and breathe it through the fragrance and color of the flowers. Did you notice?

I shout to you in the thunderstorm and the blast of a snowy day. I give the birds love songs to entertain you. I clothe you with warm sunshine and perfumed air. My love for you is deeper than the universe and bigger than the largest want or need you could ever have.

I want to spend eternity with you. I have a beautiful house prepared for you. I know you are afraid. I can see that your heart is broken. I know you don't think you measure up. I know how hard it is on earth. I really do know, because I was on earth too. I was homeless and suffered also and I want to help you.

Let me ask you a question? Let's say you had a child who did some of the bad things that you have done and worse. Would you still love that child and forgive that child if they asked? Would you? I know you would and that is the way I feel about you. I love you so much that you are worth dying for.

My Father wants to help you too, that's the way he is you know. Just call me, ask me, reach for me, I yearn to hear you call my name. It makes me cry when you ignore me. It is your decision. I have chosen you because of this I will wait... I am waiting... Because I love you. You are my friend.

YOUR FRIEND, JESUS

LISTEN AND TRY TO UNDERSTAND

A person can never fully understand what others are going through or how they feel, but one can try. What most people want is someone to listen to them and to show them that this person is trying to understand. A Person-Centered Approach to counseling is one of the best ways to build a rapport and to gain the trust of the person. Perhaps no other human has ever taken the time to really listen to the hurting person. Even though the counselor doesn't have a magic wand to make the person better, listening and understanding are like fresh air to many clients. However, at times, counselors may have their own agenda, and start preaching to the client, which blocks communication, instead of working to gain trust and bonding. One big mistake that counselors make is that they act as if they have all of the answers and are more interested in what they are going to say, rather than in listening to what the client has to say.

You cannot impose your values on someone. As a therapist you can't come with a "holier than thou" attitude and impose your own agenda upon another person. Kirwan (1984) explains that much damage can be done by an "evangelical therapist who is so concerned with changing the patient that one often fails to empathize effectively." If a client makes it clear that he or she does not want to hear any of that religious stuff, the therapist must back off and listen to what is being said. Simply by showing a person genuine acceptance, no matter what the individual's beliefs, you are demonstrating God's Love. **"Be devoted to one another in brotherly love. Honor one another above yourselves." (Rom.15:2)**

Remember that the Christian counselor also has a helper that most non-Christians know nothing about and that is the Holy Spirit. **"Whoever does not have the Spirit cannot receive the gifts that come from God's Spirit. Such a person really does not understand them; they are nonsense to him because their value can be judged only on a spiritual basis." (1 Cor. 2:14)** The Bible explains in Corinthians 12 how the

Holy Spirit gives powers and spiritual gifts to those that believe. The Holy Spirit is the Christian counselor's guide and friend.

THE COUNSELOR'S SELF DISCLOSURE

There is controversy within the psychological profession as to whether a counselor should self-disclose. In Alcoholics Anonymous and Narcotics Anonymous self-disclosures by the peers in the group have been one of the powerful sources in helping another abuser become substance free. Self-disclosure that is used appropriately can be very motivating for a client.

In the Bible St. Paul did much self-disclosing when he called himself the greatest of sinners and explained, **"I am content with weaknesses… For when I am weak…" (2 Cor. 12:10) "for even though the desire to do good is in me, I am not able to do it… what an unhappy man I am!" (Rom.7:18–24) "Therefore confess your sins to each other and pray for each other so that you may be healed. The prayer of a righteous man is powerful and effective." (Jas. 5:16)**

A counselor should self-disclose to a degree. If the counselor has personally triumphed over a therapeutic issue it is appropriate to share this experience and past struggle with the client. However, it is not appropriate for the counselor to monopolize a therapy session with these experiences. Second, the counselor should think about the ramifications of a particular self-disclosure. Obviously, the counselor should not disclose present drinking behaviors with an alcoholic client. Psychologist Tori DeAngelis (1997) explains self-disclosure in this way, "Express your vulnerability—when appropriate—to clients who will appreciate it." This approach tends to validate the counselor by showing his or her humanity, and thus creating a more honest bond between counselor and client.

EMOTIONS

The Bible contains many lessons on the full spectrum of individual emotions. Some of the most significant include:

LOVE

God's greatest commandment is **"Love one another, as I have loved you." (John 15:12)** When a person is motivated by love, his or her relationships with others become more helpful and healing. The Bible explains that if we have the love that comes from God, we will tend to do right by ourselves and for others.

"Love is patient and kind; it is not jealous or conceited or proud; love is not ill-mannered or selfish or irritable; love does not keep a record of wrongs; love is not happy with evil, but is happy with the truth. Love never gives up; and its faith, hope, and patience never fail. Love is eternal…. These three remain: faith, hope and love and the greatest of these is love." (1 Cor. 13) Think of someone that has had a positive impact on your life. Is this a person who shows love? Remember love is a gift from God.

When Eben Alexander, M.D., had a near death experience, the power of God's love was revealed to him. In his book *Proof of Heaven*. Dr. Alexander shared, "You are loved. Those words are what I needed to hear as an orphan, as a child who'd been given away. But it's also what every one of us in this materialistic age need to hear as well, because in terms of who we really are, where we really came from, and where we're really going, we all feel (wrongly) like orphans. Without recovering that memory of our larger connectedness and of the unconditional love of our Creator, we will always feel lost here on earth." (p.171)

SELF-ESTEEM

Many non-Christians believe that the Bible tears down self-confidence, and also spoils their fun. This certainly is not true. The Bible is full of reassuring passages such as, **"Therefore there is no condemnation for those who are in Christ Jesus" (Rom. 8:1),** and **"We should be called children of God" (1 John 3:1),** and **"So you are no longer a slave, but a son; and since you are a son, God has made you also an heir through Christ." (Gal. 4:7)**

Most psychological disorders are associated with low self-esteem. Often the person feels inferior, alienated and alone. Many people with severe psychological disorders believe no one really cares for them or tries to understand them. Very often they have experienced substantial rejection from significant figures in their lives (i.e. a father or mother). Their needs have not been met, and they are frustrated and angry. They often lash out, hurting themselves or others in vain attempts to fulfill their needs.

Rogerian therapists know the power of rejection and criticism in breaking down a person's self-confidence, which is why they strongly promote unconditional acceptance by the therapist. The Bible also promotes building a strong self-worth through acceptance when it says, **"Him that cometh to me I will in no wise cast out." (John 6:37)** In the story of the Prodigal son, God shows how He will accept his children back if only they ask. God also reassures the believer in **Hebrews 13:5: "I will never leave you or forsake you."**

Another thing that contributes to low self-confidence is guilt. Generally, the person will start talking about guilt when an unconditionally accepting and trusting relationship is formed. Talking and crying about the guilt in a therapeutic Christian environment can begin to heal a lagging inward self-esteem. **"Be ye kind to one another. Tenderhearted, forgiving one another, even as God for Christ's sake hath forgiven you." (Eph. 4:32)**

Recent studies suggest that empty self-esteem is next to useless. One study compared the self-esteem of people in prison with college students. The imprisoned inmates had much higher self-esteem than their college counterparts. Antisocial, narcissistic and paranoid personalities have higher outward self-esteem than the general population and yet the people with these personality disorders have severe interpersonal problems. As hostility raises a person's self-esteem artificially, both the *Bible* and psychological literature testify its detrimental effects. **"Get rid of all bitterness, rage and anger, brawling and slander, along with every form of malice." (Eph. 4:31).** Likewise, in **James 1:20, "because human anger does not produce righteousness that God desires."**

Finally, resilient people do not have high self-esteem, but can humble themselves before others. **"Blessed are the poor in spirit, for theirs is the Kingdom of Heaven." (Matt. 5:3)**

SOCIAL SUPPORTS AND RELATIONS

Dean Ornish and Geoffry Crowley address studies that show how people live better, more fulfilled, healthier lives when they love and are loved and have social support. Crowley summarizes, "Love and intimacy are at the root of what makes us sick and what makes us well...those with the strongest commitments to church and family have the longest and healthiest life and...the people who reported the least social contact died at nearly three times the rate of those report the most." Crowley continues, "People who talk or even write about things that are upsetting them, their immune systems perk up and they require less medical care... When you consider what chronic stress can do to us, the long-term benefits of friendship are not hard to fathom. The stress hormones (adrenaline, noradrenaline and cortisol) switch the entire body into emergency mode. Anything not involved in fighting or fleeing—(i.e. digestion, immune function, bone production, sexual function goes on hold) ... People who lack social support tend to stew in stress hormones all the time… When research at Carnegie Mellon University exposed volunteers to a cold virus, the most isolated got sick at four times the rate of those with the most social ties."

Ornish wrote that "If you can help people express their feelings and attend to their relationships, they can change the chemistry that feeds their illness…togetherness can help to keep people alive…It is clear that reaching out to others can help our bodies to thrive." (1998, pp. 56–57)

Ornish and Crowley agree that loneliness can be isolating and isolation is a health hazard. Some statistics for questions posed to various groups include:

WOMEN: "Do you feel isolated?"
Those that said yes were three and one-half times more likely to die of breast, ovarian or uterine cancer over a 17-year period.

MEN: "Does your wife show you her love?"
Men who said no suffered 50 percent more angina over a five year period than those who said yes.

MALE MEDICAL STUDENTS: "Are you close to your parents?"
Those who said no were more likely to develop cancer or mental illness years later.

HEART PATIENTS: "Do you feel loved?"
Those that felt the least loved had 50 percent more arterial damage than those who felt the most loved.

UNMARRIED HEART PATIENTS: "Do you have a confidant?"
Those who said no were three times likely to die within five years.

HEART ATTACK SURVIVORS: "Do you live alone?"
Those who said yes were more than twice as likely to die within a year. (Crowley 1998)

Today's American families and social gatherings are becoming increasingly isolated due to technology—the television, computer, computer games, and especially the cell phone. Not only are statistics cautioning us on the amount of screen time healthy for the developing brain, but also counseling has become available for media addictions. There is a need to return to face to face communications within the family, friendships and social groups. **"Not forsaking the assembling of ourselves together…." (Heb. 10:25)**

In some religious circles, as well as in psychology, the feminist perspective has often been overlooked with overt and covert biases against women in research methods and in the recognition of their roles. The Bible validates women and encourages all persons toward fulfilling their potential. **"And it shall come to pass afterwards, that I will pour out my spirit upon all flesh; and your sons and your daughters shall prophesy, your old men shall dream dreams, your young men shall see visions: and also upon the servants and upon the handmaids in those days will I pour out my spirit." Joel 2:28–29, Acts 2: 17–18)**

The Bible illustrates this need for community and social relationships clearly. **"If anyone does not provide for his relative, and especially for his immediate family, he has denied the faith and is worse than an unbeliever (I Tim. 5:8) 1 John 2:10** also says, **"Whoever loves his brother lives in the light, and there is nothing in him to make him stumble."** Finally, **1 John 4:11** explains, **"Dear friends, since God so loved us, we also ought to love one another."**

HOPE

Hope is one of the driving forces in life. A person without hope tends to be despairing and pessimistic. Most people with a variety of psychological disorders have had their hopes and dreams shattered, or are afraid to hope because of problems or inferiority feelings. People who are terminally ill and dying see nothingness after death if they have no hope. These clients are difficult to counsel.

By contrast, the Bible provides hope. **"We who have found safety with Him are greatly encouraged to hold firmly to the hope placed before us. We have this hope as an anchor for our lives. It is safe and sure and goes through the curtain of the heavenly temple into the inner sanctuary. On our behalf Jesus has gone in there before us and become a high priest."** (Heb. 6:18–19)

HURT AND PAIN

People are afraid of anxiety and pain. Some believe that our society is phobic towards pain. There are all kinds of medications to alleviate pain. Addicts are constantly trying to gain pleasure as they attempt to self-medicate away the physical, psychological and emotional pain.

When you cut yourself, if you keep the cut clean, the area heals itself naturally. Our emotions are the same way. Gestalt Therapy teaches people to experience the pain and let their bodies heal by crying out hurt feelings. When people hurt, they talk and cry out the feelings to feel better. (There is an unhealthy type of crying, however, and that is manipulative crying. This occurs, for example, when young children cry because they can't get their way all of the time.) A healthy person cries out with hurt feelings to release pain.

Studies show that when people feel hurt, their tears secrete toxic chemicals. Researchers injected these chemicals into other people who felt normal and found that these chemicals made these people feel depressed and anxious. It seems, therefore, that crying is nature's way of eliminating from the body toxic chemicals that create bad feelings. It is a natural biological function.

Society, however, tends to teach people that crying is a sign of weakness. In the military or in jail people are labeled as weak and are preyed upon if they cry. Men especially are taught to repress their hurt feelings and not let them out. Authorities believe that one reason men commit suicide at a three times higher rate than women is because men change hurt into anger.

Men in our society tend to reflexively react with hostility when hurt. This could be one of the reasons why men cause wars and are more likely to commit violent crimes and murder. In the over 40 years working with ex-convicts right out of jail, I have found that when they learn to talk and cry about their feelings, their aggressiveness decreases and they become more in touch with the more tender feelings of love and loneliness. Psychologists continue to try to get people to understand that crying is healthy. Crying is not babyish or feminine, it is <u>human</u>. Most crying gets hurt feelings out, softens the heart, and makes a person feel better.

Some men are taught to convert hurt feelings into anger and hostility. In the military the sergeant purposely hurts soldiers' feelings and teaches them to repress hurt feelings and turn them into controlled rage. The sergeant wants the soldier to become a good "killer," and wants the person somewhat suicidal and homicidal because, if not, the commander reasons, the soldiers wouldn't charge enemy lines. General Patton during WWII said, "Get mad and stay mad at the enemy!" (Coincidentally, when a country is at war, the suicide rate goes down.)

David, one of the greatest soldiers in the Bible, knew how to cry. David, as a small boy, fearlessly killed Goliath when the other brave soldiers of the army were afraid. Later King David wrote, **"The Lord hears my weeping; he listens to my cry for help and will answer my prayer. My enemies will know the bitter shame of defeat; in sudden confusion they will be driven away."** (Ps.9:9–10)

Not only does the Bible show that it is acceptable to cry (**Jesus wept. John 11:35**), but also even commands people to weep. **"Blessed are you who weep now; for you will laugh" (Luke 6:21)**, and **"weep with those that weep." (Rom. 12:15)** The Bible offers a healthy way of showing hurt feelings.

ANGER AND HOSTILITY

Anger is a familiar emotion. While the Bible recognizes anger as a human emotion, it also cautions how dangerous it can be. **"No more lying, then! Everyone must tell the truth to his fellow believer, because we are all members together in the body of Christ. If you are angry, do not let your anger lead you into sin, and do not stay angry all day. Don't give the Devil a chance. The man who used to rob must stop robbing and start working in order to earn an honest living for himself and to be able to help the poor. Do not use harmful words, but only helpful words, the kind that build up and provide what is needed, so that what you will do good to those who hear you." (Eph. 4:25–29)**

In the 1960's, some psychologists taught that anger was healthy and that it should be expressed. More recent studies suggest that expressing anger might, in fact, tend to increase the amount of anger a person holds. Expressing anger freely is like throwing gasoline on a fire. Indeed, violent individuals find that the more they do antisocial things, the angrier they become. People in jail are angry and have done antisocial things against society. **"If someone has a hot temper, let him take the consequences. If you get him out of trouble once, you will have to do it again." (Prov. 19:19)**

Psychologists have found that depressed people are angry and they are taking the anger out mainly on themselves. Conversely, some that are unsuccessful and inept in society tend to externalize or project their feelings. They are looking outside of themselves and this is dangerous. Clearly it is important to help clients learn to talk, learn to cry out their hurt feelings and learn to be very careful about their anger and hostility. The only person we can change is ourselves, which is why most therapies stress that people take responsibility for their own actions.

HONESTY

Delusions are common among people with severe psychiatric disorders. A delusion is defined as a false belief that is maintained in spite of evidence to the contrary. A person can believe some pretty bizarre things, including people plotting against one's life, that one has died, or that one is God. Delusions don't even have to be bad to affect a person's behavior adversely. Maintaining the delusion can cause a person to run into trouble in reality.

In working with ex-offenders and ex-addicts it became evident that many are very manipulative and often tell lies reflexively. They are not always aware of when they are stretching the truth. One client in a drug program on a weekend pass home smoked marijuana under pressure from friends. She did not talk about it when she came back to the program and the guilt and lack of honesty from that behavior caused her to relapse back to hard drugs.

Honesty is important for trust. A client must be truthful to get help. If someone lies to you in one situation, you start to doubt other things that have been said. **"Do not lie to one another." (Col.3:9) "His truth shall be thy shield." (Ps. 91:4) "You shall know the truth and the truth shall make you free." (John 8:32)** Truth helps people trust more and really does set us free.

DEMON POSSESSION

One issue that is largely ignored with psychology circles and schools is the topic of demonic possession and psychological healing. Most psychologists state that all mental illness is psychological and biological. That supposition is mainly true but the Bible says that some cases of mental illness are demonic. The Bible tells us that Satan was a celestial angel who rebelled against God and was cast out of heaven, along with other rebellious angels that teamed with him. ((Revelation 12:7–9) The Bible identifies Satan as "The God of this age." Satan and his fallen angels are called the powers of this dark world and the spiritual forces of evil. (Ephesians 6:12) These spiritual forces can possess people, and cause them spiritual and physical harm, and cause them to do evil. (Matthew 12:22; Mark 1:1–2; Luke 22:3–4)

Even though everyone, even Christians, are influenced by evil desires and pride, some are actually indwelled by demons. The Bible says that to be effective in this life against the ways of the devil people need to put on the "whole armor of God" and that is:

1. The Belt of Truth (Ephesians 6:14)
2. The Breastplate of Righteousness (Ephesians 6:14)
3. The Gospel of Peace (Eph. 6:15)
4. The Shield of Faith (Eph. 6:16)
5. The Helmet of Salvation (Eph. 6–17)
6. Sword of the Spirit (Eph. 6:17)

With all of this in place Jesus tells us that with prayer and fasting, we too can cast out demons like he did. (Mathew 17:21)

PRAYER and PRAISE

"Men ought always to pray." (Luke 18:1) Prayer is a powerful tool. Christians are instructed to **pray without ceasing. (1 Thess. 5:17) "Pray for those that despitefully use you." (Matt. 5:44)** Prayer works.

How should one pray? **"For we do not know how we ought to pray; the Spirit himself pleads with God for us in groans that words cannot express. And God who sees into our hearts, knows what the thought of the Spirit is; because the Spirit pleads with God on behalf of his people and in accordance with his will." (Rom. 8:26–27)** We should pray, just like the Lord's Prayer says, that "God's will would be done" for our clients.

When we pray, how do we know what God's will is? **"God works for the good with those who love him. (Rom. 8:28)** Our prayers activate God's ability to work in this world with our clients. God knows what is better for a person than we do. Therefore, it is vital to pray for all of the persons in our charge.

There are documented scientific studies by Dossey (1996) and others that point to the miraculous healing power of prayer. Studies have divided seriously ill clients into two groups—the prayed for (experimental group) and the not prayed for (control group). Study after study document that the prayed for group (even though they didn't know they were being prayed for) needed significantly fewer medical interventions (i.e. procedures or medicines) than the group that was not prayed for.

Also necessary is praise. To have greater power in this world we are commanded to praise God. After watching Jesus ascend into heaven his disciples **went back to Jerusalem, filled with great joy, and spent all their time in the temple giving thanks to God." (Luke 24:52–53)**

David wrote many psalms of praise to God. In **Psalms 145:21** he says, **"I will always praise the Lord; let all his creatures praise his holy name forever."** God is more likely to hear our prayers and petitions when we praise and thank him. Perhaps God is similar to us in that He responds to those who are grateful.

It has been documented that Christian believers have better health, less drug addiction and better marriages. One study strongly suggests that prayer is good for marriage. The study found that couples that pray together daily have less than one percent divorce rate. With the divorce rate now over 50% in America we should take notice of how God blesses marriage.

Love, prayer and praise gets our minds off of ourselves and it is somewhat of an unselfish act. God hears our prayerful requests and praises. From the Christian point of view, we are lost without Christ. We are like a microwave oven. Yes, a microwave is a magnificent machine but without the energy to run it, a microwave is useless in and of itself. Just so, without Christ and the empowering of the Holy Spirit, we are prideful, ineffective creatures, but with Christ and the Holy Spirit we are tapped into the power of the one true universal God.

A final word of caution needs, however, to be stated. Students of psychology are confronted with the fact that practicing their Christian faith in their profession is restricted by law. In fact, Christian counselors can offer Christian counseling aligned with their Christian beliefs only within a Christian setting and only if they offer their services as Christian Counseling. When one operates within a secular setting, the counselor may only discuss the Bible and his or her faith if the client initiates the conversation and if the client's problems relate to the Christian belief. While it is widely accepted that infusing faith and hope in the therapeutic process are rewarding and tend towards greater success, many stay on the side of caution and omit the Bible's truth in the counseling process. Likewise, when the client processes and overcomes therapeutic issues, one is usually more open to the Gospel. When you are equipped with the whole armor of God and have techniques that can help heal people. Open Christian based inpatient and outpatient programs in America. Pray for great revival and massive healing in the United States. God knows that we need it. Amen.

References

Alexander, E. (2012). *Proof of heaven.* New York: Simon and Schuster.

Besteman, M. (2012). *My journey to heaven.* Grand Rapids, MI: Revel Publishers.

Collins, G. (1988). *Can you trust psychology?* Downer's Grove, IL: InterVarsity Press.

Cowley, Geoffrey. (1998, March 16). Is love the best drug? *Newsweek.*

Dossey, Larry. (1996). *Prayer is good medicine.* San Francisco: Harper Collins Publishers.

DeAngelis, Tori. (1997, October). Tips for surviving and thriving in today's practice. Washington D.C. *American Psychological Association Monitor.*

Drakeford, J. (1961). *Counseling for church leaders.* Nashville, TN: Broadman Press.

Kirwan, W. (1984). *Biblical concepts in Christian counseling.* Grand Rapids, MI: Baker Book House.

Ornish, Dean. (1999). *Love and survival: The Scientific Basis for the Healing Power of Intimacy.* New York: Harper Collins.

Rawlings, Maurice. (1993). *To hell and back.* Nashville, TN: Thomas Nelson Publisher.

Seamands, David. (1985). *Healing of memories.* Wheaton, IL: Victor Books.

Swihart, J., & Richardson, G. (1987). *Counseling in times of crisis.* Waco, TX: Word Books.

White, J., & Blue, K. (1985). *Healing the wounded.* Downer's Grove, IL: InterVarsity Press.

Will, George. (1999, June 3). Believers truly setting prisoners free. Newark: *Star Ledger,* 21.

Study Questions

1. What are some important virtues that a good Christian counselor should have?
2. Have you ever experienced God working in your or someone else's life? Explain.
3. How would you work with a person that is terminally ill?
4. What do you think God wants most from us?
5. If someone tells you emphatically that they absolutely do not want to hear anything about God, what would you do?
6. Find five Bible verses that you think are psychologically sound.
7. Analyze your views on abortion, birth control, divorce, homosexuality, euthanasia. How would you counsel a person involved with one of these issues?

GLOSSARY OF TERMS

ACQUIRED FAMILY The family a person formulates later in life. This family typically includes husband, wife, and sometimes children.

ACUTE A mental or physical illness that has a sudden onset but is usually of short duration. Often it has intense symptoms, such as panic attacks.

ADJUDICATION A decision made by the courts in certain states concerning a person's mental competence.

ADVOCATE A person that is designated to defend the cause of another person. There are numerous advocate associations that defend the rights of the mentally delayed and the mentally ill.

AFFECTIVE DISORDERS A type of psychotic mental disorder characterized by thought disorders and disturbances in mood. For example, bipolar disorder.

ALZHEIMER'S DISEASE A presenile dementia that usually starts when the person is between 40 and 50 years old. It causes severe personality and intellectual deterioration.

ANXIETY A feeling of fear or apprehension. Anxiety is often caused by repressed thoughts, feelings and memories that are trying to become conscious.

ANXIETY HIERARCHY A list of anxiety producing stimuli used in systematic desensitization therapy to help people recover from phobic disorders.

APHASIA A disorder where a person is unable to speak. It could be caused by a brain dysfunction or by a psychological disorder.

APRAXIA Loss of the ability to make purposeful motor movements.

ATOMISM A theoretical approach that regards something as interpretable through analysis into distinct, separable, and independent elementary components.

ATTENTION DEFICIT DISORDER Severe and frequent problems with attention to talk and/or impulsive behavior.

AUTISM A severe mental disorder in children characterized by severe withdrawal and inability to relate to reality appropriately.

AVERSION THERAPY A type of behavior therapy where noxious stimuli are used on a subject to help stop certain behaviors.

BEHAVIOR THERAPY A type of therapy that is based primarily on the principles of classical and operant conditioning.

BEHAVIORAL CONTRACT An agreement between two parties about what behavior will be performed and what the positive or negative consequences of this behavior will be.

BID This is a Latin abbreviation that means "twice a day"; it usually refers to the frequency that medication should be taken.

BESTIALITY The term used for having sex with animals.

BIOFEEDBACK A technique where people are hooked up to a machine that gives feedback on their biological functions (blood pressure, brain waves, heart beat and respiration.) This feedback helps the person with learning to control bodily functions and with learning to relax.

BIPOLAR DISORDER An affective disorder characterized by extreme under activity (depression) and extreme over activity (mania).

BLENDED FAMILY A family that is not a nuclear family, but has an outside member added, such as an adopted child, or the combining of two divorced families with children.

BOUNDARIES A concept in marriage counseling which means building walls in a relationship. Boundaries are positive or negative depending upon where they are. A healthy family has reasonable and flexible boundaries.

CARDIOPULMONARY RESUSCITATION (CPR) A method of reviving a heart attack victim through cardiac massage and artificial respiration.

CATATONIC SCHIZOPHRENIA A severe type of psychotic disorder characterized by withdrawal from reality. Hallucinations and delusions are common.

CHRONIC Referring to a disorder of long duration.

CLASSICAL CONDITIONING Respondent conditioning occurs when a previously neutral stimulus becomes a conditioned stimulus because it becomes associated with an unconditioned stimulus.

CLINICAL PSYCHOLOGIST A professional psychologist who usually has a PHD or Psy.D. This doctor has advanced training in assessing and treating persons with maladaptive behaviors. Generally, the psychologist is licensed by the state.

COGNITIVE BEHAVIOR THERAPY A school of behavior therapy that helps people recognize irrational thinking and convert it to more rational thinking.

COLLECTIVE UNCONSCIOUS Part of the unconscious mind discussed by Carl Jung. It is the most deeply unconscious and common to all people.

COMPENSATION A defense mechanism where an undesirable personality trait is repressed and the person covers it with a more desirable trait.

COMPLEX A group or constellation of thoughts, feelings, or memories that are usually associated around a basic theme in the personality. Complexes are usually unconscious.

COMPULSION An irrational behavior that the person believes he or she must perform.

CONFIDENTIALITY A requirement to keep secret information that is told to you.

CONFRONTATION A technique used in counseling where the person is asked to look at the inconsistencies in his or her behavior.

CONGENITAL Refers to a defect that is present at or before birth, for example, a congenital heart defect.

CONSCIENCE Part of the Freudian superego. The part of the personality that tells people when they have done something morally wrong. It can also punish a person with guilt, shame and anxiety.

CONSCIOUSNESS The state of awareness where perceptions are interpreted.

CONVULSION Uncontrolled muscle movements that are usually associated with epilepsy.

CO OCCURING DISORDERS A diagnosis for persons who have a substance abuse disorder (drugs or alcohol) as well as a mental health disorder. This is also called a dual diagnosis.

COUNTERTRANSFERENCE The inappropriate feelings that are aroused in the psychotherapist toward the client.

CREATIONISM The belief that the universe and living organisms originate from specific acts of divine creation, as in the biblical account, rather than by natural processes, such as evolution.

CYCLOTHYMIC DISORDER A less severe form of bipolar disorder characterized by extreme swings in mood.

DAILY LIVING EXPERIENCES The functions that individuals must master in order for them to live on their own (cooking, dressing, bathing, etc.)

DECOMPENSATION When a person's personality becomes increasingly disorganized, many times because of excessive stress.

DEFENSE MECHANISM Unconscious ways in which a person tries to make him or herself look better or defend him or herself. Defense mechanisms are used to reduce anxiety and distort reality. Examples include repression, rationalization, and projection.

DEINSTITUTIONALIZATION A movement to help reintegrate people back into the community with the help of support services.

DELIRIUM TREMENS An acute disorder that is associated with alcohol withdrawal characterized by extreme anxiety and hallucinations. Also called the DT's.

DELUSION A false belief that is maintained in spite of evidence to the contrary.

DENIAL A defense mechanism characterized by not facing realities and not believing that they exist.

DEPRESSION An affective disorder characterized by under activity, dejection and sometime suicidal wishes.

DETOX To withdraw from alcohol or drugs.

DETERMINISM The doctrine that all events, including human action, are ultimately determined by causes external to the will. Some philosophers have taken determinism to imply that individual human beings have no free will and cannot be held morally responsible for their actions.

DEVELOPMENTAL DISABILITY A physical handicap or deficit that happens before the age of 18 and is expected to continue throughout the person's life.

DIAGNOSIS A process to determine the nature of a person's illness.

DIRECTIVE THERAPY A form of psychotherapy where the therapist gives direct advice and takes part of the responsibility for the outcome of therapy.

DISABILITY An impairment in emotional, intellectual, or physical functioning.

DISCHARGE PLANNING Planning for the release of a client to help insure support services for the client upon discharge from a program.

DISENGAGED FAMILY or DISJOINTED FAMILY A family that has too many boundaries and does not show responsibility to each other.

DISORGANIZED SCHIZOPHRENIA Hebephrenic type. A form of schizophrenia distinguished by incoherent speech and flat, incongruous, or silly affect. Often associated with extreme oddities of behavior, such as gesturing or grimacing.

DISORIENTATION Mental disorientation with respect to time, place, and identity.

DISPLACEMENT A defense mechanism where a person unconsciously substitutes another goal or object for one that is either blocked or unattainable.

DISSOCIATION Separation within the personality where parts of the personality lose their integration.

DISSOCIATIVE DISORDER A psychological disorder characterized by amnesia, multiple personality, or fugue.

DOUBLE BIND Communications that are contradictory or opposite in meaning.

DOWN'S SYNDROME A type of mental retardation caused by a genetic abnormality. Also called mongolism.

DSM V. DIAGNOSTIC AND STATISTICAL MANUAL OF MENTAL DISORDERS Reference book used by professionals to reach a psychiatric diagnosis.

DUAL DIAGNOSES Term is used for diagnosing a person with two severe illnesses, for example, Mental Illness + Chemical Abuse Illness (MICA.)

DYSLEXIA A severe deficit in the ability to read.

DYSTHYMIC DISORDER A milder form of depression than psychotic depression.

DYSPAREUNIA Painful sexual intercourse for females and sometimes males.

ECLECTIC An approach that draws from a variety of techniques and ideas.

EGO A term used for the part of the personality that is reality oriented. Many psychologists believe this is where the major part of a person's identity derives.

EGO-DEFENSE MECHANISM See defense mechanism.

EGO IDEAL The part of the Freudian personality that both tells a person when he or she has done something morally right and also rewards the person with feelings of satisfaction. It is part of the superego.

ELECTROCONVULSIVE THERAPY Often a treatment for depression in which an electrical current passes through a person's brain to cause a tonic clonic seizure. This therapy is mainly used in emergencies when antidepressant drugs have been unsuccessful and the client is highly suicidal.

EMDR Eye movement desensitization and reprocessing is a fairly new, non-traditional type of psychotherapy. It's growing in popularity, particularly for treating post-traumatic stress disorder (PTSD). It does not rely on talk therapy or medications. Instead, EMDR uses a patient's own rapid rhythmic eye movements.

EMPATHY An attempt to understand and experience what another person is feeling.

ENCOUNTER A group that helps people develop personal growth through group interaction.

ENMESHED FAMILY A family with little or no rules or boundaries, which interferes with normal growth or individuation.

ENURESIS The technical term for bed wetting.

EPILEPSY A disorder causing lapses in consciousness and sometimes convulsions.

ETHICS A code that tells one how to act in society and within different professions.

ETIOLOGY The study of factors that causes diseases to develop.

EVOLUTION The process by which different kinds of living organisms are thought to have developed and diversified from earlier forms during the history of the earth.

EXISTENTIAL THERAPY A type of therapy which emphasizes personal responsibility, meaning in life, and freedom.

EXTENDED FAMILY A nuclear family plus any or all relatives living nearby.

EXTERNAL LOCUS OF CONTROL See locus of control.

EXTINCTION The situation where a conditioned response disappears because it is no longer reinforced.

FAMILY LEGACY The traditions and expectations that a particular family holds sacred.

FAMILY OF ORIGIN The family into which a person is born.

FLOODING A technique used in implosive therapy where the person is exposed to an anxiety producing stimulus.

FREE ASSOCIATION A technique used in psychoanalysis where patients talk about whatever is on their mind without censoring their thoughts. This brings up repressions and integrates them into the consciousness.

FLAT AFFECT When a person shows lack of emotion.

FUGUE A dissociative disorder characterized by loss of memory and running away from a stressful situation.

GERONTOLOGY The study of the effects of aging on the individual.

GESTALT THERAPY A type of therapy promoted by Fritz Perls that stresses the present and focuses on the integration of the whole personality.

GRAND MAL EPILEPSY A severe tonic clonic seizure.

GUARDIANSHIP The legal responsibility to have the right to direct the welfare and health of another person.

IMPLOSIVE THERAPY A technique in behavior therapy where a person is required to face an anxiety arousing situation.

IMPOTENCE The inability of a male to achieve an erection.

INCONTINENCE The inability to control urination.

INFANTILE AUTISM See Autism.

INFERIORITY COMPLEX Strong feelings of inadequacy; a concept discussed by Adler.

INPATIENT A patient that is hospitalized.

INSTINCT A complex unlearned behavior. Some animals have them; humans do not.

INSTRUMENTAL CONDITIONING See Operant conditioning.

INTEGRATION The intermingling of functions to make a whole.

INTERNAL LOCUS OF CONTROL See locus of control.

INVOLUNTARY COMMITMENT The act of admitting a person into an institution against his or her will, often because the person is deemed to be harmful to self or others.

KORSAKOFF'S PSYCHOSIS An organic psychotic disorder that is usually associated with chronic alcoholism.

LATENT CONTENT In psychoanalysis the repressed content or the hidden meaning of a dream.

LOCUS OF CONTROL Personality characteristic in which an individual believes with that he or she has the power to affect the outcome of situations (internal locus of control) or that he or she has little control over what happens (external locus of control.)

LONGITUDINAL STUDIES Research strategy based on observing and recording the behavior of people over periods of time. It involves obtaining measures on the same population, either continuously or at specific or regular intervals.

MALINGERING To consciously and deliberately fake physical or mental illness.

MANIA A type of affective disorder characterized by extreme overactivity.

MANIC-DEPRESSIVE DISORDER An older term for bipolar disorder.

MANIFEST CONTENT In psychoanalysis, the part of the dream that the dreamer remembers.

MANIPULATIVE Attempting to get one's own needs and wants fulfilled from others without regard for the feelings and needs of others.

MARATHON GROUP A psychotherapy group that is run for 24 hours or more.

MATERIALISM A philosophy which holds that matter is the fundamental substance in nature, and that all things, including mental states and consciousness, are the result of material actions. Materialistic philosophers discount the influences of the spiritual.

MEDICAID A federal and state funded program that pays for the medical needs of the poor.

MASOCHISM A sexual disorder where the person gets pleasure from having pain inflicted on him or herself.

MENTAL RETARDATION Below normal intelligence. Defined as an I.Q. below 68.

METHADONE An orally administered synthetic narcotic that takes away the craving for heroin.

MICTURATE To urinate.

MILIEU THERAPY An institutional setting where the whole environment is set up and oriented toward the rehabilitation of the clients.

MINDFULNESS A mental state achieved by focusing one's awareness on the present moment while calmly acknowledging and accepting one's feelings, thoughts, and bodily sensation; can be used as a therapeutic technique.

MINNESOTA MULTIPHASIC PERSONALITY INVENTORY (MMPI) A 500 question true/false personality test that helps diagnose depression, anxiety and other disorders.

MODELING A type of imitative learning where a person learns certain behaviors from watching others perform them.

MORPHINE An addictive drug derived from opium.

MULTIPLE PERSONALITY DISORDER A dissociative disorder characterized by two or more personalities in the same person. Also called dissociative identity disorder.

MUTISM Inability or refusal to talk.

NARCISSISM Self-love.

NARCISSISTIC PERSONALITY DISORDER A disorder where the person acts with a great sense of entitlement and self-importance.

NARCOLEPSY A disorder characterized by involuntary compulsive states of sleeping.

NARCOTICS Drugs that cause physical dependence and cause withdrawal symptoms.

NATURALISM The philosophical belief that everything arises from natural properties and causes, and supernatural or spiritual explanations are excluded or discounted.

NONDIRECTIVE THERAPY A type of therapy in which the therapist will not give advice or direction to the client.

NON-RAPID EYE MOVEMENT SLEEP (NREM) The part of sleep when the eyes are not moving. During this time the person cannot recall any dreams.

OBSESSION A useless or irrational thought that the person cannot get rid of.

OBSESSIVE COMPULSIVE PERSONALITY A disorder characterized by both irrational thoughts that the person cannot shed and irrational acts that the person feels must be performed.

OPERANT CONDITIONING A behavioristic technique of reinforcing voluntary behavior and making it more likely to occur. Also called instrumental conditioning

OPIUM A depressant narcotic drug derived from the poppy plant.

OUTPATIENT An ambulatory patient that visits a hospital or clinic for treatment.

OUTREACH The way agencies let people know what services are available and to encourage people to participate.

PANIC DISORDER A disorder characterized by acute anxiety.

PARANOID PERSONALITY A person who uses the defense mechanism of projection, and is very often over sensitive and jealous.

PARANOID SCHIZOPHRENIA A type of schizophrenia where delusions of persecution and/or grandeur are present. This person uses the defense mechanism of projection excessively.

PARAPROFESSIONAL Someone who works with a professional to aid him or her. Usually the person holds a bachelor's degree or less.

PARKINSON'S DISEASE An organic disorder characterized by degeneration of the nervous system. It is progressive and continues into complete paralysis of the voluntary muscles.

PASSIVE AGGRESSIVE PERSONALITY A hostile person who resists demands from others for adequate performance and in this way expresses hostility.

PEDOPHILIA A sexual deviation where an adult has sex with children.

PEER GROUP A social group of about the same age and background.

PERCEPTION The interpretation of sensory input.

PERSON-CENTERED THERAPY A non-directive form of therapy founded by Carl Rogers that believes the client knows best how to resolve his or her own problems.

PHOBIA An irrational fear that is out of proportion to the actual danger.

PHYSIOLOGICAL DEPENDENCE A dependence on drugs. When the drug is discontinued, the person has withdrawal symptoms.

PLAY THERAPY The use of toys and games with children in the therapy process.

PLEASURE PRINCIPLE The desire of the id to get the greatest amount of pleasure and the least amount of pain.

POSITIVE REINFORCER A reinforcer that strengthens the probability of a given response.

POST-TRAUMATIC STRESS DISORDER A mental disorder that follows excessive environmental trauma.

PRN A Latin abbreviation meaning "as needed." This term is commonly used in medical settings regarding the taking of medication.

PROJECTION A defense mechanism where a person attributes his or her own unacceptable thoughts, feelings, and actions to others.

PSYCHIATRIST A medical doctor who works in the treatment of those with mental disorders, and can prescribe medication.

PSYCHOANALYSIS A theory of personality developed by Sigmund Freud.

PSYCHOPHYSIOLOGICAL DISORDERS A group of physical disorders that are brought on by environmental stress.

PSYCHODRAMA A therapy group in which people act out their feelings as if they are actors on a stage.

PSYCHOSIS A severe personality disorder that usually requires hospitalization.

PSYCHOSOMATIC DISORDERS See psychophysiological disorders.

PUNISHMENT Giving the organism a noxious stimulus in an attempt to eliminate an undesirable behavior.

RAPE An act of aggressively forcing another to have sexual relations with a person.

RAPID EYE MOVEMENT (REM) SLEEP A stage of sleep where the eyes move. Often associated with dreaming sleep.

RATIONAL EMOTIVE BEHAVIORAL THERAPY A school of psychotherapy founded by Albert Ellis that teaches that if one wants to change one's feelings and behavior, he or she must learn to think more empirically to resolve these emotional and behavioral problems.

RATIONALIZATION A defense mechanism where the person gives at least partly false excuses for his or her behaviors.

REACTION FORMATION A defense mechanism where the person acts the opposite of the way he or she really feel.

REALITY PRINCIPLE A Freudian term where the ego attempts to know reality. Freud said that the ego works under the reality principle.

REALITY THERAPY A school of therapy founded by William Glasser which helps people learn to fulfill their needs in a responsible manner.

RECIDIVISM A slipping back to old, less adaptive ways of acting after having been under treatment or through rehabilitation.

REENTRY Returning to mainstream society after a period away, such as being institutionalized or hospitalized.

REFERRAL Sending a person or a group of people for treatment or testing.

REGRESSION A defense mechanism where the person acts in a more childish or primitive way.

REHABILITATION The use of treatment, instead of punishment, to help a person.

REINFORCEMENT Anything that causes conditioning or learning. Usually a reward.

REMISSION An improvement in a person's condition that may not be permanent.

REPRESSION The most common defense mechanism where conscious thoughts, feelings or memories are forced into the unconscious mind.

RESISTANCE The tendency to be uncooperative in a treatment as a result of fear.

RESPONDENT CONDITIONING See Classical Conditioning.

RESPONSE COST A procedure in behavior therapy where the person is "fined" or punished for negative behaviors by having reinforcers taken away, such as money, or freedom.

ROLE PLAYING A method of psychotherapy where a person play acts a different way than he or she would normally behave.

RORSCHACH TEST A projective diagnostic test in which a person looks at a series of inkblots and tells the examiner what he or she sees in the inkblots.

SADISM A sexual deviation in which the person gains sexual pleasure by inflicting pain on another.

SCHIZOID PERSONALITY A disorder characterized by reclusiveness and lack of emotional responsiveness.

SCHIZOTYPAL PERSONALITY A person that has schizoid personality characteristics but also acts peculiar, and shows a lack of interest in social relationships. This person tends to be solitary, secretive, detached, and apathetic.

SECONDARY GAIN The "advantages" to be gotten out of a psychological disorder.

SECONDARY PREVENTION Preventative measures to detect as early as possible psychological predispositions in people and to help them overcome these problems before they get too severe.

SECONDARY PROCESS The ego is said to work under the secondary process, which is learned and is reality oriented.

SELF The personality in Jungian theory after it has been integrated into a more balanced, mature human being. Also sometimes used to refer to ego.

SELF-ACTUALIZATION To fulfill one's unique potentials. To attain the self in Jungian theory.

SELF-ESTEEM A sense of personal worth or well-being.

SELF-MONITOR To take note of one's own behavior.

SELF-REINFORCEMENT To reward one's self for positive appropriate behaviors.

SELF-STATEMENTS What a person says to him or herself about his or her own behaviors or personality.

SENSATE FOCUS A technique used in sex therapy where sexual partners learn to pleasure their partner by touching them.

SEROTONIN One of the group of chemical neurotransmitters that implement neural transmission across the synapse.

SEXUAL DYSFUNCTION An impairment of the ability to experience or receive sexual gratification.

SHAPING A technique used in behavior therapy where successive approximations of the desired behavior are achieved by using reinforcement.

SHOCK THERAPY The use of electrical shock in treating mental disorders.

SIBLINGS Offspring of the same parents.

SOCIAL WORKER (MSW) An individual with a Master's Degree in social work and clinical training.

SOCIOPATHIC DISORDER See antisocial personality disorder.

SOMNAMBULISM Sleepwalking.

STATUTORY RAPE Sexual intercourse with a minor.

STIMULANT A drug that increases a person's metabolic functions.

STIMULUS GENERALIZATION When an organism acts the same way to similar stimuli.

STRESS INOCULATION A cognitive therapy technique that helps a person cope with stress by preparing him or her for the stress.

STRESSOR An adjustive demand made upon a person with which the person must learn to cope.

STUPOR A situation where the person is lethargic and unresponsive.

STUTTERING Speech disorder where the person is unable to say certain words or repeats the initial sounds of words.

SUBLIMATION A defense mechanism consisting of those displacements that are more socially acceptable.

SUICIDE To kill oneself.

SUPEREGO According to psychoanalytic theory the moral arm or internalized parent of the personality.

SUPPRESSION To consciously push unwanted thoughts, feelings and memories into the preconscious mind. Unlike repressed materials, suppressed memories can be retrieved at any time.

SYMBOL Something that is used to represent something else.

SYMPTOM The physiological or psychological manifestation of a disease. Often symptoms come in groups or clusters called syndromes.

SYSTEMATIC DESENSITIZATION A behavior therapy technique where a person is taught deep muscle relaxation and then reviews a hierarchy of anxiety producing images. This technique is particularly effective with anxiety and phobic disorders.

TACHYCARDIA Rapid heartbeat.

TARDIVE DYSKINESIA Involuntary muscular movements caused by antipsychotic drugs called phenothiazines that patients have taken for extended periods of time.

THEMATIC APPERCEPTION TEST A diagnostic projective test in which a person is asked to tell a story to a given picture. Also called the TAT.

THERAPY The treatment of a problem or disorder.

TID A Latin abbreviation for three times a day. Usually refers to the frequency that medication should be taken.

TOKEN ECONOMY A behavior therapy technique frequently used in institutional settings where a behavior of a client is reinforced by giving tokens which can later be traded for something that the person wants.

TOLERANCE A physiological condition where a greater dosage of an addictive drug is needed to get the same effect as a smaller dose did before.

TONIC CLONIC EPILEPSY A severe convulsive disorder where the person involuntarily also loses consciousness.

TRANSFERENCE In therapy the feelings that a client displaces onto the therapist, especially the feelings that this individual may have toward a significant person in his or her past, such as, mother.

TRANSSEXUAL A person who believes that he or she is the opposite sex from the sex into which he or she was born, and often wishes to have sex change therapy.

TRANSVESTISM A person who usually gets sexually aroused by dressing as a person of the opposite sex.

TRAUMA A severe environmental or psychological stress that has a lasting effect on a person.

TRICYCLIC DRUG An antidepressant drug.

UNCONDITIONED POSITIVE REGARD The attitude that a person centered therapist is to have toward a client. The therapist is to convey a sense of total acceptance toward the client.

UNCONDITIONED STIMULUS (UCS) A stimulus that elicits an unconditioned response, such as eye blinking to a particle in the eye.

UNCONSCIOUS The part of the mind that people are unaware of and repress their thoughts, feelings and memories into.

WAXY FLEXIBILITY A conditioned common in catatonic schizophrenia where the limbs are moved into a variety of positions and stay there for extended periods of time.

WITHDRAWAL Physiological changes, varying from mild to extremely unpleasant, that take place after an individual's discontinuation of a habit-forming substance.

WITHDRAWAL FROM REALITY To retreat psychologically and physically from life. A symptom of many psychoses.